James Fenimore Cooper
versus the Cult of Domesticity

James Fenimore Cooper versus the Cult of Domesticity

Progressive Themes of Femininity and Family in the Novels

SIGNE O. WEGENER

McFarland & Company, Inc., Publishers
Jefferson, North Carolina, and London

LIBRARY OF CONGRESS CATALOGUING-IN-PUBLICATION DATA

Wegener, Signe O., 1945–
  James Fenimore Cooper versus the cult of domesticity :
progressive themes of femininity and family in the novels /
Signe O. Wegener.
    p.   cm.
  Includes bibliographical references and index.

  ISBN 0-7864-2128-2 (softcover : 50# alkaline paper) ∞

  1. Cooper, James Fenimore, 1789–1851—Characters—Women.
2. Cooper, James Fenimore, 1789–1851—Political and social
views.   3. Women and literature—United States—History—
19th century.   4. Domestic fiction, American—History and
criticism.   5. Femininity in literature.   6. Family in literature.
7. Women in literature.   I. Title.
PS1442.W6W44   2005
813'.2—dc22   2005003510

British Library cataloguing data are available

©2005 Signe O. Wegener. All rights reserved

*No part of this book may be reproduced or transmitted in any form
or by any means, electronic or mechanical, including photocopying
or recording, or by any information storage and retrieval system,
without permission in writing from the publisher.*

*On the cover: (top) James Fenimore Cooper (Clipart.com);
(bottom) "The Promised Land," William Smith Jewett, 1850
(Pictures Now.com)*

Manufactured in the United States of America

McFarland & Company, Inc., Publishers
  Box 611, Jefferson, North Carolina 28640
    www.mcfarlandpub.com

Contents

Preface	1
1 • The Courtship Novel	5
2 • The Domestic Matrix	35
3 • Marriage and Motherhood	54
4 • Fatherhood	92
5 • Daughters	123
Conclusion	170
Chapter Notes	173
Bibliography	183
Index	189

Preface

Regardless of aspirations, no writer truly escapes his or her cultural and socioeconomic context. No matter where in time the writer chooses to pitch a literary tent, the contemporary cultural matrix remains, flavoring subject matter, plot, and character development. And for the early to mid-nineteenth-century American, male and female alike, an important part of this cultural matrix was what can best be termed "the cult of domesticity"—a set of values aimed at shaping private and public life in the rapidly changing nation. From 1820 to 1860, fiction and nonfiction alike sought to promote the cult's ideals in the areas of religious, domestic, and personal development. Consciously or subconsciously, positively and negatively, writers reacted to the cult's tenets, promoting or challenging them, presenting markedly woman-centered texts. Among them were popular women writers like Lydia Maria Child, Catharine Maria Sedgwick (both authors of woman-centered "Indian Tales"), Susan Warner, and Maria Cummins—and the equally prominent male writer James Fenimore Cooper. All wrote in response to the predominant cultural climate, and all created texts with women as an integral part of the plot line.

Critics have, over the years, paid relatively scant attention to the issue of family in Cooper, for the most part shying away from any "feminine" interpretation of Cooper's representations of family dynamics. Instead, the tendency in the critical exploration into Cooper's families has been decidedly masculine and autobiographical, with a strong emphasis on the role of the patriarch. Even Jay S. Paul, who in "Home as Cherished: The Theme of Family in Fenimore Cooper" (1973) at least initially links Cooper's interest in family to contemporary concerns and the popularity of domestic fiction in the nineteenth century, ignores any possibility of Cooper responding to "feminine" impulses, claiming instead the "desire to father a race" and "the sense of identity resulting from long habitation of a place" as primary incentives (Paul 39). William E. Cosgrove, in

"Family Lineage and Narrative Pattern in Cooper's Littlepage Trilogy" (1974), comments that the "narrative patterns" of the works "are based on an archetypal feminine impulse, the desire to form a family through marriage" (3) but limits his discussion to the three Littlepage novels—*Satanstoe, The Chainbearer, The Redskins*.

My text provides a more comprehensive discussion of Cooper's view of family dynamics. It explores the textual relationship and similarities found in the works of Cooper, Child, Sedgwick, Warner, and Cummins. It demonstrates that from the very outset of his career, James Fenimore Cooper, who took from the popular books of his day, using "whatever plot devices seemed useful to him" (Ringe 4), presented himself as a writer of domestic, i.e., women's fiction. More importantly, like his female contemporaries, he used the value system provided and promoted by the cult of domesticity. Even so, he never accepted the cult's ideals without qualifications; instead, he sought to simultaneously present and critique the forces shaping the emerging nation. In order to establish Cooper's relationship to the cult, to the domestic matrix providing raw materials for character development, this book will address how the cult manifested itself in fiction and nonfiction alike.

When I started working on my doctoral dissertation, on which this book is based, in the early 1990s, I had long been interested in nineteenth-century domestic life, mainly because so many of our own values and notions originate there. I had also long been aware of Cooper's woman-driven plots. Significantly, the scene I remember best from my childhood reading of *The Deerslayer* is the title character's "psychological evaluation" of the Hutter daughters based on their room at Muskrat Castle. However, I was initially unfamiliar with the extent and impact of what I later came to see as the cult of domesticity. Two texts remedied this. The first was Harvey Green's lavishly illustrated *The Light of the Home: An Intimate View of the Lives of Women in Victorian America* (1983), a Christmas gift from cousins interested in Victoriana. Through photos, advertising, and excerpts from advice books, fiction, and personal recollections, the book presents the domestic lives of American women — and the standards they were urged to emulate. The second was Barbara Welter's excellent discussion of these standards in her reading of early to mid-nineteenth-century ladies' magazines and other nonfiction in the 1973 article "The Cult of True Womanhood 1820–1860." In it, she sets down the cornerstones of nineteenth-century female behavior: piety, purity, obedience, and domesticity, and demonstrates how nineteenth-century advice literature and fiction sought to inculcate its readers. I am greatly indebted to both writers for their insights.

My study examines representations of Victorian domesticity and family dynamics in ten Cooper novels—*Precaution, The Spy*, the five Leatherstocking novels (*The Pioneers, The Last of the Mohicans, The Prairie, The Pathfinder*, and *The Deerslayer*), *Homeward Bound* and *Home as Found*, the Littlepage trilogy, especially *Satanstoe*, and *The Wept of Wish-Ton-Wish*—against the backdrop of the cult of domesticity and as critical response to it. To do so, I have put Cooper's texts into the context of popular nineteenth-century nonfiction and domestic women's novels: Lydia Maria Child's *Hobomok*, Catherine Maria Sedgwick's *Hope Leslie*, Susan Warner's *The Wide, Wide World*, and Maria Cummins's *The Lamplighter*. Each chapter approaches one particular aspect of the cult and aims at establishing Cooper within this woman-centered context.

Each of the study's five chapters discusses one specific aspect of family life as it appears in these novels. Within each chapter, I follow a three-pronged approach, juxtaposing Cooper's novels to a selection of nineteenth-century advice literature and private papers as well as to Child's, Segdwick's, Warner's, and Cummins's texts. Each chapter therefore falls into three separate parts. First, I discuss the particular issue as it appears in nonfiction. Second, I trace the ideas outlined in part I in the works of Child, Sedgwick, Warner, and Cummins. Third, I demonstrate how Cooper's novels approach the issue discussed in the chapter and how his representations compare to those crafted by women writers and to the standards propounded by the cult of domesticity.

Chapter 1, "The Courtship Novel," opens my discussion, demonstrating how Cooper initially chose this genre as his vehicle and how the courtship paradigm remained a constant in his later novels. Chapter 2, "The Domestic Matrix," presents an overview of the cult of domesticity in fiction and nonfiction alike, delineating the origins and effect of nineteenth-century domestic life. Chapter 3, "Marriage and Motherhood," discusses and critiques representations of mothers in nineteenth-century society and literature and the standards that ruled their lives. Chapter 4, "Fatherhood," provides insight into how the cult of domesticity and contemporary novelists present and critique fathers and their responsibilities in fiction and nonfiction. Chapter 5, "Daughters," treats the central character in domestic fiction, providing behavioral standards and literary treatment of the role of daughters in family life.

I am greatly indebted to Professor Philip Beidler at the University of Alabama for initially suggesting that I work with James Fenimore Cooper's novels, and also to the other members of my dissertation committee—Drs. Claudia D. Johnson, Sara de Saussure Davis, Don Noble, and Ralph Bogardus—for advice and encouragement.

The main part of this work was researched at the Gorgas Library at the University of Alabama and written at the Department of English at the University of Alabama under the direction of Dr. Philip Beidler. As presented here, it is a revised version of a doctoral dissertation presented to the faculty of the Graduate School of the University of Alabama in December 1995.

1

The Courtship Novel

> It is a truth universally acknowledged that a single man in possession of a good fortune must be in want of a wife.
> — Jane Austen, *Pride and Prejudice*, 1813

> ...for you well know that no gentility, no husband; and it's dull work to you young ladies without at least a possibility of matrimony...
> — James Fenimore Cooper, *Precaution*, 1820

Young John Moseley's comment on women's specific interest in marriage and marriage prospects in Cooper's first novel, *Precaution*, evokes Jane Austen's opening lines in *Pride and Prejudice*. The words also signal Cooper's familiarity with the plot conventions of the courtship novel, a genre intimately intertwined with the domestic novel in subject matter and plot development. Like many other nineteenth-century writers of domestic fiction, Cooper often closes his novels with a marriage prospect, a wedding, or an epilogue detailing the characters' future. His preoccupation with the issues this feminized genre discussed are as central to Cooper's literary *corpus* as they are to works by Lydia Maria Child, Catharine Maria Sedgwick, Susan Warner, and Maria Cummins.

Katherine Sobba Green, in her 1993 study *The Courtship Novel, 1740–1820: A Feminized Genre,* observes, "Although not all courtship novels were written by women, the genre itself, with its domestic setting, was an ideal medium for expressing middle-class women's values and issues" (13). More importantly, Sobba Green shows that writers of courtship novels deliberately feminized their texts to appeal to the growing female readership. This "feminizing" followed a specific formula. First, the authors made the prudent middle-class lady the central figure in the plot, relegating male characters to supporting roles. Second, they placed the heroine in a domestic setting, an environment familiar to their upper- and middle-class readers. Third, the novels' heroines, settings, and issues combined to produce a gendered text, specifically designed to reach and appeal to a female audience who could identify with the novels' characters and situations. Fourth, as Paula Marantz Cohen notes, writers of courtship novels avoided the prolonged sexual pursuits typical of, for instance, the gothic novels.[1] Finally, the courtship novels, like conduct books and stories and articles in women's periodicals, were openly and unashamedly didactic: the objective was always to shape female conduct, whether they espoused patriarchal views or questioned accepted gender roles.[2] Combinations of these five conventions appear in a wide variety of British and American novels.

From his female predecessors and contemporaries, Cooper appropriated certain key plot elements. Among these were didacticism, the insistence on the heroine's middle-class respectability, her moral superiority to other characters in the text, and her right to marry for love, regardless of parental or societal demands. The latter element was clearly a subversive act: the heroine openly rebelled against patriarchal society. Casting the heroine as the central figure in the plot, Cooper, like the women who wrote similar tales, among them Child, Sedgwick, Warner, and Cummins, created feminized texts that challenged ruling gender roles and gender expectations. Even in the Leatherstocking tales, some of the most memorable characters are the young women. More often than not they are the very characters whose presence propels the plots of the novels, as in the cases of the best known of Cooper's female characters, Elizabeth Temple, Mabel Dunham, Cora Munro, and Judith Hutter. In her discussion of the female characters in the Leatherstocking tales, Nina Baym argues that women are indispensable to the meanings of Cooper's novels. Because marriage forms the matrix of Cooper's romances, women are of "central significance" in his works.[3] Baym's assertion is equally true of Cooper's other novels. Despite the "undomestic" settings, such as the frontier or the ocean, and the capture and escape and pursuit plots, Cooper's tales center on courtship: the main plot involves joining the heroine to an eligible suitor — i.e., to the "heroine's hero," as Kay S. House calls him (22).[4] This suitor faces a daunting task; he has to prove himself worthy of the morally superior heroine. He has to overcome all doubts, all questionable behaviors and attributes. By choosing this feminized approach, Cooper, like other writers of courtship novels, created works that he knew would appeal to readers eager to identify with his heroines. To such readers, the female behavior exemplified in the courtship novels and advice literature was familiar territory, as was the courtship advice that Cooper's novels dispensed so freely.

※ ※ ※

> Flirting is to marriage what free trade is to commerce. By it the value of a woman is exhibited, tested, her capacities known, her temper displayed, and the opportunity offered of judging what sort of wife she may probably become.
> — *Godey's Lady's Book and Magazine*, July 1860

> In no other country, is the same freedom of intercourse between the unmarried of the two sexes, permitted, as in America.
> — James Fenimore Cooper, *Notions of the Americans*

As Cooper's statement points out, the young republic also saw a change in courtship behaviors. Chaperoning, a "must" for "respectable" middle- and upper-class young women in England at various activities, was relative unusual. The historian Harvey Green notes that in the United States, "unchaperoned social activity was the norm, and young people had more social freedom than their English counterparts." This "was in part the result of the less rigid class structure ... and, in part, of the less secure and respected position of older single women in American culture" (12).[5] Yet this freedom did not mean licentiousness and impropriety: advice books and articles sought to prescribe appropriate courtship behavior, recommending everything from the minimum age requirement for young ladies to what gifts she could or could not receive from a suitor. Flowers were acceptable, jewelry was not.[6] And at every step in the courtship phase, the young woman had to show she possessed the qualities that would make her an excellent wife and mother.

Despite this greater freedom in male-female relationships that Cooper emphasizes in *Notions of the Americans*, the young American girl's behavior and self-expression meet with noticeable restrictions in fiction and nonfiction alike. At his time, a plethora of etiquette books and ladies magazines consistently expounded on appropriate female behavior, prescribing the best methods for conducting one's education or the search for a prospective spouse. Advice literature had long been a staple in the offerings to the sophisticated female reading public of eighteenth-century London, a result of the emerging idea that a marriage should be both companionate and affectionate, not merely a political or financial transaction. However, the nineteenth-century editions aimed at a different readership than their eighteenth-century counterparts: the burgeoning crop of middle-class female readers in a nation trying to find its feet morally and socially. Initially, most advice manuals were written by men and, like most literature of this kind, dispensed varied and often contradictory advice, advocating either female intellectual growth or female subjugation. Some, like Eliza Haywood, hoping to make learning fashionable, even promoted studies in philosophy, geography, history and mathematics, areas reserved for men.⁷ Two advice manuals were well known in America at Cooper's time: Edward Moore's *Fables for the Female Sex* (1787; eleven editions by 1815) and James Fordyce's *Sermons to Young Women* (1766; five editions by 1809), providing the parameters for social interaction between the sexes, for instance while calling on somebody at home, or in the ballroom.⁸

Dances and balls—despite often being denounced as a distraction for young women—provided young people with excellent opportunities for private conversation and physical closeness. The dancing, however, had to be, as Fordyce suggests, "moderate and discreet." The author defends his position, claiming, "It seems to me, there can be no impropriety in it, any more that in modulating the voice into the most agreeable tones in singing; to which none, I think, will object."⁹ Propriety reigned also in this venue: the young woman could not dance more than twice with one man unless she wanted to invite gossip. Men had the initiative—they were the ones asking young women to stand up with them. Advice books also aimed at helping the young woman develop proper ballroom skills. *The Young Lady's Book: A Manual of Elegant Recreations, Exercises and Pursuits* (1830) instructs the readers on "proper carriage of the arms" while dancing, claiming this aspect is "one of the greatest difficulties in dancing" and that it "therefore demands the utmost attention on the part of the pupil" (409). Moral deportment eclipses physical grace: "Accomplishments, however desirable and attractive, must always be considered as secondary objects, when compared to those virtues which form the character and influence the power of woman in society" (23).

Cooper eagerly participates in the discussion of American manners and female deportment. In the two volumes of *Notions of the Americans* (1828), in many ways Cooper's own advice book, the author lets his traveling Belgian narrator provide his European readers with a wealth of information on American behavior and *mores*, among them courtship manners. These the European traveler, unfamiliar with American social *mores* and the cultural context, completely misinterprets. Although young, well bred, and well connected—qualities apparently guaranteed to meet with female favor in Europe—the Belgian to his surprise finds himself rebuffed by Isabel, a young female American fellow passenger. When the narrator, obviously drawn by her *joie de vivre*, approaches her, he finds to his disappointment that all her "joyous, natural and enticing merriment" instantly metamorphoses into "the cold and regulated smiles of artificial breeding" (26). She is polite and aloof. His American friend, the much older Cadwallader—perhaps Cooper's *alter ego*—is easily accepted by the same lady. "With Cadwallader," the narrator admits grudgingly, "every thing was reversed. In his society she laughed without ceasing; chatted, disputed, was natural and happy" (Vol. I. 26). Naturally, the jealous young man believes nuptials between the two are imminent; however, Cadwallader soon clarifies the situation by a statement which sums up Cooper's beliefs. Any lasting, successful marriage had to be based not only on carefully guided "taste and inclination" but, more importantly, on an equality in age, rank, wealth, religion, and nationality. This demand for equality he presents as an inherently American — and *democratic*— tradition. Rejecting any European notion of the benefits of May–December marriages, Cadwallader calmly observes that he due to his age is considered harmless to "young ladies of seventeen" (Vol. I. 27). "Unequal matches," he asserts, "are of exceedingly rare occurrence among us.... Taste and inclination, rather guided, than controlled, by the prudence of older heads, form most of our matches; and just as much freedom as comports with that prudence, and a vast deal more than you probably deem safe, is allowed between the young of the two sexes" (Vol. I. 27–28). Because Cadwallader is a fellow American capable of reading her behavior as she intends it to be read, Isabel can behave in a natural, straightforward manner with him. He is a threat neither to her reputation nor to her virginity; she may talk with him without fear of compromising her reputation. However, having traveled, both she and her grandfather have familiarized themselves with European manners and know that a European is apt to misread the signals a freer behavior transmits, hence the young girl's coldness toward the narrator.

Like many a contemporary magazine article, *Notions* repeatedly returns to the topic of the young American female and her manners—and her effect on the opposite sex. Cooper presents a veritable catalogue of ideal female qualities exemplified in the properly raised upper- and upper middle-class American woman. These qualities, when sufficiently internalized, supposedly make her eminently marriageable. This female's distinguishing feature, the narrator asserts, is "nature"; furthermore, she is both "decidedly handsome" and "delicate" (Vol. I. 191). Besides rhapsodizing over the beauty of the American girl, the narrator conscientiously records his emotional response to this phenomenon, responding as a potential suitor. He appears particularly interested in American courtship practices, patiently delineating what works and what does not work in the discourse between the sexes. It is a discourse marked, for example, by its decorum and its absence of gallantry — i.e., flirting: "The language of gallantry is never tolerated. A married woman would conceive it an insult, and a girl would be exceedingly apt to laugh in her adorer's face.... He who addresses an unmarried female in this language, whether it be of passion or only feigned, must expect to be exposed, and probably disgraced, unless he should be prepared to support his sincerity by an offer of his hand" (Vol. I. 195). Cooper was not alone in his condemnation of flirting. *Titcomb's Letters to Young People, Married and Single* (1858) claims, "To become a flirt is to metamorphose into a disgusting passion that which by natural constitution is a harmless and useful instinct.... Coquetry, which makes a woman a thing to be won ... is not a thing to be cultivated or developed, at all" (100). Still, flirtation had its uses: it provided women with "the opportunity to broaden that network of eligible and interesting men, enabling her to make a wiser choice about which man she would allow to court her and which proposal she would accept" (Green 12).

The principles the "Belgian" here notes underlie all of Cooper's "courtship novels" from *Precaution, The Spy, The Pioneers,* and *The Last of the Mohicans* to *Homeward Bound, Home as Found, The Pathfinder, The Deerslayer* and the Littlepage trilogy. Cooper saw these principles as of profound interest and importance not only to himself but also to his female and male readers. More importantly, they are principles worth emulating, as the phrase "between ourselves, rightly believes" indicates; Cooper intends *Notions of the Americans* as a prescriptive, not a descriptive, work: the text presents American manners not as they *are*, but as they *ought* to be.

※ ※ ※

> Must I then become an avowed prude at once, and refuse him admission, if he call, in compliance with the customary forms? By no means. I am sensible, that even the false maxims of the world must be complied with in a degree. But a man of Major Sanford's art can easily distinguish between a forbidding, and an encouraging reception. The former may, in this case, be given without any breach of the rules of politeness.
> — Hannah Webster Foster, *The Coquette*, 1797

When Cooper, in 1820, sat down to write *Precaution*, the courtship novel had been popular for more than half a century. It was, as Sobba Green notes, an eminent teaching tool: "Although not all courtship novels were written by women, the genre itself, with its domestic setting, was the ideal medium for expressing middle-class women's values and issues" (13). Among the genre's early practitioners were Samuel Richardson, Eliza Haywood, Frances Brooke, Charlotte Lenox, Susanna Rowson, Hannah Webster Foster, Franny Burney, Mrs. Opie, Maria Edgeworth, and Jane Austen. In nineteenth-century America, Lydia Maria Child, Catharine Maria Sedgwick, Susan Warner, and Maria Cummins produced similarly gendered texts.

The reader immediately recognizes several of the conventions Sobba Green emphasizes in Child's *Hobomok*. Despite being named for a *male*—the heroine's Native American suitor and later husband—the narrative itself is woman centered, with an upper-class heroine and hero, a domestic setting, a deliberate downplaying of sexual pursuit, and an implicit didactic goal. Although outwardly "masculine"—the novel's frame narrative coyly posits both a male narrator and a male editor—the novel focuses on the life, courtships, and marriages of the heroine, Mary Conant. Beside her, the two suitors, the titulary "hero" Hobomok and his rival for Mary's favor, the English gentleman Charles Brown, become supporting actors indeed; they appear only in relationship to her. So does the narrator, who feels so drawn to the heroine that he comes across almost as a besotted third suitor. Although merely a visitor to New England, he admits to wanting to stay in the colony from "earthly motives" which he links to the "childish witchery of Mary Conant" (12). Thus there is a distinct courtship flavor to the narrator's watching over Mary while she conducts her witchcraft rite: he purports to stay for her safety, claiming that a "mixed feeling of diffidence and delicacy" induce him to remain hidden (14). However, he is a *voyeur* spying on his beloved, not an objective observer. Intrigued by her beauty and actions, he never attempts to stop her, nor does he report the event to the Puritan authorities.

Mary's two courtships, then, interwoven with loss of mother and lover, and her struggle against paternal directives take center stage throughout the clearly feminized text. Like any true sentimental heroine, Mary's love never dies, even when it is thwarted by her unrelenting father and by Charles's supposed death. Mary's relationship to Charles Brown, her only "real" courtship, takes a subversive but familiar course: with Brown denied access to the Conant household, the lovers have to resort to secret, nocturnal meetings and professions of love. To Charles, Mary has become the center of the universe. As he confides to Mary: "My life was full of enjoyment before I met you in Lincolnshire; and now, when I try to think of any source of happiness in which you have no share, I am forced to acknowledge that you are, in some way or other, connected therewith" (49). The meetings show the tenderness of courtship, but Charles never displays the kind of idolatrous reverence for Mary that Hobomok exhibits around her. When the lovers meet, Charles "gaily imprint[s] a kiss upon her hand" (48) and quotes Spenser; he plays the suave, courtly lover to Mary's equally courtly chaste maiden. Little is said of reverence in this relationship: to Charles, Mary is socially and spiritually an *equal*, not a superior being. Hobomok, on the other hand, looks upon her "with reverence, which almost amounted to adoration" (33). *He* sees her as being almost goddess-like, and thus far superior to himself. However, Hobomok in a way deceives himself. Because of his adoration for and attraction to Mary — which he rejects as "a kind of blasphemy" when Conanchet points it out — his affection for her still leads him to betray his people and his social responsibilities. He leaves the Native American woman he is expected to marry, "Pokanecket's daughter." In fact, he finds "he loathed the idea of marriage to her" (33).

But Child does not stop there. She cleverly incorporates even the country house setting into the narrative: Mary's maternal grandfather belongs to the English upper class, and Mary has been raised in his home and according to his aristocratic, worldly principles. Child uses sentimental terms to describe her heroine and her mother, adroitly setting them apart from her inferiors. Mary, full of "gentleness and beauty" (9), possesses a "sylph-like" figure, whereas her friend Sally is "buxom" (16). Mrs. Conant, once beautiful, now exemplifies "decaying elegance" (17).

The refinement of Mrs. Conant's and Mary's upper-class background constantly shines through, a refinement inspiring respect and reverence in the men surrounding them, from fellow colonists to Hobomok. In a scene reminiscent of Cooper's courtship novels and their examples of "good" and "bad" courtships, Child juxtaposes Hobomok's behavior to that of "one Mr. Thomas Graves" who has been "deeply smitten with the comely countenance" of Sally Oldham, Mary's social inferior. Sally clearly inspires a different behavior in men than Mary does; Mr. Graves refuses to stop at mere distant admiration of his beloved. His interest in Sally is physical; he expects her to respond in kind. Full of cocky male self-confidence, and "never for a moment doubting that the fascination was reciprocal," he becomes "somewhat obtrusively officious" (17). Hobomok's demeanor, the narrator observes, manifests a very different attitude, one familiar to nineteenth-century readers: male admiration and reverence for the morally superior female. In this respect, Hobomok behaves like the "ideal" Christian suitor. The narrator observes this distinction between the two men: "It was singular to observe the difference of deportment between him [Mr. Graves] and the Indian. Whenever Hobomok gazed upon Mary, it was with an expression in which reverence was strikingly predominant" (17). Nevertheless, the narrator ignores that not only the males, but the object of their desires, differ socially.

Despite dabbling in witchcraft to find out whether she will marry Brown, Mary is basically a prudent and disinterested young lady, without even "half an eye for other folks' affairs," as Sally observes (21). Mary is well behaved and domestic and especially attentive to her ailing mother; in short, she possesses some of the most indispensable qualities of the ideal nineteenth-century daughter. Those who surround her, even the "savage" Hobomok, respond to her refinement and moral superiority, treating her with the respect due a socially and morally superior being. A noticeable class bias surfaces in Child's representations of men's treatment of women. In Child's fictional world, only upper-class women meet with respectful treatment; lower-class women are exposed to sexual harassment from superiors and equals alike. Charles Brown, Mary's "favoured lover," offers her respect and protection, as does Hobomok. The more "common" Sally, on the other hand, finds herself pursued not only by the odious Mr. Graves, but also by the lecherous and aptly named minister Mr. Lyford, about whom she declares to Mary, "many a sly look and word he'd give me, when his good-woman was out of the way" (19). By showing Mary's and Sally's courtships, Child provides her readers with a courtship manual complete with examples of good and bad courtships.

The conventions of the courtship novel also inform Sedgwick's *Hope Leslie*. This woman-centered adventure story has been designed to appeal to a female readership. Not only one, but three sympathetically drawn women characters vie for the readers'—and the hero's—attention, each one embodying variations of the nineteenth-century domestic ideal. Following the demands of the genre, her female characters are members of the upper classes. Hope Leslie is the grandchild of Sir William Fletcher, "an eminent lawyer" (7), Esther is the niece of Governor Winthrop, and even Magawisca is the daughter of a noble Indian chief. Also, in keeping with the genre, even the strong-willed and lively title character exerts herself for the good of others, not for herself. By presenting several courtships, the novel provides the readers with examples of what to look for and what to avoid in similar situations. The novel argues for love, common background, and common interests as the basis for a successful marriage; these are indispensable qualities that tie the hero and heroine together. However, the heroine Hope Leslie, who eventually marries her "brother" Everell Fletcher, first has to rebuff a clearly unsuitable suitor. Everell also has to extricate himself from his engagement to Mrs. Winthrop's ultra-religious niece Esther, a commitment into which he has been maneuvered partly by Hope Leslie and partly by the Winthrop family. In the context of the novel, courtship and marriage are public, not private matters, decided on by the colony's governor and the young persons' parents or guardians, an idea the novel clearly rejects. The heroine causes turmoil in the Puritan society; hence Governor Winthrop wants "to enforce the necessity of a stricter watch over this lawless girl" (154). And, he believes, the only way to quell this female rebellion is through marrying her off, to "consign her to some one who should add to affection, the modest authority of a husband" (154).

Ironically, the one courtship the Puritan leadership encourages for the young heroine is a potentially disastrous one: Hope Leslie is pursued, with Governor Winthrop's approval, by the story's villain, Sir Philip Gardiner, a disguised Roman Catholic who, it turns out, even has a shipboard mistress masquerading as his cabin boy. Governor Winthrop, who despite his exalted position in the colony clearly lacks the ability to discern human nature, finds Sir Philip "an uncommon personable man" who "hath that bearing that finds favour in maidens' eyes" (155). In fact, Winthrop interprets Sir Philip's propitious arrival as the workings of divine Providence (155). Eager to "put jesses on this wild bird ... while she is our perch," the governor sees the older man as a means to control the spirited young lady who has caused the Puritan elders so many "perplexities" (155). Although Hope's guardian protests—he is obviously a shrewder judge of character than the governor—on the grounds that Sir Philip is, as he points out, "a new-comer today! and old enough to be the father of Hope Leslie," Governor Winthrop considers Sir Philip "The fitter guide for her youth," eagerly urging what the reader knows would be a disastrous marriage (155).

To complicate the romantic plot, Hope Leslie is not the only female the text casts in the mold of the conventional courtship heroine. The writer also deploys the conventions of courtship literature to create the young Indian woman Magawisca, who loves Everell and sacrifices an arm to save his life, specifically to appeal to female readers. Magawisca, more so than the title character Hope Leslie, is a dutiful daughter, obedient to her father and his way of life, save in this one instance when she disobeys paternal directives to rescue the man she loves. Despite this sympathetically drawn Native American woman, Sedgwick rejects any possibility of a love relationship between Magawisca and Everell—propriety, religion, and cultural differences, she demonstrates, create insurmountable obstacles.

She also rejects the idea of a marriage between Everell and Esther Downing, the third woman who loves him and whom he initially is to marry. Like Magawisca, Esther is a sympathetic character, and—most importantly—she is the epitome of the "angel in the house": pious, humane, sensitive, generous, and selfless. Foreshadowing Esther's fate, Sedgwick chooses some lines from Milton's "Il Penseroso" to characterize her: the young "pilgrim damsel" is a "pensive Nun, devout and pure, / Sober, steadfast, and demure" (Milton ll. 31–32, Sedgwick 133). However, she is no suitable mate for Everell: he needs somebody more adventurous and decisive than this mild-mannered creature. Significantly, the relationship between Everell and Esther also lacks the requisite "master-passion." As in *Hobomok*, distance, misunderstandings, and difficult family members who wish to control the young man or woman's choice of spouse are standard obstacles on the path towards marriage. Both works explicitly aim at shaping female behavior and advocate piety, common background, and common interest, as well as love, as prerequisites for a successful marital relationship.

One element needs to be added to the discussion of the conventions of the courtship novel and the domestic novel: Child, Sedgwick, Warner, and Cummins all portray what some twentieth- and twenty-first-century critics see as a quasi-incestuous relationship between heroine and hero. In *Hope Leslie*, the young lovers Hope and Everell have for years considered one another "sister" and "brother" and Magawisca was in part raised with Everell. In *Hobomok*, Mary meets Charles at her grandfather's Lincolnshire mansion and Hobomok under her father's New England roof. Long familiarity and physical proximity, the novels seem to argue, is in fact the best guarantee for a successful marriage. Warner's *The Wide, Wide World* and Maria Cummins's *The Lamplighter* promote similar ideas. In the former, Ellen Montgomery eventually marries John Humphreys, the brother of her surrogate mother, Alice; in the latter, Gerty becomes the wife of Willie Sullivan, quite literally the boy next door and son of Gerty's surrogate mother. Cooper shares these literary tendencies. In *The Spy*, *Home as Found*, and *Lionel Lincoln*, the heroines marry their cousins. G. M Goshgarian, in *To Kiss the Chastening Rod: Domestic Fiction and Sexual Ideology in the American Renaissance* (1992), at length discusses the incestuous implications he sees as underlying nineteenth-century women's fiction. In his discussion of *Ernest Linwood*, *Lena Rivers*, and *The Lamplighter*, he argues that "domestic fiction engenders the incestuousness whose persistence it attests." He then adds, "if the scribbler's heart, as Kelley affirms, 'directs her pen,' the pen itself conjures up the incestuous 'inner truth' of the directing heart" (181). The above novels themselves, one feels compelled to add, appear to see nothing wrong in such matrimonial arrangements. Still, one must ask: are these "brother" and "sister" marriages necessarily "incestuous"? Legally speaking, of course, they do not fit the definition of incest, hence nothing impedes such marriages.

※ ※ ※

> ...had I a daughter, I would follow a similar course. Give her delicacy, religion, and a proper taste, aided by the unseen influence of a prudent parent's care, and the chances of a woman for happiness would be much greater than they are; and I am entirely of your opinion, "that prevention is at all times better than cure."
> — James Fenimore Cooper, *Precaution*

These didactic words, spoken by the Rev. Dr. Ives, one of the novel's father figures, end *Precaution*—Cooper's first foray into the literary arena—with a text that expressively concerns itself with courtship and marriage. A critic striving to ignore Cooper's woman-centered narratives may claim, as does James D. Wallace in *Early Cooper and His Audience* (1986), that *Precaution* is male centered and that its main character is Denbigh, Emily's suitor, who must undergo several tests to show his true character. Wallace asserts that the novel "is not really 'about' the consequences of improper training. Instead, it is about Denbigh's ability to create himself in the violent transitions to which his author subjects him" (76). Yet Wallace, in his eagerness to include *Precaution* in Cooper's later—and ostensibly more male-oriented—literary *corpus*, fails to see the reasons for and trajectory of Denbigh's development. In doing so, he ignores the fact that Denbigh's trials are there for a specific courtship purpose and that his behavior very much is the result of a superior kind of training. Denbigh appears reactive rather than active; he does not "create himself" as much as he responds to a crisis on the basis of the training he has received from (among others) General Wilson, Mrs. Wilson's late husband. What is at stake for Denbigh is not to prove himself a strong, independent male, but to prove himself worthy of the heroine Emily. Specifically, he has to show himself as a Christian gentleman. *Her* demands for a suitable spouse have to be met, not his. Denbigh has to remove the mysteries surrounding his character—a mistaken identity, suspicion of deceit, and even attempted rape—in order for Emily and, more importantly, her mentor Mrs. Wilson to accept him. He has to prove himself worthy of admission to the domestic world. Ironically, Denbigh creates his own problems: he has, with the help of his relatives the Rev. Dr. and Mrs. Ives, concocted an elaborate masquerade to plumb the depths of the heroine's feelings. His ploy recalls a similar masquerade enacted in Oliver Goldsmith's 1766 novel *The Vicar of Wakefield*. In both works, a suitor arrives incognito to find out if the young lady is attracted to him or to his money. Predictably, the hero barely avoids being hoisted by his own petard: he almost destroys his chances due to problems arising from his assumed identity.

Bearing in mind the conventions of the courtship novel when approaching *Precaution*, we see the degree to which Cooper has succeeded in constructing a markedly woman-centered text. The reader easily recognizes the prudent upper-class heroine, the domestic settings, the didactic tone, and the gendered plot designed to appeal to a female audience. The movement of its main plot, for instance, appears decidedly feminized. Not only is Emily the *de facto* center of the novel, but all the male characters have been pushed out toward the wings. The readers for the most part see the men as they interact *with* the female characters, or they see the men and their actions through the eyes of women characters. The female matrix, then, rules character and plot development: the novel's ultimate concern is to guide the characters to the domestic haven. This is a particular female issue: for a woman, the book argues, the only source of happiness is a good marriage. The novel also attempts to answer a question of special interest to women: how does one go about achieving this important prize? Cooper's text not only calls for an answer, but provides it. According to the narrator, the novel functions as the "unseen influence of a prudent parent's care" (418). It does so by didactically discussing a variety of courtship options.

All Cooper's heroines face a dilemma presumably familiar to his female readers: how to attract the right kind of suitor and take advantage of what Royall Tyler in the 1787 play *The Contrast* had labeled the "main chance." In *Precaution*, Cooper accomplishes this through a strategic doubling. He juxtaposes a number of good and bad courtships and marriages. I.e., they are appropriate (good) or inappropriate (bad) according to societal ideals. Taking his cue from, among others, Jane Austen, Cooper presents a variety of courtships and marriages. In doing so, he deftly challenges both parental involvement in the process—read manipulation—and lack of involvement equally. Either approach has the potential for disaster for the woman. The novel repeatedly asserts a woman's right to choose her spouse and provides the reader with the tools needed to make an informed choice. In this respect, *Precaution* goes a step further than Austen's *Persuasion* where the heroine, Anne Elliot, claims only men have the right to choose; women only have the right to accept or decline the offer.

The novel centers around the Moseley family and the courtship and marriages of its four marriageable children and various relatives; however, neighbors and acquaintances provide examples of good (and especially *bad*) courtships and ensuing marriages as well. Three daughters grace Sir Edward's and Lady Moseley's country estate—Clara, Jane, and Emily—and one son, John, although it is the young women who receive the most attention from the narrator. John is a rather amiable, but shallow, country gentleman, fond of his pointers, hunters, and guns, knowledgeable about hunting and seasons, but clearly lacking a spiritual core. Clara, the eldest, is already engaged to the fledgling minister Francis Ives, typically, a childhood friend. Their relationship appears loving and devoted but rather tame; even the narrator appears to have some doubts as to the depth of their feelings, commenting that their "passion, if so gentle a feeling deserves the term" (6) comes from "an attachment which had grown with their years" (6). However, when the narrative opens, their courtship is already a *fait accompli*; it is therefore not part of Cooper's discussion. Besides, Clara's choice of partner, as well as her docility and malleability, is not due to any principled education but rather, the narrator informs us, somehow damning the arrangement with faint praise, to a certain lack of imagination: "If Clara's weaknesses were less striking than those of Jane, it was because she had less imagination, and that in loving Francis Ives she had so long admired a character, where so little was to be found that could be censured, that she might be said to have contracted a habit of judging correctly, without being able at all times to give a reason for her conduct or her opinions" (13).

This is not the case with the heroine: the reader here realizes the very characteristic that distinguishes Emily from her siblings: she is the only one who has been exposed to what the narrator considers a superior education. This education has not only made her eminently fit for this life and for eternity, it has also — and this is an essential quality in a young woman — enabled her to recognize optimal "husband material" when she encounters it. On the surface, the courtship that Emily and Denbigh conduct appears almost as passionless as the one presented by Clara and Frances Ives: Cooper presents a quiet and above all decorous relationship, emphasizing it is a union of *spiritual* equals. If we read the text as a courtship manual, it provides the following prescription for courtship: the prospective spouses must behave piously, modestly, and decorously and avoid impropriety at all cost. Denbigh and Emily, the text shows, suit one another because they both possess the same qualities. Ironically, although strangers, there is an important connection between the two: they have been shaped by conscientious mentors. In fact, they have been influenced and guided toward adulthood by the partners of another successful relationship: Emily has been molded by her aunt Mrs. Wilson, Denbigh has been trained by his commanding officer, General Wilson, Mrs. Wilson's late husband. Clara, Jane, and John, the other Moseley children, on the other hand, have been under the care of their biological parents and, presumably, the customary nannies and tutors, and therefore have received no such instruction.

In this respect, Sir Edward and Lady Moseley differ noticeably from the parents in *Hobomok*. Where Child lets her heroine's parents recreate the rigidity and lack of understanding to which they themselves have been exposed, Cooper shows parents who, because their own marriage has been successful despite opposition from Sir Edward's family and friends, *refuse* to control or manipulate their children. The narrator observes that objections from friends and "the protracted and inconsequent opposition of his parents had left ... an aversion ... to the exercise of parental authority in marrying their own descendants" (4). Consequently, the Moseleys have become well-meaning but ineffectual parents incapable of instilling proper values in their children; Lady Moseley at the most *encourages* her daughter's interest in the suave Colonel Egerton, who is in line for a baronetcy, but goes no further in securing such a match. In the case of the third sister, Jane, Cooper allows no development of the kind found in Samuel Richardson's *Clarissa*; this well-bred young lady avoids Clarissa's fate. Yet Jane's aborted romance with the villainous Egerton, who as "heir to his uncle, Sir Henry" initially appears to be a good "catch," nevertheless proves disastrous to her. Egerton is, the text reveals, not only a would-be rapist but "the greatest latitudinarian amongst the ladies, of any man in England" (15, 263). Although his pursuit of Jane ends when he elopes with Mary Jarvis, their incipient romance still mars Jane's life. It proves impossible for her to overcome the failed romance. Or rather, Cooper, always opposed to young women who show unsolicited love for a man, cannot allow Jane to rise above the circumstances. Although not unsympathetic to her plight — the perfidious Egerton is hardly the kind of suitor a good pre–Victorian would wish for — he still wants to show the wages of this kind of one-sided attachment: lack of self-worth and perpetual self-reproach. For the duration of the novel, Jane wallows in self-pity and shame; she becomes "reserved and distant to most of her friends" (246). Not only does she cast herself as a victim, but she continues to victimize herself by insisting that her romance with Colonel Egerton makes her unfit to become the wife of a more suitable man.

Cooper is far less inclined to show sympathy for another jilted lady, Caroline Harris, who cavorts through fashionable Bath on an unsuccessful search for a husband and whose antics in the marriage market make her the laughingstock of the fashionable world, the *ton*. Jane, at least, has the good sense to behave with decorum. Miss Harris, on the other hand, flirts frivolously and even stoops to attempting to purchase a suitor, the despicable Captain Jarvis; or rather, she proposes to buy him a baronetcy if he marries her, but to no avail. Cooper knows where to put the blame for her behavior, though, the indiscriminating Miss Harris has always been spoiled by an indulgent father. Again, the fault is the lack of a proper education and of parents who do not understand their responsibilities *vis-à-vis* their children. Since she has not been fortunate enough to have a female mentor like Mrs. Wilson, Miss Harris lacks the knowledge to recognize a suitable spouse in the men surrounding her. She lacks the education and self-awareness necessary not only to make an informed choice, but to make *herself* a suitable choice as well. Modesty and self-control are prerequisites for a marriage, not frivolity and self-abandonment. Miss Harris transgresses notably in the face of this code of behavior, leaving herself open to ridicule and social censure. The emphasis, then, in those of Cooper's works that are most indebted to the courtship novels, is on female mentorship and the inculcation of so-called domestic values. The bases for successful courtships and marriages appear surprisingly simple: modesty and decorum in behavior and similarity in age, rank, religious faith, and interests. This message, often dramatized through juxtaposing "good" and "bad" relationships, he was to repeat in his succeeding works, demonstrating it through choice of characters and plot. Throughout Cooper's literary career, the reader sees these principles at work. *The Spy* and *The Pathfinder*, for example, have strong central female characters and also provide examples of successful and failed courtships for the reader's emulation or avoidance. The success or failure of each courtship depends, in part, upon the heroine's education and upon the extent of parental interference.

Like other writers of courtship novels, Cooper subscribes to the adage that "familiarity breeds contentment," not contempt. Even when he creates lovers without consangual ties to one another, they often turn out to be connected through family-like associations. Colonel Munro and Sergeant Dunham, respectively, see Duncan Heyward and Natty Bumppo almost as sons and, for this reason, find them eminently suited to wed their daughters. *Precaution*'s Emily and Denbigh have been educated by spouses; *The Pioneers*' Elizabeth Temple marries the son and heir of her father's good friend. The ties are even closer in other works: in *Homeward Bound* and *Home as Found*, Eve Effingham meets and marries her cousin Paul; in *Lionel Lincoln*, the hero marries his cousin Cecil; in *The Spy*, Frances Wharton, her cousin Peyton Dunwoodie, and so on. Although strangers, even *Satanstoe*'s Corny and Anneke find that they are distantly related.[10]

The Spy, like *Precaution*, juxtaposes examples of successful and failed courtships, its characters' development and courtship plot closely paralleling those Cooper created for his first novel. In Frances and Sarah Wharton, the reader recognizes Emily and Jane Moseley, whereas Isabella Singleton, Frances's "rival," corresponds to the misguided Miss Harris. Cooper skillfully teaches his "courtship lesson" by delineating the fates of these three women—from the perspective of the women involved. Two of them, Frances and Isabella, are in love with the same man. The text focuses primarily on Frances's, Sarah's, and Isabella's emotions and actions. Peyton Dunwoodie's opinions on the matter hardly enter into the process. He has already chosen Frances and therefore his desires seem of little interest to the narrator. Colonel Wellmere receives similar treatment. Cooper's manipulation of the courtship plots demonstrates his connection to the cult of domesticity: in the "courtship battle" between Frances and Isabella, the values that ultimately secure Frances the "victory," to use Isabella's term, are the ones espoused by the cult. There is no real "battle" between the contenders; instead, Cooper focuses on showing the devastating effect "improper" behavior has on women, regardless of who initiated the courtship process. Yet the reader ought to remember that male demands decide what makes a woman worthy of pursuit: in this novel, the man, not the woman, ultimately becomes the beneficiary of the carefully inculcated domestic values. Although — or perhaps precisely *because*— she is motherless, Frances is the end result of careful female mentoring. Her aunt, Miss Jeanette Peyton (a Mrs. Wilson clone) has been carefully training her young charge to become the kind of woman who will appeal to discerning men, those who will build a democratic society.[11] Ironically, an unmarried woman has imparted this training. Furthermore, as in *Precaution*, the hero must prove himself worthy of the heroine's love: Peyton Dunwoodie has to remove the misunderstandings that raise obstacles between him and his beloved. His military prowess and democratic values are never in doubt; his morals are. The main obstacle to future marital bliss is the suspicion that he is deceitful and interested in somebody else.

Cooper focuses not only on the ideal daughter and the rewards of her virtues; he is even more preoccupied with the wages of sin heaped upon those who fail to live up to the domestic female ideal. One must presume that the elder sister Sarah has benefited from the same training as Frances has. However, in Sarah's case, this instruction clearly has failed: not only are her sympathies with the British, but she cannot recognize a cad when she sees one. There is no genuine reciprocal affinity between the two actors in this drama. When they first meet in the social circles of New York, Colonel Wellmere makes so deep an impression on Sarah that she keeps him in her heart from then on; he experiences no such attraction. To him, she is indistinguishable from other young women he meets; he scarcely remembers her when they meet later at The Locusts. Sheltered as she has been, Sarah might believe she is experiencing a grand passion; the worldly colonel harbors no such illusions. Adding fuel to the fire of infatuation, the ineffectual Mr. Wharton, out of selfishness and fears for his material future, encourages Sarah's emerging relationship with the English officer. Of course, in his relative isolation in the country, Mr. Wharton has no way of knowing that the man he welcomes as a prospective son-in-law is a would-be bigamist and in his own way as great a "latitudinarian" as *Precaution*'s Colonel Egerton. The attachment climaxes in a disastrous wedding scene where Harvey Birch's intervention, combined with an attack by the Skinners, saves Sarah by the skin of her teeth just before the couple take their vows. Birch reveals that the colonel's common-law English wife has arrived in New York and is now looking for him. Only one solution remains for the well-bred eighteenth- (and nineteenth-) century young lady: when Sarah sees Birch's accusation confirmed in her fiancé's features, "the room whirled round, and she fell lifeless into the arms of her aunt" (265). The scenario recalls the outcome of Jane Moseley and Colonel Egerton's romance in *Precaution* but visits an even harsher sentence on the woman involved. Although one can scarcely blame Sarah personally for Wellmere's perfidy — she is at the most guilty of being a poor judge of character — Cooper nevertheless punishes her for her inability to discern her fiancé's true character by relegating her to insanity and lifelong celibacy. The insanity appears almost instantaneously: when she awakens after having fainted at the wedding, she thinks she is in heaven, administered to by angels, not by her sister: "This, then, is heaven — and you are one of its bright spirits.... I had thought the happiness I have lately experienced was too much for earth. But we shall meet again; yes— yes— yes— we shall meet again.... Hush, ... you may disturb his rest — surely, he will follow me to the grave. Think you there can be two wives in the grave? No— no— no; one — one — only one" (275). A twenty-first-century reader recognizes Sarah's retreat into denial: although suffering from severe mental trauma, she clings to her belief in Wellmere's love for her. The reader also notices that Sarah may be in shock; however, this shock has not erased her knowledge of what preceded it. Furthermore, the traumatized young woman fully expects her lover to choose her over his common-law wife and even follow her in death: death will, so to speak, sanctify their union. She represses the memory of the disastrous wedding scene, remembering instead her own immense happiness— it was "too much for earth" — not the unsavory reasons behind its destruction.

Frances's rival, Isabella Singleton, makes the same mistake as *Precaution*'s Miss Harris had made. Due to lack of mentoring — she has grown up in various military installations surrounded by men — she openly pursues the man of her choice, blithely unaware that he fails to reciprocate her attachment. The narrator praises Isabella's beauty; she is "young, and of a light and fragile form, but of exquisite proportions," like any heroine of her day. Yet conventional beauty alone is not enough to attract and keep a man's attention: Cooper manages, with three ordinary words, to foreshadow Isabella's eventual demise: "Her eye was large, full, black, piercing, and at times *a little wild*" (155, emphasis mine). Her wildness proves her undoing. The dying woman confides in Frances, "I was born under a burning sun, and my feelings seem to have imbibed its warmth; I have existed for passion *only*" (294, emphasis mine). Since her forward behavior is wrong according to both the cult of domesticity and the conventions of the courtship novel, the narrator cannot condone her behavior; however, he can deploy her death as a powerful judgment on female passion and lack of self-control. Such impropriety, the novel emphasizes, has its price. Significantly, Isabella, suffering the detrimental effects of lack of solid female mentoring, pleads the most eloquently for this kind of assistance: she sees Dunwoodie's choice of Frances as the result of the younger girl's superior upbringing. Female mentoring, in other words, gives an otherwise equal contender for male attention an indisputable edge. On her deathbed, Isabella comforts herself with this thought. Like Jane Moseley, she considers herself a victim of circumstance, not a participant in her own life; her lack of success in winning Peyton Dunwoodie's affection can be attributed to outside influences, not to any personal lack. This is how she assesses her failure to capture Dunwoodie's heart: "here is the innocent, the justifiable cause. We are both motherless; but that aunt — that mild, plain-hearted, observing aunt, has given you the victory. Oh! how much she loses, who loses a female guardian to her youth. I have exhibited those feelings which you have been taught to repress. After this, can I wish to live?" (295). Interestingly, neither love nor affection enters Isabella's equation; she reduces courtship to a mere matter of cause and effect, or rather, to payment for proper behavior. When looking for a spouse, the right kind of man responds, her words imply, to a specific set of domestic stimuli: modesty and decorum. Only a woman who possesses these qualities, one who has been taught to repress her emotions (at least in public), will receive a man's love and admiration. Isabella, although obviously a devoted sister and daughter, has learned neither self-control nor self-abnegation in the course of her young life. Immodest and willful, she deserves no husband. But the novelist damns her further: he adds sexual awareness and confidence to her lack of decorum. Sure of her own sexual power over men, it simply never enters her mind that Dunwoodie may already be attracted, let alone betrothed, to somebody else. Such unwarranted self-assurance in a woman, the novel opines, must be punished. Yet if Cooper preaches repression of female emotions, he also emphasizes that a successful courtship must be based on reciprocity. Isabella's primary transgression, then, is not only that she has shown her passions openly, but that she has given her heart to a person already in love with someone else. Her punishment is therefore harsher than the one meted out to Miss Harris. As befits the fate of a dramatic woman, the novelist gives her ultimate punishment a notably dramatic — and ironic — flair. In keeping with both her military family tradition and the fact that the event takes place during the Revolutionary War, Isabella is hit by a bullet intended for her admirer Captain Lawton and dies. Yet the dark-haired beauty does not die in vain: the narrator utilizes her death with a vengeance, prolonging her deathbed scene as if to allow her to plead eloquently for female mentoring and domestic values like dependence and self-control: "Woman must be sought to be prized; her life is one of concealed emotions; blessed are they whose early impressions make the task free from hypocrisy, for such only can be happy with men like — like Dunwoodie" (295). What Cooper in *The Prairie* was to call the "master-passion" falls outside Isabella's perception of courtship *mores*. Still, the reader ought to observe that the text does not argue against passion *per se*, but it castigates the woman who shows her passion immodestly, i.e., without knowing whether or not it is reciprocated.

Satanstoe, narrated by the protagonist, Corny Littlepage, makes its domestic intentions clear already in the first chapter. Corny confides in his readers that he has "come to the determination, however feeble it may prove, to preserve some vestiges of household life in New York" (5). He provides domestic details, and also presents several scenes of American courtship rituals: at home calling, visits to the theater, dinner parties, and even an outing by sleigh. All properly chaperoned, of course. The sleigh outing — one of the most dramatic parts in Corny's courtship — ends with Corny reaffirming his position as hero in Anneke's eyes.

His successful courtship of Anneke Mordaunt forms a very important part of this literary effort. Predictably, the two young lovers are appropriately upper class. Corny is the heir to his family's land, and the heroine is the pretty daughter of Herman Mordaunt, "a man of considerable note in the colony," the son of a British major who "had married the heiress of a wealthy Dutch merchant" (50). Mordaunt has "talents, a good education, a very handsome estate ... and is well-connected" both in America and "at home" (77). To complicate courtship matters, Anneke is sought not only by Corny, but also by the suave English officer Major Bulstrode, "the oldest son of a baronet, of three or four thousand a year" (80); he is Anneke's cousin. Bulstrode, realizing Corny's intentions, warns his rival off, explaining that he has the prior claim. Although he has "no reason to believe Anne Mordaunt" prefers him, he has the support he needs. Herman Mordaunt, he explains, "likes my offers of settlement; he likes my family; he likes my rank, civil and military; and I am not altogether without the hope that he likes *me*" (241). However, in proper British upper-class fashion, he does not approach Mr. Mordaunt to offer for her until his father, Sir Harry, has "authorized" the settlement. To Bulstrode, affection is not the key to marital success; wealth and position are. Marriages—an economic union—cannot be left to the vagaries of affection. They are to be determined by men. The father's approval eclipses the daughter's emotions. Ultimately, as is the case with any courtship text, the novel rejects this way of arranging a marriage—Anneke makes her own choice based on her affection and admiration for Corny.

The Spy and *Precaution* aim at reinforcing the cultural demand for female piety, modesty, and decorum by presenting these qualities not as ends in themselves but as means to entice an eligible suitor. Cooper sends the same message in both *Homeward Bound* and *Home as Found*: female piety, modesty and decorum are more important than beauty when it comes to a man's choice of spouse. Eve, "polished and courteous" (*HF* 5), is so accomplished that she "could become the wife of a gentleman only" (*HF* 300). The novels' two upper-class courtships demonstrate this important lesson: Eve Effingham's and Grace van Cortland's suitors, Paul Powis and Sir George Templemore, respectively, are attracted as much to the women's *behavior* as to their *physical attributes*. More importantly, Cooper makes both young women—and their lovers—paragons of modesty and decorum; all four always behave like proper ladies and gentlemen, conscientiously avoiding placing themselves in compromising situations. Neither man, for instance, proposes until he knows the woman's feelings, nor is he alone with her before the moment of proposing. The narrator grants them some *reprieve*, though: Grace and Sir George are left alone by accident, "as much as design," on the day he "poured out his love in a language that her unpractised and already favorably disposed feelings had no means of withstanding" (*HF* 298). Similarly, Eve and Paul, despite "a secret sympathy" for one another, have not been alone "under circumstances that admitted of an uninterrupted confidential conversation" until the moment of Paul's proposal of marriage (*HF* 320–21).

However, not satisfied with showing how ladies and gentlemen conduct their courtships, Cooper juxtaposes their decorous behavior to that of the upstart Aristabulus Bragg who proposes to Eve as soon as they are alone—completely overlooking Eve's coldness toward him. Bragg, Cooper shows, is attracted to Eve's fortune, not her domestic and spiritual qualities. Whereas he leaves Paul's and Sir George's proposals of marriage to the reader's imagination, Cooper gleefully reproduces Bragg's indelicate offer of marriage to emphasize the man's churlishness and incompatibility with the sophisticated Eve. The proposal is the height of inappropriate behavior:

> Ah! Miss Eve, such another opportunity may never occur again, for your foreign ladies are so difficult of access! Let me then seize

> this happy moment here, beneath the hymeneal oaks, to offer
> you this faithful hand and this willing heart. Of fortune you will
> have enough for both, and I say nothing about the miserable
> dross. Reflect, Miss Eve, how happy we might be, protecting and
> soothing the old age of your father, and in going down the hill
> of life in company; or, as the song says, "And hand in hand we'll
> go, and sleep thegither at the foot, John Anderson, my Jo" [300].

Eve responds to Bragg's proposal as befits a lady assured of her own self-worth: the man is so far beneath her that she cannot take the offer seriously.[12] And, although Bragg claims similarity in age and habits, Eve calmly rejects this claim. When Bragg asserts that "Our ages are perfectly suitable, our dispositions entirely consonant, our habits so similar as to obviate all unpleasant changes, and our fortunes precisely what they ought to be to render a marriage happy, with confidence on one side, and gratitude on the other," Eve coolly observes that they are "sufficiently different" for Bragg not to see the impropriety in his behavior toward her (301). Furthermore, in keeping with the advice given to young ladies placed in a similar situation, Eve gives her suitor an answer "as distinct as the proposal. I decline the advantage and happiness of becoming your wife, sir" (301).[13] So polite is her rejection, though, that Bragg feels "considerably encouraged" (302). However, Cooper allows Bragg to succeed in finding a wife — as soon as he lowers his sights toward a person on his own level. He proceeds to propose to Eve's French maid Annette, who accepts, perceiving it to be "a legitimate means of bettering her condition in life" (430). A woman, then, can marry "above" her station; a man cannot. Although this courtship affirms the demand of equality in choice of spouse, Cooper still provides this lower-class variant of the courtship plot with a negative touch: Bragg proposes to Annette only as a last resort; she accepts for ulterior reasons, not because of any affection for the uncouth Bragg.

The two last of the Leatherstocking tales, *The Pathfinder* and *The Deerslayer*, written in 1840 and 1841, respectively, rely heavily on the conventions of the courtship novel for character and plot development, but they also have distinctly different courtship plots. *The Pathfinder*, in particular, argues forcefully for a woman's right to choose, explicitly rejecting paternal manipulation. Yet the novel shows the daughter's difficulties in asserting herself vis-à-vis paternal desires and self-interest, and it demonstrates how much gratitude may influence a woman's choice of spouse. *The Pathfinder* ought rightfully to have been called *The Courtship of Mabel Dunham*, since this is the basis for all of the novel's events. At the center of the courtship plot is the pretty, vivacious, and adventurous Mabel, or "Magnet," as her doting uncle Cap calls her, "in allusion to his niece's personal attractions" (9). Ironically, the sailor expects his niece to be oblivious to the implications of this significant epithet. But Mabel is not merely physically appealing, she also satisfies, albeit rather circuitously, the courtship novel's demands for appropriate — i.e., middle-class— social standing. Despite her rather humble origins as the daughter of a non-commissioned officer, the narrator emphasizes she is superior to other young women of her class. This is not entirely a chance occurrence, however; her "natural character" has been improved by a certain measure of female instruction: "she had been taught much more than was usual for young women in her own station in life; and in one sense certainly, she did credit to her teaching" (109). Under the tutelage of the "widow of a field-officer who formerly belonged to the same regiment as her.... She had lost the less refined habits and manners of one in her original position, without having quite reached a point that disqualified her for the situation in life that the accidents of birth and fortune would probably compel her to fill. All else that was distinctive and peculiar in her belonged to natural character" (109). Here the narrator illuminates the class- and gender-based inequity in colonial education: Mabel has been educated beyond what is customary for women and for someone of her social class. The text also registers a certain ambiguity as regards education: on the one hand, education appears a benefit; on the other, it might prove a detriment — at least for the lower classes— too much education will make the educated person unfit for his or her lot in life.

Four men show considerable interest in the attractive woman: Natty Bumppo, the only suitor condoned and encouraged by her father; the dastardly Quarter Master Muir, discouraged from pursuing her not only by his superior Major Duncan but also by the wives of the other officers at the fort; the treacherous Indian Arrowhead; and the young sailor Jasper Western, the one who succeeds in winning the girl, although not entirely on his own merit. Cooper presents courtship "case histories," clearly distinguishing between "proper" and "improper" forms and providing his readers with models to emulate. Utilizing comparisons, the text repeatedly emphasizes that certain basic demands have to be met in order to secure a successful marriage; when three of the four suits fail, they do so because they fail Cooper's courtship litmus test — equality in all areas. Natty Bumppo, albeit — as all readers of Cooper's Leatherstocking tales by then knew — a skilled woodsman and a man of the utmost integrity and "scarcely in the prime of life" (15), is clearly too old and unsophisticated for the young woman. Muir, with four marriages under his belt, is both too old and too experienced. He is also of higher military rank than her sergeant father. The Tuscarora Arrowhead is the wrong race. All these characteristics are disqualifying factors in Cooper's books: birds of a feather flock together in all his aviaries. Similar age, similar social rank, similar faith, and similar values are indispensable demands which will guarantee future happiness. No December–May marriages occur in any of Cooper's plots although both Sergeant Dunham and Muir argue for them. According to the latter, no man is ever too old to marry a young woman: "there is such a thing as a husband's being too old for a wife" (159). However, Muir clearly does not see himself as an "older man" vis-à-vis Mabel; he is merely in his "middle age" and therefore eminently suited to guide a young woman. He relentlessly presses his suit, arguing, "The happiest marriages are those in which youth and beauty and confidence on one side rely on the sagacity, moderation, and prudence of years" (159). Ironically, Muir comes across as sorely lacking in all these areas.

In *The Pathfinder*, Cooper adds a new dimension to his treatment of Natty Bumppo, titillating the reader with the possibility of a marriage for his woodsman, although the only suitable wife for a man with his lifestyle would have been an Indian one.[14] Mabel, for all her domestic ability and love of the outdoors, clearly would not do. Natty knows this and tries to explain the circumstance to her scheming father, but without success. Although he loves Mabel, he also sees insurmountable obstacles. One such obstacle is what the twentieth-century reader recognizes as an inferiority complex: Natty considers himself "beneath her in idees"; furthermore, he is "a poor ignorant woodsman, after all" (129–30). Another obstacle is the question of reciprocity; Natty correctly fears Mabel may disagree with her father's choice: "the daughter may not be so likely to view a plain, ignorant hunter as favorably as the father does" (132). Their different backgrounds obliterate even a superficial similarity in social rank. Natty, acutely aware of his own "worthlessness," muses: "Mabel and I are so nearly alike that I feel weighed down with a load that is hard to bear, at finding us so unlike" (130–1). He voices all his misgivings to Sergeant Dunham only to be won over by his friend's persuasive argument that Mabel really *wants* to marry him. Cooper expends much energy on presenting Natty as a would-be lover, showing that even the sensible Pathfinder has a longing for a home and for someone to come home to. It is almost as if he has his character experience a midlife crisis: marrying Mabel is his last chance to acquire his own family and domestic happiness. The sergeant, whom the reader by now knows has his own personal welfare at heart as much as he has his daughter's, is a master manipulator, cleverly hinting to Natty about Mabel's love for him — "the girl as much as told me so herself" (131). The operative phrase here is "as much as told me so herself"; the sergeant twists

Mabel's words to entice Natty. Such arguments, presented to a romantically very inexperienced — and infatuated — lover by an old friend, clearly work. Of course, as the earlier Leatherstocking tales all had presented Natty as a confirmed bachelor, there is only one outcome. Still, Cooper dangles the prospect of a possible marriage for his hero in front of his readers' eyes.

Yet Cooper has disqualified the Pathfinder for another reason than eternal bachelorhood: Mabel does not love him the way a woman should love a prospective husband. Of course, she is hardly indifferent to him; however, she feels gratitude and respect but not love. Already from the first meeting with Natty and Jasper Western in the forest, she is drawn to the younger man, whom she ultimately marries. Meeting Natty with "steadfastness," she has a different reaction to his young companion: "when her eyes encountered those of the young man at the fire, they fell before the gaze of admiration with which she saw, or fancied she saw, he greeted her." Then the narrator adds, foreshadowing the ultimate outcome of the meeting: "Each, in truth, felt that interest in the other, which similarity of age, condition, mutual comeliness, and their novel situation would be likely to inspire in the young and ingenuous" (16). However, the novel's courtship drama involves no confrontation between rivals, or even the faintest hint of rivalry: the loser always yields respectfully in Cooper.

Mabel's struggle with herself adds poignancy to Cooper's characterization. Although not openly defiant, the fact that she even entertains thoughts that differ noticeably from her father's is rebellious in itself. And Mabel does not give in without at least an internal struggle: the working of her mind records her personal — and opposing — preferences even when she is subordinating her desires to those of her father. Still, the good daughter always has her parent's well-being at heart, regardless of parental manipulation and self-interest. Several scenes in the book show Mabel pondering her situation and, despite her love for Jasper, ultimately yielding to her fathers demands: "to render him happy there was no proper sacrifice which she was not ready to make.... Trained like a woman to subdue her most ardent feelings, her thoughts reverted to her father, and to the blessings that awaited the child who yielded to a parent's wishes. 'Father,' she said quietly, almost with a holy calm.... 'I will marry whomever you desire'" (311–12).

Cooper further complicates the courtship plot by giving Mabel — and everybody else for that matter — knowledge of Jasper's feelings toward her. Combined with the fact that no Cooper heroine gives her heart to someone without knowing that the other person reciprocates, one can see Mabel's quandary and her unwilling submission to her father's wishes.

Filial love and obedience speak here, not personal preference: Mabel's only concern is to "render him happy" by sacrificing her own happiness on the matrimonial altar. It is Natty himself who finally releases Mabel from the promise her dying father extracted from her. Here Cooper chooses a conclusion quite consistent with Natty's character: he puts the welfare of others before his own. This is also very much the way Child's Hobomok behaves when he divorces Mary and disappears into the forest. Besides, Cooper had already, in the earlier Leatherstocking tales, committed himself to a celibate Natty Bumppo and has to extricate his character from romantic entanglements. A marriage would chain him to a family and to domesticity but would destroy his function as a facilitator of cultures and civilizations.

The Pathfinder, then, qualifies as a courtship novel in that it not only discusses courtship *mores* but also asserts a woman's right to follow her own heart. It forcefully rejects parental involvement in choice of spouse but also shows how manipulative and persuasive parental involvement can be. Although the novel appears to promote a woman's right to choose, it also discusses how difficult it is for an obedient girl to withstand paternal directives, especially if these directives take the form of a deathbed wish.

As far as courtships are concerned, *The Deerslayer* truly holds a special place among Cooper's novels. The work not only shows Natty's coming of age through the killing of his first enemy; it also shows his coming of age in a different manner: interwoven into the plot is Natty's first courtship. Yet Cooper, so often formulaic in his approach, suddenly surprises his reader. Where he in *The Pathfinder* had posited Natty Bumppo as an initially hesitant, but then very willing, suitor, in *The Deerslayer*, he reverses the scenario. He presents Natty as the *object* of courtship; at long last, Natty has, as Grossman has observed, "achieved the hero's right to be the object of love" (148), albeit a very reluctant one. Throughout the work, the attractive Judith Hutter eagerly pursues the hero; however, the negative outcome of her quest is a given.[15] Cooper's casting of Natty in female position underscores his androgynous characteristics. He is kind, religious, and self-effacing (all characteristics typical of the ideal nineteenth-century woman); these qualities set him apart from the other men in the novel and make him the novel's moral center. *His* are the only worthwhile opinions, *his* behavior the standard for moral conduct. Physically, the text presents him in near feminine terms: like many a nineteenth-century heroine he is "light and slender," his face expressing "guileless truth, sustained by an earnestness of purpose and a sincerity of feeling that rendered it remarkable" (20–21). In fact, Cooper uses rather similar terms to describe Judith's younger sister Hetty. Harry March, another contender for Judith's favors, claims Deerslayer is "young and thoughtless" (25); again, these are terms often used about women. Furthermore, the text shows that Natty is more "attuned" to women; he "knows how to esteem and treat" them (63). His attitude appears as a novelty to Judith, making him almost irresistible; he is, she tells him, "the first man I ever met who did not seem to wish to flatter — to wish my ruin — to be an enemy in disguise" (98). Such a man is worthy of pursuit; he is a trophy worth fighting for and displaying for others to envy. Judith, displaying a much more active female role in courtships than other Cooper heroines, asserts: "The girl that finally wins you, Deerslayer, will at least win an honest heart, one without treachery or guile; and that will be a victory that most of her sex ought to envy" (140). Based on prior experience, Judith correctly evaluates her own chances of emerging victorious — and resents her own assessment: her face has "a resentful frown on it; while a bitter smile lingered around a mouth that derangement of the muscles could render anything but handsome" (140). Judith wants other women to envy her; she wants a "trophy husband." Aware of her own worth, she does not want to be only "the plaything of an idle hour," but "an equal and a friend" to her lover (161).

The Deerslayer's courtship plot works itself out in a circular motion: Harry March, "Hurry Harry," chases the attractive Judith, although he finds her a little too flighty; Judith chases Natty who rejects her because of her tainted past and her lack of decorum. Natty, on his side, is drawn to the more simpleminded Hetty, who reminds him of his mother and who in her turn loves Harry. Critics, for instance Joyce Warren, have chastised Cooper for his treatment of Judith, but despite his admiration for her courage and ingenuity she is clearly not nineteenth-century marriage material.[16] Nina Baym has pointed out that the Hutter sisters are "unmarriageable" because they are illegitimate; they are tainted by their parents', and especially their mother's, sins and therefore lack the proper family background to contract a marriage.[17] However, other characteristics also disqualify them in the marriage market: Hetty, for all her piety and domesticity, has mental flaws, repeatedly stressed in the text; Judith, for all her beauty, strength, and intelligence, fails not only due to her moral flaws but just as much to her lack of nineteenth-century "domestic" values. "Vanity" and "self-love," not the mandatory selflessness, characterize Judith (161).[18] The denouement of the courtship plot — Deerslayer's rejection of Judith — makes the most sense if we read the novel in the context of ideal nineteenth-century female behavior.

In The Deerslayer, then, Judith has to prove herself worthy of Deerslayer, just as the hero in other courtship novels has to prove himself worthy of the heroine. She fails miserably, primarily because she has no idea of how to behave in a manner that meets with male approbation, or at least not in a manner that can show her as potential wife. Besides, Natty considers her "sworn" to Harry March, although, as we learn, this is March's and Hutter's, not Judith's, idea of their relationship. She not only forcefully asserts her right to choose and acts out her choice, but, by openly professing her interest in Deerslayer, she violates two of Cooper's demands for a successful courtship. First, love has to be reciprocal; and second, no decent girl may declare her love without knowing the recipient's feelings for her. Furthermore, her interest in Natty stems from pride, not from love. Deerslayer's failure to respond to her charms "piqued the pride of the girl and gave him an interest that another, seemingly more favored by nature, might have failed to excite" (161).

As Cooper in *The Pathfinder* had presented the traits that disqualified three of Mabel's four suitors, he in *The Deerslayer* provides a series of examples of Judith's lack of suitability. Although she in many ways is Cooper's strongest and most resourceful heroine, she is also hopelessly flawed morally. Cooper, the reader knows, was first and foremost a moralist intent on conveying what he considered indispensable moral values, in this case through Deerslayer. Ironically, although he presents Natty's superior moral qualities as much as a result of a beneficial nature as of Moravian principles, Judith, for the most part raised in an equally beneficial nature, on the beautiful Lake Glimmerglass (Lake Otsego) and by her apparently religious mother, has the manners and values of a tainted civilization, a civilization from which Deerslayer recoils. She might possess extraordinary *external* beauty, but she is divorced from *inner* beauty, i.e., from natural moral purity.[19] Throughout the novel, Cooper focuses on Judith's shortcomings *vis-à-vis* the domestic ideal of the time. He highlights her interest in finery and personal beauty and emphasizes her lack of consideration for the feelings of others. Words like "self-control" and "self-abnegation" have no place in Judith's vocabulary; neither have "passivity" and "domesticity." Yet by creating a woman so at odds with the nineteenth-century domestic ideals, Cooper has contrived to create a perfect foil for Deerslayer's possession of these qualities; Judith is "a means for the glorification and purification of Leatherstocking" (Davis 20). In this reversal of the traditional courtship novel, there can be no joining of hero and heroine; no marriage can bring the plot to a close. Cooper, then, again affirms his view of marriage and physical and spiritual compatibility, rejecting the possibility of marriage if there is no mutual love, or if the heroine or hero fails to live up to the prescribed moral standards. He also clearly rejects a more active role for the woman in a courtship.

The novel is remarkable in another manner as well: it is the first example of a truly Native American romance in American literature. The whole reason for Natty Bumppo's presence on Lake Glimmerglass is that he and his friend Chingachgook, "the best of loping red-skins ... respected ... but of a fallen race, and belonging to a fallen people" (33–34), are to rendezvous by the lake, by "a small round rock, near the foot of the lake, where ... the tribes are given to resorting to make their treaties, and to bury their hatchets" (23). From there the two will infiltrate the Huron camp to free Wah-ta!-Wah, Chingachgook's betrothed, from Mingo captivity and the threat of an enforced marriage. Again, Cooper adheres to his principles of spiritual and physical compatibility: the two are clearly well suited. Both have the same faith and gifts and similar "social" background. Chingachgook, whom Natty describes as "a comely Injin" and "much look'd upon and admired by the young women of his tribe, both on account of his family and on account of himself" (138), is a young chief. Wah-ta!-Wah, his betrothed, is "the rarest gal among the Delawares, and the most sought a'ter and craved for a wife, by all the young warriors of the nation" (138). Of course, both are appealing physical specimens as well: Wah-ta!-Wah is an Indian beauty, "whose smile was sunny as Judith's in her brightest moments, whose voice was melody itself, and whose accents and manner had all the rebuked gentleness that characterizes the sex among a people, who habitually treat their women as the attendants and the servitors of the warriors" (174). The narrator confides that "the original owners of the country were not unlike their more civilized successors, *nature* appearing to have bestowed that delicacy of mien and outline that forms so great a charm in the youthful female, but of which they are so early deprived; and that, too, as much by the habits of domestic life, as from any other source" (174–75). In other words, Wah-ta!-Wah is the Native American version of the *ingénue* familiar from domestic fiction. She is also intelligent, and "having succeeded in lulling their [her captors'] suspicions, was permitted to wander around the encampment" (175). Chingachgook is, according to his lover, a "bold and handsome warrior" (176), and the narrator — and Wah-ta!-Wah — repeatedly stresses his courage and deployment of his natural gifts, such as the honor that comes from taking an enemy's scalp, "scalp make his honor" (177).

Cooper's "courtship novels" affirm the author's abiding interest in middle-class domesticity. In his feminized texts, Cooper repeatedly places women at the center of his plots and focuses on female concerns, such as the search for a suitable spouse. Significantly, the heroine's demands had to be met if marriage was to be an option; the hero had to live up to her moral standards. Furthermore, Cooper, like the women who wrote similar texts, advocates a companionate relationship based on love. He also promotes equality in age, rank, wealth, and interests as prerequisites for a successful relationship. By creating strong, moral women who marry the men of their choice, Cooper asserts a woman's right to choose and forcefully rejects the notion of parental manipulation in the courtships of their children. In doing so, he deliberately challenges nineteenth-century family rule. More importantly, his use of the conventions of the courtship novel explicitly links him to the pervasive woman-centered domestic ideals of his day, what I have termed "the cult of domesticity." These ideals Cooper credited with civilizing the frontier.

2

The Domestic Matrix

If there is harmony in the home
There will be order in the nation
If there is order in the nation
There will be peace in the world.

— Scottish Blessing

Each family is a world in miniature; and all the necessary trials of the temper and of the character, are usually found within its circle.
— William A. Alcott, *The Young Woman's Guide*, 1840

...individual families are the building blocks out of which the larger units of social organization are fashioned.
— John Demos, *Past, Present, and Personal: The Family and Life Course in American History*, 1986

The United States of the nineteenth century was a nation in flux. Geographically, the young republic expanded its land mass from the Atlantic to the Pacific, from the Gulf of Mexico to the Great Lakes. The nation's population spread, first beyond the Appalachian Mountains, then beyond the Mississippi River and on westward. The migrants sought a better life for themselves and their families than they had known either on the eastern seaboard or in Europe. Migrations, though, often meant a sundering of traditional family ties. Adventurous men and women left parents and other family behind and sought their own personal future far from their native soil. Due to this development, "family" increasingly came to mean parents and children. The extended family, with several generations living together under one roof, became less common.

The nation also transformed in other ways: the decades leading up to the Civil War saw the beginnings of the Industrial Revolution, a phenomenon which would eventually lead to the separation of place of work and home, thereby neatly dividing the American society into a public and a private sphere and profoundly changing the nation's view of how it saw the family, family interaction, and the home. As John Demos asserts, in the early decades of the nineteenth century, "American family life acquired an extremely sharp image" (30).[1] The new nation needed a *new* kind of family, an institution that would provide a measure of harmony and balance and contribute to the nation's physical, industrial, and moral growth, and reformers of many kinds strove vehemently to accomplish this goal.

For my own discussion, the most interesting result of this demand for a new kind of family is the cult of domesticity, a set of ideas which from 1820 to 1860 was instrumental in shaping the idea of "family" in the modern sense of the term and whose impact could be felt in fiction and non-fiction alike. The conventions of this cult solidified the image of the modern (i.e., "nuclear") family, positing its version of this institution as the only stable element in a rapidly changing — and exceedingly competitive — industrial and commercial world. The family, over the preceding centuries taken more or less as a given, was now viewed more self-consciously, its functions and dynamics more clearly defined, its family members' roles delineated and differentiated. Striving to establish a bulwark against what they considered malignant societal forces, concerned clergy, educators, and domestic writers created a powerful myth: a myth that presented — but also constructed — a highly idealized view of the family, a persuasive myth of origin. The myth still exists as seen in our nostalgic longing for an unattainable ideal, a golden past: a stable and nurturing family founded on solid old-fashioned "family values." Large segments of the American population, Demos asserts, "appear still to believe that there is some ideal state of domestic life which we have tragically lost" (Demos 30). No wonder, then, that we, as inhabitants of a world even more unstable than that of the nineteenth century, seek for more peaceful, uncomplicated times and look for them in our imagined domestic origins. Faced with the grim reality of domestic violence, child abuse, and dysfunction, as well as crime, social and political upheaval, torture, and wars whenever we consult the media, we create fictions to cover what we perceive as our own failures. For instance, we still maintain that the domestic violence and child abuse reported must be "unnatural," implying that family relations were more "natural," i.e., more harmonious, earlier. Yet in romanticizing and mythologizing nineteenth-century family life, we blithely overlook the fact that *we*, like our ancestors, perpetuate a utopian domestic *myth*, taking advice literature and fiction at face value, as descriptive rather than prescriptive texts. The domestic myth of origin we still cling to is firmly rooted in the nineteenth-century cult of domesticity.

Seemingly more matriarchal than patriarchal, the cult of domesticity presented a restructuring of family life and a redistribution of parental control from the father to the mother, as the middle-class father spent his days at his place of work. As Nancy Cott notes, "the emphasis placed on and agencies attributed to the family unit were new, and the importance given to women's roles as wives, mothers, and mistresses of households was unprecedented" (2). As this family philosophy was new, connected to this cult and promoting its values from the 1820s onward was a canon of writings—novels, advice books, sermons, and magazine articles—aimed at shaping male and female attitudes towards family and society.[2] Major nineteenth-century writers, among them James Fenimore Cooper, Lydia Maria Child, Catharine Maria Sedgwick, Susan Warner, and Maria Cummins, reacted consciously to the cult's prescriptions, deploying the cult's conventions to shape characters and plots. This created a peculiar tension in their works. While ostensibly adhering faithfully to a particular set of cultural signifiers, these writers through woman-centered narratives and truncated family constructs managed to simultaneously *fashion* and *critique* the emerging middle-class American family. Although the authors cunningly cloaked their ideas in conventional garb, their works can be seen as strikingly subversive.

✳ ✳ ✳

> If anything from the pen of the writer of these romances is at all to outlive himself, it is, unquestionably, the series of "The Leather-Stocking Tales."
> —James Fenimore Cooper, 1851

James Fenimore Cooper's assessment of his future reputation, as seen in this excerpt from his preface to the 1851 edition of *The Leather Stocking Tales*, has proved uncannily astute. Many readers—scholars included—base their evaluation of Cooper's writing almost exclusively on these tales, among the first "American" fictional epics. Cooper may indeed have heavily mined this "original" American ore, but in both quantity and quality there is more to his literary output than Natty Bumppo's adventures in the American wilderness. More importantly, all Cooper's fictional works, disparate as they may appear temporally and spatially,[3] express the writer's complex moral philosophy; they are, as Donald Ringe has observed, "remarkably unified in the moral vision of life" (7). Central to this vision, which fueled Cooper's fiction and non-fiction alike, is the preoccupation with domesticity, family dynamics, and the home.

Furthermore, Cooper aims not merely to *entertain*; his primary objective is always to *instruct*. Eager to promote an American society based on democratic values, he insists on families as the building blocks of this sociopolitical edifice. When Cooper through his novels lectures on manners, he does it through demonstrating how democratic values — or their absence — manifest themselves in the emerging American character. He does so not only through the solitary woodsman Natty Bumppo but through his representations of the American family, consistently working out his ideas within a specific social matrix, a matrix provided by the cult of domesticity.

Cooper's representations of middle-class American domesticity become especially intriguing when we consider that his total literary career, from the 1820 *Precaution* to the 1851 *The Way of the Hour*, falls within the parameters of the heyday of this domestic cult. His literary output amply demonstrates that the cult had a profound and inescapable impact on Cooper himself. By focusing on domestic issues and utilizing plots familiar from courtship novels and sentimental domestic novels, albeit mostly in a decidedly non-traditional domestic setting, Cooper positioned himself within the canon of texts which served to reinforce the ideological underpinnings of the cult of domesticity.

The cult not only elevated woman to the rank of man's moral superior, it credited her with *national* importance. One of Cooper's contemporaries, Arthur Freeling, in *The Young Bride's Book* (1830), observes "Home duties are the peculiar duties of woman, and are those in which she shines pre-eminently, and from the execution of which she derives her highest influence" (29). This influence stretched beyond the front door. "Even statesmen," Freeling states, "have owed some of their finest bursts of eloquence — their most lucid reasonings, to the influence of a superior wife" (35). Josiah G. Holland, writing as "Timothy Titcomb," succinctly summarizes the cult's view of the mother's importance: "The foundation of our national character is laid by the mothers of the nation" (200–1).[4] Furthermore, the wife had a decisive influence on her husband's spirituality. Magazines such as *Godey's Lady's Book* projected this image, stating that, "The perfection of womanhood ... is the wife and mother, the center of the family, the magnet that draws man to the domestic altar and makes him a civilized being, a social Christian. The wife is truly the light of the home" (Qtd. in Green 56). But what twenty-first-century readers tend to overlook is that the canon of domesticity, promoted through sermons, novels, essays, and poems, simultaneously *created* and *perpetuated* this ruling domestic myth — it *prescribed* certain roles and behaviors it considered beneficial.

James Fenimore Cooper, eager to help shape his country's morals and manners, enthusiastically participated in the creative process through fiction and non-fiction alike, through characterizations and plot development. Central to his work, Donald Darnell asserts in his discussion of Cooper as a novelist of manners, is his "abiding concern with social purpose" (ix). This concern remains as a constant throughout Cooper's literary career. Even when the author lifted the action of his novels out of the drawing room, the parlor, or the kitchen and placed it in the forests or on the seas, the underlying assumptions prevailed: home was a sanctuary, a bulwark against the encroaching outside world, and women were its keepers and moral core. Since Cooper in every respect "took from contemporary fiction whatever plot devices seemed useful to him" (Ringe 94), the domestic scenes and plots deployed in his works need to be put into this specific woman-centered context. Cooper's families have to be held up to the Victorian ideal of the family, as exemplified in advice literature and in texts by, among others, Catharine Maria Sedgwick and Lydia Maria Child. Like Cooper, these women were popular writers placing their characters in frontier settings, and, like him, they authored a species of fictional "guidance books," providing their readers with models for proper moral and spiritual behavior. Cooper's representations of family life also align him with authors like Susan Warner and Maria Cummins. Like Cooper, they all shaped their texts—even subversive ones—according to the conventions prescribed and eagerly advocated by the proponents of the cult of domesticity.

To fully understand Cooper's literary and cultural accomplishment, his works must be put into this particular domestic matrix: they must be compared to the domestic philosophy of his day and to the works of women writers of domestic fiction. One must, so to speak, enter Cooper's world and simultaneously enter the world of the mother. Or, as is often the case with nineteenth-century texts, the reader must enter a world deliberately constructed to fulfill the conventions of the cult of domesticity yet for the most part devoid of actual mothers. Cooper, "writing about American manners and attitudes at the very period in which they were undergoing a profound change" (Grossman 22), readily dispenses with the supposed indispensable core of the cult. Leslie Fiedler's comment, therefore, that Cooper subscribed "literally" to the cult's tenets, yet at the same time revenged himself upon women, offers an intriguing perspective.[5] As I will demonstrate, Cooper's vision of the family is far from idealized; he is far too conscious of domesticity's dark side to create an idyll. His families often are amputated and markedly "dysfunctional" to critical modern eyes. His is a world of weak, ineffectual fathers and more often than not absent mothers; he shows parents as incapable of creating a nurturing and safe environment for their offspring. This brings a particular question to light: how can a new society be built on such imperfect ground, leveling or democratic as it might appear? Cooper argues for a democratic society established through marriage and domesticity. In particular, he appears to focus on a new kind of woman, one better qualified to raise democratic daughters and sons than the stereotypical mother of the cult of domesticity. He does not create women that today's feminist would consider strong, independent role models[6] because he knew the social reality of his audience well and was himself part of it. Characters that were too new and revolutionary might not invite the same reader identification and response — i.e., emulation — or as brisk sales as more conventional and familiar characters would.

In order to evaluate Cooper's representations of nineteenth-century American domesticity, then, the reader has to move beyond the notion that Cooper's world is one of "Solitary Man and Superfluous Woman" (Warren 91).[7] My reading strategy reveals Cooper's ambiguous relationship to the cult of domesticity: his is, in fact, a world of "Social Men and Indispensable Women." And while he consistently moves his heroines and heroes toward matrimony and domesticity, he just as consistently challenges, even subverts, the prescribed norms for Victorian family life.

※ ※ ※

> It is at home, where man ... seeks a refuge from the vexations and embarrassments of business, an enchanting repose from exertion, a relaxation from care by the interchange of affection: where some of his finest sympathies, tastes, and moral and religious feelings are formed and nourished — where is the treasury of pure disinterested love, such as is seldom found in the busy walks of a selfish and calculating world.
> —1827 address on female education, New Hampshire.[8]

The above statement, taken from an address on *female* education but appropriately delivered by a man, neatly encapsulates the controlling conventions of the cult of domesticity — and its ultimate goal. It juxtaposes the two different spheres of society, the public and the private one, and it posits the affectionate marriage as a counterbalance and corrective to the pernicious influence of the world of business. Significantly, the speaker opines that the home functions to satisfy *male* needs: women are expected to provide "man" with a "refuge" from business-related problems. They are also expected to stimulate his mind and religious sensibility. Yet to him the home is only an escape. The family is part of but never his whole existence; he seeks and finds self-fulfillment in the outside world. In the words of a young law student of 1820: "it is upon his *employment* that he depends almost entirely for the happiness of his life" (Qtd. in Cott 79, my emphasis). Job satisfaction is everything. For the middle- and upper-class woman, on the other hand, the only means of self-realization and happiness lies in the home: her husband and family constitute *her* whole existence, the goal toward which her life is directed. She, the commencement address implies, has no needs of her own. That is, her only non-familial activity came in the form of close female friends.[9]

Many writers sought to camouflage this reality, insisting that the separation of spheres was a boon to women and encouraging the societal division. Within the walls of the home, they were safe from the pollution of the "busy and calculating world." Sarah Josepha Hale, then editor of the Boston *Ladies' Magazine*, in the January 1830 issue echoes this concern when she urges her readers to "keep our women and children from the contagion as long as possible" (42, qtd. in Cott 68). The world of commerce was an infectious disease only the walls of the home could keep at bay. Yet proponents of the cult did not challenge the modern organization of work and the pursuit of financial success. They were aware, as Mary P. Ryan observes, that "structural changes in the household, economics, and class were entangled with the idiosyncratic episodes of evangelism and reform" (15).[10] Instead of sharply denouncing the rampant industrialization and commercialization taking place in the United States, they strove to temper the male sphere, inoculating the *paterfamilias* against societal and occupational "disease." After all, the husband's financial success was needed to uphold the ultimate goal: the support and preservation of the domestic *sanctum*.

The controlling convention of the cult of domesticity was the contrast between the home and the world. Often, its defenders described the home in biblical terms: it was an "oasis in the desert," a "sanctuary," and a place where "disinterested love is ready to sacrifice everything at the altar of affection" (Cott 66–67). The cult demanded a lopsided arrangement: only *women* were expected to sacrifice everything at this particular altar, whereas men received the blessings for this. Implicit in the popular convention of two opposing societal spheres was the belief that the world of industrialism, commerce, and politics had the ability to corrupt its people. Cott asserts that writers of domestic works, especially the women writers, "denigrated business and politics as arenas of selfishness, exertion, embarrassment, and degradation of soul" (Cott 67). This writing strategy should come as no surprise: business and politics were the two arenas to which women had no access. Ironically, the cult offered job opportunities for women in the world outside the home as journalists, writers, and teachers, thereby recruiting them to uphold a system that discriminated against their gender.

The cult of domesticity was, as promulgated through nineteenth-century novels, magazines, advice books, and sermons, primarily an urban, Northern, middle-class phenomenon, contingent on the growth of the middle class during and after the Industrial Revolution.[11] Yet the cult was not limited to the United States. Industrialization was the key: western Europe felt its impact as surely as America did. This middle-class ideology expressed "a cultural preference for domestic retirement and conjugal-family intimacy over both the 'vain' and fashionable sociability of the rich and the promiscuous sociability of the poor" (Cott 92). The Victorian family's position placed it parallel to public life yet firmly attached to it. Although promoted as a "walled garden" or a "haven," the family "both reflected the outside world and prepared people to participate in it" (Mintz 5). In the new republic, the family — and the home — fulfilled the need for perceived traditional values.[12]

Because of this new ideology, the concept of "home" took on a new meaning. Even the word itself, as Demos writes, "became highly sentimentalized" and "was pictured as a bastion of ... unwavering devotion to people and principles beyond itself" (21). It was a sanctuary, an embodiment of the family's moral standing, a place for inculcating religious and ethical values, and a repository for "the ways and values of an older America that was fast disappearing" (Demos 31). It forged a much-needed link with the past, establishing an idealized, sentimentalized domestic heritage for the emerging industrial nation. The prosperous, upwardly mobile businessman ensconced his wife and children in the home, safely removed from the place of production because it was no longer necessary for them to participate in securing the family income. Instead, the businessman's private residence, his wife, and his daughters and sons became the public gauges by which his financial success as well as his family's moral status was measured. The cult of domesticity attempted to shape the physical environment of the members of the American middle class as well as the psychological and moral environment. And, as Josiah G. Holland's *Titcomb's Letters* indicate, there was a good reason for this creativity: unlike the French, who "have the thing without the name ... a large portion of the American people have the name without the thing." And he continues, "There are comparatively few who have an adequate idea of what home is, as an institution." He finds it "not unjust to say, that half of the young married people of America have no higher conception of home than this. What they call their homes are simply boarding-houses, where, for purposes of economy and convenience, they board themselves." To the writer, the home is "an institution of life ... both an outgrowth of life, and a contributor to its development" (219–220).

Holland was not alone in his opinions. The middle-class nineteenth-century home incorporated a variety of functions—and symbols.[13] The cult made the home into a place of rest, education, and religious instruction; the family's residence, inside as well as outside, manifested these elements physically. Inside, furniture, books, and decorations emphasized the home's sacral and educational function. An exemplary house and immaculate grounds, rich, constraining clothes, and proper behavior testified to both the family's *moral* and its *financial* fortitude. The physical environment mirrored *moral* standing: neatness was next to godliness. Hence the fear of slovenliness that we meet in works such as Cummins's *The Lamplighter* and Warner's *The Wide, Wide World*; morally corrupt women have untidy houses, good women have tidy ones.

The family home not only transmitted recognizable signals to the world at large, the exterior of the home also was believed to be influenced by and in return able to influence the family's moral life. Shirley Murphy expressed the cult's ideas when she, in *Our Homes and How to Make Them Healthy* (1883), asserted that "A clean, fresh, and well-ordered house exercises over its inmates a moral, no less than physical influence, and has a direct tendency to make members of a family sober, peaceable, and considerate of the feelings and happiness of others" (312, qtd. in Green 59). Even less pretentious households could meet the exacting standard the cult prescribed. Lydia Maria Child argues in *The Frugal Housewife* (1829) that "Neatness, tastefulness, and good sense may be shown in the management of a small household ... these qualities are always praised, and always treated with respect and attention" (5). Several of Cooper's works, among them *Precaution*, *The Pioneers*, and *Home as Found*, attest to the author's awareness of this moral tenet.

The domestic myth so carefully constructed and upheld in early- to mid-nineteenth century fiction and nonfiction alike, soon showed signs of wear. After mid-century, writers of domestic fiction produced a less favorable representation of domestic life. The cult's proponents had for decades promised domestic bliss, yet the popular literature of the day increasingly presented domesticity's darker side, arguing that the family was, in fact, disintegrating. Cott explains that "divorce and desertion were increasing; child rearing had become too casual and permissive; authority was generally disrupted; the family no longer did things together; women were more and more restless in their role as homemakers" (30). The domestic dream had turned into a domestic nightmare. But perhaps nothing else could have been expected in a society that had tried to live up to both the cult of domesticity and the cult of the self-made man.

✼ ✼ ✼

> ...the writer of these pages is a man — one who has seen much of the other sex, and he is happy to have an opportunity of paying a tribute to female purity and female truth. That there are hearts so disinterested as to lose the considerations of self, in advancing the happiness of those they love; that there are minds so pure as to recoil with disgust from the admission of deception, indelicacy, or management, he knows; for he has seen it from long and close examination.
> — James Fenimore Cooper, *Precaution*, 1820

It may, initially, seem far-fetched to link James Fenimore Cooper not only with domesticity but with the works of the "female domestics," the women writers of his day who wrote domestic, sentimental novels, looking to the cult of domesticity for ideas. However, the above lines, taken from Cooper's first novel, encourage this reading, one alien to those who have customarily read his work solely in a male context, as chronicles of the American wilderness. If Cooper's representations of family dynamics have been discussed at all, it is in terms of his relationship to his father. Warren Motley does this when he asserts that the writer uses "familial images" in the frontier novels "to negotiate between the powerful childhood presence of Cooper's father and issues of social and political authority he faced as an adult," both in connection with his own family and that of his wife, the de Lanceys (3).[14] Such a reading belittles Cooper's creativity — and his literary contribution to the formation of a new nation. Cooper does not limit his interest in the American family to the depiction of father figures of various kinds, acting out his own unresolved conflicts and emotions concerning his father. Instead, a wide range of family configurations and family dynamics provide the extensive fibers of his narratives. Central to Cooper's "new" look at the family and domesticity is the cult's insistence on separate spheres and the importance of women as moral and religious instructors. Further, Cooper also utilized another of the cult's tenets: he presented the home's interior and exterior as a gauge of a family's (or a person's) moral standing.

Cooper's first novel placed him irrevocably among the domestic women writers of his day. *Precaution* (1820), a novel of manners set in rural England around 1815, with excursions to Bath, the most popular spa and "watering-hole" of the day, concerns itself chiefly with marriage and domesticity. The author highlights the process involved in choosing a spouse and discusses and rejects the idea of parental management in the process. Its title and plot evoke two of Jane Austen's works, *Persuasion* and

Pride and Prejudice. Cooper himself, according to his daughter Susan, leaned more to "the school of Mrs. Opie," a moralistic writer who was immensely popular in the British Isles and in America in the 1820s.[15] Cooper's interest in domesticity was to remain with him for the duration of his literary career. And, although male critics like Grossman, Spiller, et al. may see Cooper's first foray into the literary world as a *misstep* before the author found his "true" course and created the great American epic, the Leatherstocking tales, Cooper deliberately *chose* the domestic novel as his venue. These critics overlook the ironic fact that even the first of his stories involving Natty Bumppo is a *domestic* novel. This ought to come as no surprise: it was, after all, the kind of literature with which Cooper was well acquainted and where he knew he would find an established audience if he were inclined to have the text published.[16] Even if one wants to say, as does James D. Wallace, that Cooper deliberately crafted a *new*— i.e., *male*—kind of audience, since "his readers demanded a new kind of fiction suited to the continent" (184), Cooper never ignored his female audience.[17] Besides, during his first decade as an author, Cooper repeatedly presented himself as a writer of domestic fiction: when he published *The Pioneers*, for example, the title page immediately stressed that this was a new work by the author of *Precaution*, not of the more masculine *The Spy*, a novel set during the American Revolution. The domestic novel eclipsed the historical one — domesticity was a better marketing ploy than revolution, or so Cooper (or his publisher) seemed to think. And central to the events in *The Pioneers* is a strong, appealing young woman, Elizabeth Temple, who when the novel opens is returning home after four years at school in New York to take on her domestic duties.

In *The American Democrat* (1838), Cooper's "primer" for the citizenry of the United States, he defends the separation of spheres and women's exclusion from political activities. He asserts, in a curious comment from a militant litigant, that women's interests are "thought to be so identified with those of their male relatives as to become, in a great degree, inseparable." Because of this, "females are, almost generally, excluded from the possession of political rights. There can be no doubt that society is greatly the gainer, by thus excluding one-half of its members, and the half that is best adapted to give a tone to its domestic happiness, from the strife of parties, and the fierce struggles of political controversies" (42). Note that the "interests of women" are "thought" to be the same as those of their male relatives. In *The Pioneers*, the novel's two fathers appear to see such ideas as literal truths, however, the novel's daughters do not wholeheartedly subscribe to this. Significantly, the excerpt from *The American Democrat* emphasizes instruction and inculcation of domestic values. Women merely are best "adapted" to be homemakers: they do not perform these functions intuitively; their behavior is a result of training, of "necessity," all for the good of society.[18] Although Cooper saw women as "the natural agents in maintaining the refinement of the people" (*American Democrat* 122), he also realized and repeatedly dramatized that different needs, such as life on the frontier, would call for a different and more physically active and adventurous kind of woman than was the norm in "standard" domestic novels.

In his works, Cooper repeatedly operates within the domestic matrix by settling on families as both the backdrop and core of his romantic plots: in *Precaution*, the Moseleys; in *The Spy*, the Whartons; in *Homeward Bound* and *Home as Found*, Mr. Effingham and his daughter Eve; in *Satanstoe*, the Littlepage family but also the Mordaunts. The pattern also emerges in *The Last of the Mohicans*, Colonel Munro and his daughters Cora and Alice; in *The Pioneers*, Judge Temple and his daughter Elizabeth, Rector Grant and his daughter Alice; in *The Pathfinder*, Sergeant Dunham and his indomitable daughter Mabel, in many ways the most vibrant and appealing of Cooper's females; in *The Deerslayer*, Tom Hutter and his daughters Judith and Hetty; and in *The Prairie*, the Bush clan, but also Inez and her father, Don Augustin. Interestingly, all but one of the above examples presents families that explode the conventions of the cult of domesticity: they are not nuclear in our sense of the term, but amputated. The favorite family constellation, so to speak, is either a father-daughter dyad or, as in *The Spy*, *The Last of the Mohicans* and *The Deerslayer*, a father-daughter triad. By choosing this particular plot device, Cooper inserts the American family, with all its virtues, vices, and foibles into what at first appears an unlikely arena: the frontier novel. Not even the lonely woodsman Natty Bumppo remains untouched: the narrator makes it clear that Natty keeps his family alive in his thoughts and shows that it has left its indelible imprint on his character.

Yet in most cases Cooper, like his contemporaries, dispenses with the very core of Victorian domestic life — the mother. And when she emerges, as in *Precaution*, *The Prairie*, and *Satanstoe*, her influence is limited. In *Precaution*, she leaves mothering to others. In *Satanstoe*, Cooper provides the hero Corny (Cornelius) Littlepage with a close-knit, loving and complete nuclear family: the speaker is an only child, as is his love interest, Anneke Mordaunt. The heroine's family exemplifies the father-daughter dyad: Anneke is motherless. *The Prairie* has a wide sampling of families, nuclear, amputated, and extended, white and Native American. Predictably, the heroine Inez is motherless. However, the sharpest criticism of the family — and the mother — is directed at the intact Bush clan, especially against its lawlessness and the fact that the parents' lack of respect for the laws of the nation and for private ownership of land is passed on to younger generations.

By deploying amputated families and orphans, especially orphaned daughters, Cooper again links his works to those of contemporary women writers. The orphaned girl is, according to Alfred Habegger, a "staple" of nineteenth-century women's fiction.[19] Maria Cummins's *The Lamplighter*, Susan Warner's *The Wide, Wide World*, Child's *Hobomok* and Sedgwick's *Hope Leslie* all show amputated and dysfunctional families and orphaned or semi-orphaned daughters, young women who must find and/or adjust to their places in society. Cooper, though, gives the orphan motif a new twist. Not interested in providing a female *Bildungsroman* à la Cummins and Warner, but in the end results of the process—his young females take the stage at the cusp of womanhood—he nevertheless creates heroines that often seem to be the very embodiment of the cult of domesticity: they are obedient, domestic, pure, pious, and must be protected from unseemly influences. Because of their innocence, they make the men around them behave like gentlemen. The use of the sexually inexperienced daughter as a primary character is a strategic move: the author avoids having to deal with any sexual implications. Yet Cooper's texts demonstrate that this strategic move often fails: insisting on female innocence, the narrator instead emphasizes the daughters' sexuality: characters like Alice and Cora Munro, Inez Middleton, Mabel Dunham, and Elizabeth Temple are clearly sexual and thus elicit more than tender and fatherly or brotherly feelings from the men surrounding them.

Cooper not only utilizes the conventions of separate spheres and of female purity; he also deploys another of the cult's conventions to great effect: he makes effective use of the home as a gauge of the family's moral and religious status. In the texts, even *names* of houses become important indicators of moral standing. The Wharton country estate is "The Locusts," a name which not only indicates the stately trees surrounding the retreat but also immediately conjures up images of hordes of insects devouring everything in their path. Perhaps this is Cooper's indictment of Mr. Wharton's self-absorbed and avaricious behavior. The estate also falls prey to the two-legged infestation of marauding Skinners who metaphorically "skin" their victims. By comparison, the Mordaunt country estate in *Satanstoe* is called "Lilacsbush," a name which evokes domesticity and peace—lilacs were often planted by the front doors of colonial residences. The residence Herman Mordaunt has constructed on the patent he owns in the wilderness, on the other hand, has a name that links it to acquisitive carrion birds: "Ravensnest." The name "Satanstoe" receives particular attention: Corny, the novel's narrator, clearly feels the need to "say a word concerning its somewhat peculiar name," perhaps in order to forestall any negative associations. He claims the family property has had the name "from time immemorial" and that it supposedly originated in its proximity to a sound called "Hell Gate," confiding that a "fancied resemblance to an inverted toe (the devil being supposed to turn every thing with which he meddles, upside-down) has been imagined to exist in the shape and swells of our paternal acres; a fact that has probably had its influence in perpetuating the name" (7).

Cooper deploys the strategy successfully in *The Pioneers* in his description of Judge Temple's residence. Although detailing a building designed to overtly display the owner's wealth, authority, and superiority, Cooper's words nevertheless imply that this superiority rests on a shaky foundation: it is clearly *not* a home. When Elizabeth approaches the building, the narrator comments on the girl's first impressions of her future home: she "reads" the building as "cold" and "dreary," not homelike and inviting: "Nothing stood before her but the cold dreary stone walls of the building." Elizabeth feels "as if all the loveliness of the mountain view had vanished like the fancies of a dream" (59). Materials have been thrown together in haste and for show, but they lack substance: the "portico" attached to the house is a "superficial construction," marred by "structural flaws," intended only to prove the fertility of its builder's imagination and its master's resources. *Luck*, not competence or skill holds it all together. The narrator comments:

> It was lucky for the whole fabric that the carpenter who did the manual part of the labor had fastened the canopy of this classic entrance so firmly to the side of the house that, when the base deserted the superstructure in the manner we have described, and the pillars, for the want of a foundation, were no longer of service to support the roof, the roof was able to uphold the pillars ... a few rough wedges were driven under the pillars to keep them steady and to prevent their weight from separating them from the pediment which they ought to have supported [60].

Not only has everything here been assembled too quickly and haphazardly, some essential part is missing: its foundation. The same can be said about the Temple family: the domestic foundation, i.e., Elizabeth's mother, has been dead for several years. Remarkable Pettibone, Judge Temple's housekeeper, is like the rough wedges that are driven under the pillars in lieu of a proper foundation. Now, with Elizabeth's return, the family residence might indeed *become* a home; it will have a solid foundation: a properly trained domestic woman.

The impression of items put hastily together continues once Elizabeth enters the building. Immediately, the narrator stresses that the homelike atmosphere is missing. The interior of the mansion is "dimly lighted" and has an incongruous stove in the middle of the living room. The furniture presents a cacophony of styles and tastes: some pieces are imported, others manufactured at Templeton. Again, the emphasis is on *show* rather than on solid workmanship, good taste and quality. Most telling, though, are the walls, "hung with a dark, lead-colored English paper that represented Britannia weeping over the tomb of Wolfe." Due to cousin Richard's domestic incompetence in lining up the pattern, "some difficulties occurred that prevented a nice conjunction; and Britannia had reason to lament, in addition to the loss of her favorite's life, numberless cruel amputations of his right arm" (64). The Temple family is similarly amputated; it needs hands better than Richard's to put it all to right.

The same belief in the home as gauge of a person's moral status appears in several of Cooper's works, for instance in *The Deerslayer* in the description of Judith and Hetty Hutter's room. In *Sensational Designs,* Jane Tompkins mentions that what she remembers from reading the novel at age nine is the image of a man on the outskirts of a vast forest. The images *I* retain from my first reading of the book at roughly the same age are markedly different: one is the image of Tom Hutter inspecting a moccasin and deciding the race, gait, and habits of the person who had worn it. The other is Judith and Hetty's bedroom at Muskrat Castle, where the narrator uses the domestic setting to highlight not only the two sisters' different personalities but, more importantly, their different moral statures. This is what Natty sees: to one side are dresses "of a quality much more superior to what one would expect to meet in such a place" and shoes, fans, and gloves "such as were then worn by females in easy circumstances.... Even the pillow, on this side of the bed, was covered with finer linen that its companion, and it was ornamented with a small ruffle. A cap, coquettishly decorated with ribbons, hung above it, and a pair of long gloves ... were pinned ostentatiously to it, as if with an intention to exhibit them there, if they could not be shown on the owner's arms" (42–3).

This part of the room belongs to Judith, the more beautiful and, we suspect, "experienced," flirtatious, and superficial of the two sisters, a young woman more concerned with earthly belongings than with her soul. Everything on Judith's side of the room emphasizes the girl's sensuous nature and her love of and desire for male attention. Even the insensitive Harry March perceives the room's significance. The decorations are, he comments, "Judith's character to a riband!" (26). Her clothes are of "superior" quality; she has an abundance of fans "of gay colors" and even long gloves. Adverbs such as "coquettishly" and "ostentatiously" add to what the reader already knows about Judith from Harry, "The hussy is handsome, and she knows it" (26). However, she is hardly proper marriage material for a man whether from the eighteenth century or from the age of the cult of domesticity; she is too flirtatious and frivolous. She is also sexually tainted; her relationship to the officers at the garrison implies impropriety. This, in addition to her colonial background, destroys her chances of marriage to an English officer.

The other side of the room exhibits a very different and unassuming personality (and gives the narrator far less to write about): Here "everything was homely and uninviting, except through its perfect neatness. The few garments that were hanging from the pegs were of the coarsest materials and of the commonest form, while nothing seemed made for show. Of ribbons there was not one; nor was there either cap or kerchief beyond those which Hutter's daughters might be fairly entitled to wear" (43).

Note that the text combines the words "homely" and "uninviting": the objects on Hetty's side of the room are what one could expect to find in many a frontier home. They are uninviting insofar that they, like their owner, do not "invite" male attention; they give no promise of sexual enticement. They have not been arranged for show but for function. They are also in keeping with Hetty's social standing. However, "its perfect neatness" appeals and is designed to be admired. The narrator thus deftly links Hetty to domestic virtues, to plainness, to renouncing things beyond one's proper station in life. In a few paragraphs Cooper, in a kind of imagist shorthand, has managed to contrast two different female personalities. A Victorian reader immediately would have understood the implications of the description, with its criticism of the flighty Judith and its praise of the more ordinary Hetty. The narrator inserts a double message: even he is enticed by his fascinating heroine although he denounces her sexuality and pretense. More important, though, is the impact the room has on Natty: the room reminds him of both his mother and his sister, the former more like Hetty (but, hopefully, less simpleminded), the latter in "the manner of Judith, though necessarily in a less degree" (43). The room triggers remembrances and these "opened a long hidden vein of sensations; and as he quitted the room, it was with a saddened mien" (43). Even Natty longs for the home and the family he has lost.

The Wept of Wish-Ton-Wish similarly exploits the tenet that the home exemplifies the family's moral rectitude — and social standing. The description of the Heathcote home clearly demonstrates this. A "bright and cheerful fire" lights her kitchen, where healthy, athletic male servants perform the "fitting employments to close the business of a laborious and well-spent day... some drawing coarse tools carefully through the curvatures of ox-bows," while "the notable and stirring industry of handmaidens busied in the more familiar cares of the household" (24). An "inner and superior apartment" adds to the impression of rank: "candles of tallow, on a table of cherry-wood from the neighboring forest; walls ... wainscoted in the black oak of the country, and a few other articles of a fashion so unique, and of ornaments so ingenious and rich, as to announce that they had been transported from beyond the sea. Above the mantel were suspended the armorial bearings of the Heathcotes and the Hardings, elaborately emblazoned in tent-stitch" (24). If cleanliness is next to godliness, all is well in the Heathcote household.

Cooper also deploys the convention that women are more religious than men, hence better equipped to educate and control the men surrounding them. Inez in *The Prairie*, Dus Malbone in *The Chainbearer*, and Mary Pratt in *The Sea Lions* belong to this category. The "desire of proselytizing" and converting the Protestant Middleton partly fuels Inez's (and her father's) interest in the suitor; when Middleton proposes, the sixteen-year-old religious enthusiast "thought it would be a glorious consummation of her wishes to be a humble instrument of bringing her lover into the bosom of the true church" (159). Dus Malbone converts her uncle Andries Coejemans, and Mary Pratt steadfastly works on Roswell Gardiner, refusing to marry him until he becomes a Christian. Cooper also presents Mary as a far more religious and charitable person than her greedy deacon uncle, who despite his position in his church has no perception of Christian charity. This does not mean that every Cooper heroine is deeply pious, but Cooper comes down firmly on the side of the Episcopal Church. Many of his characters, although churchgoing, lack evangelical fervor; they do not, for instance, necessarily resort to God in times of danger. Elizabeth, when confronting first, a ferocious panther and later, a fire, finds it impossible to pray, afterwards telling her father that she could not think of anything to say. Dus Malbone teaches her uncle to pray and impresses both Mordaunt Littlepage and the Thousandacres family with her piety. Yet when Ravensnest is under attack in *The Redskins*, a pistol comes to hand just as easily as a prayer; Dus is ready to defend herself and her home against intruders, instead of waiting to be protected, just as Esther Bush in *The Prairie* had been ready to defend herself and her family.

While Cooper appears to affirm family life and conjugal obligations, he also creates characters whose behavior consistently undermines the ruling stereotype; i.e., the characters challenge or refuse to obey parental orders. He discusses this behavior in *The American Democrat*, arguing that "the fifth commandment, then, may be said to contain the first of our social duties ... the obligation of the child to its parents ... the entire extent of the family relations are included in principle, since it cannot be supposed that those who precede our immediate parents, are excluded from the general deference that we owe to the greater experience, the love, and the care of our predecessors" (85–86).

Note that Cooper sees family dynamics from a biblical perspective; the fifth commandment is the foundation of a person's "social duties." Central to this view are the child's obligation and deference to its parents, due to the love and care it has received. Advocates for the cult of domesticity had the same idea of the parent-child relationship: Abbott's book on a mother's duty, for instance, focuses largely on the inculcation of duty and obedience; it is also a lesson the female protagonists of such works as *The Lamplighter* and *The Wide, Wide World* have to learn. Cooper, on the other hand, never argued blind obedience to parental rules; religious duty, for example, overruled even the demand for obedience. Mrs. Fitzgerald, the beautiful stranger in *Precaution*, refuses to obey her father's order and renounce her Protestant faith. The portrayal of the Bush clan in *The Prairie* also criticizes excessive parental control, but then they are lawless squatters and not bound by the rules of polite society. Children can also err out of misguided filial duty: Alice and Cora Munro defy their father's orders and travel to join him at the besieged Fort William Henry. Mabel Dunham struggles to resist her father's "retirement plan," which involves her being married off to her father's best friend Natty, and Anneke Mordaunt chooses Corny Littlepage over her father's favorite, the English officer and nobleman Bulstrode.

Writing during the "heyday" of the cult of domesticity, Cooper deploys the cult's conventions—the separation into male and female spheres; the insistence upon female purity and piety; and women's position as man's moral superior and his teacher of moral and religious values—shaping his characters and their surroundings to conform to these. More importantly, his representations of nineteenth-century domesticity follow a trajectory also found in woman's domestic literature: the "nuclear" family has been amputated, and this deviation from the Victorian norm creates tension. Cooper's vision of middle-class domesticity is hardly unequivocally idyllic: many of his representations of the American family constitute severe injunctions against the institution, especially as regards the lack of parental guidance and nurturing, the very backbone of nineteenth-century family life. In creating his domestic scenes, Cooper seems to have had a dual objective: he simultaneously helps establish and critique Victorian domesticity by presenting its absence in his truncated families. Although the home is the haven toward which his heroines and heroes move, it often falls short of the domestic ideal of Cooper's day. The same can be said of nineteenth-century women writers whose works, although affirming middle-class norms, also revealed these norms to be perpetuating a domestic myth. Where the cult of domesticity prescribed family unity and harmony built around a mother's disinterested love, Cooper and female domestic writers of his day used the tenets of the cult of domesticity in order to focus on amputated, motherless families, exploring instead the father-daughter relationship so vital to the Victorian society and promoting a new kind of American woman, one who challenges and subverts paternal authority.

3
Marriage and Motherhood

> A man by marrying places his domestic comforts in the power of his wife, and relinquishes to her all command and management of them; and she must so regulate them, as that he shall in no particular imagine or feel that anything could be better arranged.
> —Eliza Ware Farrar, *A Young Wife's Book*, 1838

> Marriage is called a lottery, and it is thought, like all other lotteries, there are more blanks than prizes...
> —James Fenimore Cooper, *Precaution*, 1820

> Careful historians now show that the greatest civilizing power all along the pathway of natural development has been found in the wisdom and tender sentiments growing out of motherhood.
> —Elizabeth Cady Stanton, 1891

When Stanton, a famous nineteenth-century feminist, made the comment above, she showed the durability and mutability of the ideals of the cult of domesticity. Throughout the century, writers had not only diligently posited the mother as the center of the family, but they had consistently endowed her, as Stanton does, with "civilizing power." Whether considered from a religious or secular perspective, the belief in this maternal power profoundly impacted society: on it rested not merely the family's, but the whole nation's, well-being. Even in 1891, four decades after its heyday, its tenets still held sway and could be evoked for political purposes.

The cult of domesticity presented marriage and maternity as the culmination of nineteenth-century womanhood. Marriage was both a private and a public concern: it provided a woman with happiness, respectability, *and* usefulness to society. Motherhood added three more tempting incentives to women: private pleasure, domestic control, and the prospect of national influence. Fiction and nonfiction alike consistently reinforced the cult's values. Explicitly and implicitly women's literature extolled the physical and spiritual benefits matrimony and maternity supposedly had for women, indicating through their very vehemence that reality often fell short of the ideal. And, as if these benefits were not enough to lead the susceptible young woman down the domestic path, texts designed to appeal to women forcefully reminded its readers of their responsibilities not only to God and family but also to the nation through the production and training of virtuous husbands and children. The writers of such literature well knew that neither marital happiness nor maternal success was a given. There were, as Cooper's *Precaution* repeatedly dramatizes, "more blanks than prizes" in the marriage lottery.

※ ※ ※

> Marriage is certainly a condition upon which the happiness or misery of life does very much depend.... To be confined to live with one perpetually, for whom we have no liking or esteem, must certainly be an uneasy state.... Marriages, founded on affection, are the most happy.
> —"Marriage." *Godey's Lady's Book*, November 1832

> The most anxious ... if not the most important duty of married life, is that which is due to children.... To accomplish ... these duties, a woman must be domestic. Her heart must be at home.
> —*The Young Lady's Own Book*, 1836

Nineteenth-century advice literature amply demonstrates that many of Cooper's contemporaries shared his belief in the importance of marriage and motherhood; however, writers worked to define and encourage what in many ways were totally new relationships. Private documents express similar preoccupations. Where the preceding centuries had seen upper- and middle-class marriages as business arrangements between families and means to improve and secure people's social and/or financial status, the late eighteenth and the nineteenth centuries increasingly saw it as an emotional attachment. In addition, for both men and women, marriage meant social respectability and signified commitment and responsibility in financial as well as sexual matters.[1] Mutual affection alone, however, could not secure the emotional, financial, or national stability the cult promised. But combined with a strong sense of duty, it might contribute to achieve this objective, or so the cult's advocates opined. Furthermore, to those influenced by the evangelistic movements of the day, marriage was increasingly seen as not only an emotional but as a religious commitment — in this world as well as in the next.

Although other Western nations experienced a similar restructuring of family life, the change in the concept of marriage was especially striking in the emerging United States. As Alexis de Tocqueville points out in *Democracy in America*, in the young nation, marriage had become more individualistic, egalitarian, and intimate than was the case in Europe.[2] As an answer to outside pressure — the competitive marketplace, industrialization, and religious doubt — marriage had come to be seen as a bulwark against all forces vying to destroy the fledgling nation. Marriage, claimed the proponents of the cult of domesticity, formed a protective circle around the endangered American civilization. Strict measures were needed to protect the ways and values of an older and ostensibly more stable America; hence, domestic writers — whether working in fiction or nonfiction — created a dichotomy still with us today, the separation of the public and private spheres of interest. The two societal spheres formed a symbiotic, indivisible relationship. By the breadwinner's daily return, the business world encroached on the domestic sphere and, more importantly, the business world provided the finances necessary to maintain this domestic *sanctum*.

Many magazine articles aimed, like Cooper's texts, at middle-class readers emphasized the importance of marriage for both individual and societal well-being. A perusal of *Godey's Lady's Book* in the period 1830–1850 reveals a significant number of articles — by and for women *and* men — with such self-explanatory titles as "Marriage," "Hints on Marriage," and "Cursory Remarks on a Wife." "Cursory Remarks on a Wife," which appeared in the July 1832 issue, demonstrates that *Godey's*, albeit ostensibly a "lady's book," also aimed at a male readership. The text advises "every young *gentleman*" (my emphasis) on the importance of accurately judging a woman's character when looking to acquire a wife. This is crucial, because a good wife, is "one of the most valuable treasures a man can possess in his life." The author envisions the following domestic rewards for the nineteenth-century husband courtesy of his devoted wife. She functions as his nurse, housekeeper, and adviser and is "his best companion in prosperity and truest friend in adversity" (8). The essay appears almost biblical in tone, reminding its readers that a good wife is a blessing, or as an old prayer has it, she is worth more than rubies. Although specific as to the *wife's* role within the family, it refrains from listing what the husband has to accomplish or contribute in order to deserve these heavenly blessings.

In a sense, Child, Sedgwick, and Cooper take up where *Godey's* leaves off, teaching men to be appreciative and worthy of their loves. Basic requirements for a successful marriage, the texts emphasized, are love — and precaution when it comes to choice of spouse. In November 1832, *Godey's* published the article "Marriage," in which the article's author cautions the magazine's readers to "Let your love advise [sic] you before you choose, and your choice be fixed before you marry" since "nothing but death can dissolve the knot." More importantly, the text argues, as Cooper consistently did, for equal matches, claiming that "especially, the temper and education must be attended to." Lack of love, the author asserts, leads to the "innumerable domestic miseries that plague and utterly confound so many families." Moreover, the article presents marriage as a stabilizing force of global proportions; a harmonious marriage is not a private issue but one which "more nearly concerns the peace of mankind." Again, the writer's words are prescriptive, not descriptive; they project an idealized vision of marriage, a view appropriate for the most ambitious of utopian undertakings, the founding of the United States. The constant reiteration of such demands indicates that reality fails to meet these expectations, but this domestic vision needs to be realized if the nation is to remain stable. Many American families, the article has to admit, fall short of this ideal, exhibiting, instead of harmony, "neglect and careless management of affairs at home, and ... profuse, extravagant expenses abroad" due to "want of love and kindness in the wife or husband." The author blames men, rather than women, for unequal matches since women "can seldom be choosers." However, the text insists that it still rests on the woman to use her "foresight and penetration" to avoid a potentially disastrous marriage (244). Considering the status of female education, and the demand for female otherworldliness, a twenty-first-century reader wonders where the cloistered woman would acquire such knowledge.

Like much advice literature, the *Godey's* article "Marriage" concludes with demands for female education and inculcation of what it sees as appropriate domestic values. Regardless of a young woman's abilities and interests, only one profession was open to the daughter of the middle-class family. Significantly, the author, addressing daughters and wives of the burgeoning bourgeoisie, takes her terms from the mercantile world: "the business of a family is the most profitable and honourable study they can employ themselves in. The best dowry to advance the marriage of a young lady is, when she has in her countenance mildness — in her spirit, wisdom — in her behaviour, modesty — and in her life, virtue" (244). Note the use of the words "business," "profitable," and "employ" in this context — even the cult of domesticity needs to deploy the language of commerce to make its point. Marriage may no longer be seen as an economic contract between families, yet as behooves a burgeoning industrial nation, the institution is still presented as a "business" and a "profitable" one at that. More importantly, marital success can all be evaluated in terms of debits and credits.

The mother stood at the center of this domestic cult. Although legally and politically inferior to her husband, and for the major part of the nineteenth century unable to control her finances, she was "intrinsically superior (from a moral standpoint) to her male partner" (Demos 32). A plethora of writings, religious and secular, strove to reinforce the concepts of matriarchal superiority and duty. It was, W. A. Alcott points out in *The Young Woman's Guide* (1840), "the peculiar province which God in nature has assigned her" (175). As Barbara Welter has shown, this female superiority rested on "four cardinal virtues—piety, purity, submissiveness, and domesticity.... Without them, no matter whether there was fame, achievement, or wealth, all was ashes. With them she was promised happiness and power" (Welter 313). Ironically, this divinely ordained female province, albeit separate from the public sphere, influenced even the world of business, "it was an irresponsible mother who did not see to it that her male children were prepared for the competitive world of their father" (Green 7). The Victorian mind obviously did not find it contradictory that a person who supposedly had no knowledge of the cutthroat business world could prepare anyone to face its problems. However, the emphasis was on her ability to form her son's character, John Abbott asserts, in his 1834 advice book *The Mother at Home* under "the principles of maternal duty," that "from her goes the most powerful influence in the formation of the character of man" (2). Two decades later, the English poet Coventry Patmore, determined to glorify conjugal love, coined the phrase "the angel in the house," neatly summarizing the presiding *Zeitgeist*. A paragon of piety, she teaches her husband how to pray; she makes him "divine." God, Patmore writes, created her for a specific purpose, male salvation:

> Marred less than man by mortal fall,
> Her disposition is devout,
> Her countenance angelical;
> ...
> The faithless, seeing her, conceive,
> Not only heaven, but hope of it [83].

Patmore asserts that God created woman last not because she is inherently inferior, but because she represented a higher spiritual level than man. Being less "marred," hence more pious, she was more able to influence and civilize man. This female piety, and its potential in regards to religious instruction, provided an alternative to organized patriarchal religion.[3]

Many advice books aimed at female readers sought to counteract the ironic gap between the female dependence on men and their dependence on her. They also offered practical advice in how to best develop and profit from this uniquely female career. "Timothy Titcomb" in 1858 assured his female readers, in words almost identical to those of Patmore, that female dependency was divinely ordained: the dependent woman was a blessing. Without women, he states, men "become savage and sinful. The purer you are, the more they are restrained, and the more they are elevated" (158). Women also were believed to be "naturally more pure than men" since they supposedly had "weaker erotic impulses" (Fishburn 22). Smith-Rosenberg attributes this belief to the reformers of the time, pointing to the fact that as the cult influenced middle-class society, the view of women's sexuality changed from sensual to naturally frigid.[4] Cooper likely subscribed to the concept of female sexuality: his heroines fulfill the demand for sexual purity and innocence and have a tempering influence on the males they encounter. The demand for sexual inexperience may also account for the lack of mothers in Victorian fiction: by focusing on daughters instead of mothers, the writers avoided the disturbing issue of female sexuality.

Purity was not the only demand. First of the cardinal virtues the cult demanded came piety: if a woman was really pious, the other virtues would follow as a matter of course. A pious wife, of course, guaranteed fidelity and domestic bliss. The insistence on piety should come as no surprise for students of the early nineteenth-century United States: the middle class participated actively in the Second Great Awakening then sweeping the nation. The cult of domesticity thus had firm roots both in the economic and religious worlds, culminating in a contradictory reverence for and severe denigration of the mother; she was considered "theoretically an angel and was practically a slave" (Laver 143).[5] In legal matters, the situation was even direr: "man" had, in the words of the 1848 "Declaration of Sentiments" from the Women's Rights Convention at Seneca Falls, "made her, if married, in the eye of the law, civilly dead." The mother might have been given an enormous power at home, yet nothing was legally her own: her privileges and responsibilities stopped at her front door. And, the declaration claimed, man "has made her, morally, an irresponsible being, as she can commit many crimes with impunity, provided they be done in the presence of her husband. In the covenant of marriage, she is compelled to promise obedience to her husband, he becoming, to all intents and purposes, her master — the law giving him power to deprive her of her liberty, and to administer her chastisement."

Some women deliberately, even gleefully, exploited the fact that they could commit crimes without fear of punishment, as did the British actress and writer Fanny Kemble, when she started teaching Aleck, a slave on her husband's plantation at St. Simon's Island, Georgia, to read. In the journal of her residence on this plantation in 1838–39, she assures herself that she cannot be punished for her activity, although teaching a slave to read is illegal. Kemble smugly writes that "it is simply breaking the laws of the government under which I am living. Unrighteous laws are made to be broken —*perhaps*— but then, you see, I am a woman, and Mr. [Butler] stands between me and the penalty" (271). Yet in flaunting the law, Kemble made the private public. She was not alone in doing so. A woman's obligation to *appear* moral — hence her responsibilities— extended beyond the domestic sanctuary and were ultimately public.

To encourage the acceptance of their circumscribed social role, or at least the appearance of it, young women were advised to be timid, dependent and perpetually childlike. What we today would consider female self-realization was firmly rejected; true women sacrificed their own non-domestic talents for the welfare of husband and family. A perusal of even a small number of prescriptive advice books shows a definite trend: they all clearly agree on the wife's function — she has no life separate from her family. And, as Mrs. Louisa Tuthill admonishes in *The Young Lady's Home* (1847): "Do not think it a mark of judgment to despise the appropriate duties of woman" (40). Her comment clearly indicates that many young women did exactly that. Caroline Gilman's *Recollections of a Housekeeper* (1834) advised the young bride always to put her husband's concerns before her own, urging her to "Reverence his *wishes* even when you do not his *opinions*" (122, in Welter 319). *The Lady's Token* (1848), although envisioning the wife as her husband's advisor, prescribed that a wife should devote herself solely to "domestic affairs" and not offer her husband advice "until he asks for it" (119, in Welter 322). *A Wife's Book: A Manual of Moral, Religious and Domestic Duties* (1838) preaches reciprocity in married life, but also insists on female obedience as a "Divine command" (12). W.A. Alcott's *The Young Woman's Guide* (1840) urges his readers to "love domestic life, and the care and society of the young, because it is, without doubt, the intention of Divine Providence that they should do so; and because home, and the concerns of home, afford the best opportunities and means of moral improvement" (175). The *Mother's Assistant and Young Lady's Friend* (1843), under the heading "Rules for Conjugal and Domestic Happiness," lists "Always Conciliate" as the first commandment in marital affairs. The text ends with a stark reminder to its young, female readers about the reality of their only career path: "Do not expect too much" (115, in Welter 319), a sad comment on a young woman's future.

Under the insistence on domesticity as both the most profitable and most honorable task for women lay a specific subtext: the cult of domesticity above all envisioned a utilitarian existence for American women.

Above all, it demanded that a woman be *useful*. Even motherhood implied usefulness and duty. No children meant no nation, no workers, and no prosperity. Hailed as her husband's moral superior she might be, yet she nevertheless existed to be *used* by him; her wisdom, modesty, and virtue all combined to satisfy *his* needs, complement *his* shortcomings, and raise *his* children to be useful members of society. Male and female writers argued that a woman's happiness depended on her usefulness, thereby affirming the patriarchal demands. These support activities, however, had to be carefully inculcated and cultivated. A plethora of manuals sought to instill missing domestic values in the American population, among them Lydia Maria Child's *The Frugal Housewife* (1829) and Catharine Beecher's *Treatise on Domestic Economy for Use of Young Ladies at Home and at School* (1841), which she expanded into *The American Woman's Home* in 1869.[6]

In her slim volume, Lydia Maria Child asserts: "Young ladies should be taught that usefulness is happiness, and that all other things are but incidental. With regard to matrimonial speculations, they should be taught nothing! Leave the affections to nature and all will end well" (13). Child's chapter on the "Education of Daughters" expresses the writer's exasperation with what she saw as the "greatest and most universal error" of this education: the exaggeration of the importance of getting married (91). Although Child concedes that it is both "natural and proper" that mothers wish to see their daughters happily married, she also argues that the female education of her day neglects to teach girls "quiet, domestic habits" (92). Instead of sending a young girl to school until the age of sixteen, Child advocates a practical domestic education of "two or three years spent with a mother, assisting her in her duties, instructing brothers and sisters, and taking care of their own clothes. This is the way to make them happy, as well as good wives; for, being early accustomed to the duties of life, they will sit lightly as well as gracefully upon them" (92). Following the dictates of the cult of domesticity, Child argues that the domestic education she proposes leads to a harmonious marriage, asserting that "indifference and dislike between husband and wife are more frequently occasioned by this great error in education, than by any other cause" (96).

Beecher and Stowe's *The American Woman's Home*,[7] although a far more comprehensive and detailed text than Child's work, has the same primary objective: it seeks to construct and prescribe a woman's domestic usefulness. However, where Child modestly had dedicated the work to those of limited means who were not afraid to learn economy, Beecher "affectionately"— and flamboyantly — dedicates her book "To the women of America, in whose hands rest the real destinies of the republic, as moulded [sic] by the maturer [sic] influences of home." The work, the title page asserts, is "a guide to the formation and maintenance of economical, healthful, beautiful and Christian homes." The introduction immediately demonstrates the authors' commitment to the cult of domesticity, claiming, "It is the aim of this volume to elevate both the honor and the remuneration of all the employments that sustain the many difficult and sacred duties of the family state, and thus to render each department of woman's true profession as much desired and respected as are the most honored professions of men" (13). The statement also adds a new facet to the issue of domesticity: family duties are a woman's *profession*. Furthermore, it ought to be treated as such: women must approach their duties in a professional manner.[8] The reasons for women's disabilities and sufferings, Beecher and Stowe assert, can be found in the nation's lack of appreciation for "the honor and duties of the family state" as well as in women's lack of training for their profession. Women from all walks of life, the text argues, will benefit from the training it offers. The work takes its readers from "The Christian Family" to "The Christian Neighborhood," from "Scientific Domestic Ventilation" to "Domestic Manners."[9] The work — adhering closely to the conventions of the cult of domesticity — prescribes the following role for the American housewife: "Her great mission is self-denial, in training its members to self-sacrificing labors for the ignorant and weak: if not her own children, then the neglected children of her Father in heaven. She is to rear all under her care to lay up treasures, not on earth, but in heaven" (19). A woman, the text asserts, has a dual usefulness. She sees not only to her family's physical needs; her chief objective is the family's growth as Christians. For completing this mission she will be rewarded in heaven. According to Beecher and Stowe, the family home becomes a temple, its exterior and interior reflecting the family's spiritual and moral standing.[10] Other writers shared their opinions: works such as *The Young Lady's Class Book* (1831) emphasized the woman's role as spiritual guide, commenting that "the domestic fireside is the great guardian of society against the excess of human passions" (166). Similarly, *The Lady at Home* (1847) asserted the importance of the domestic sphere, concluding that "even if we cannot reform the world in a moment, we can begin the work by reforming ourselves and our households — It is woman's mission. Let her not look away from her own little family circle for the means of producing moral and social reforms, but begin at home" (177–8).

Other advice literature also consistently emphasized the role of the mother, presenting motherhood as an essential component in a proper marriage — and as a spiritual and cultural power base. Mrs. Sigourney's *Letters to Mothers* (1838) asserted that "If in becoming a mother, you have reached the climax of your happiness, you have also taken a higher place in the scale of being ... you have gained an increase of power" (9). Faced with declining birthrates, advice writers stridently promoted the benefits of childbirth and motherhood to its white middle-class readers. Maternity was presented not only as a great pleasure, but as the crown of female physical and mental achievement. *Titcomb's Letters* (1858) elaborates that motherhood enabled women to reach "the highest and most harmonious development" possible for them. If they are childless, Holland asserts, one of "the most beautiful regions of [a woman's] nature must forever remain without appropriate and direct culture" (200–1). The author was even sharper in his criticism when discussing women who for some reason chose to avoid maternity. If women were childless "by cool and calculating choice," they were "either very unfortunately organized, or ... essentially immoral" (203). Motherhood allegedly had physical benefits as well as psychological ones: *Godey's Lady's Book* of December 1860 argued that motherhood provided the "fulfillment of a woman's physiological and moral destiny" (529–30, qtd. in Green 29). Later in the century, a columnist in the June 1887 issue of *Demorest's Monthly Magazine* reiterated this idea, arguing that "bearing children tends to keep beauty of form and feature — other things being equal — even increasing it sometimes, and putting old age a long way off" (500, qtd. in Green 29). The fact that a considerable number of American women never lived to see their children reach adulthood makes these statements singularly peculiar and dubious. Cooper would not have agreed with this rosy view of maternity, at least not if the mother was young. In *Notions of the Americans*, for instance, he comments that American women marry and have children at an early age; this development has "an obvious tendency to impair the powers of the female and to produce a premature decay" (Vol. I. 195). And *Home as Found*'s Eve Effingham, upon returning to Templeton after having spent eleven years in Europe, makes the same observation: she sees "that many of her own sex whom she had left children, grown into womanhood, and not a few of them at a period of life when they should be cultivating their physical and moral powers, already oppressed with the cares and feebleness that weigh so heavily on the young American wife" (178). Words such as "oppressed," "cares," "feebleness," and "heavily" attest to a negative view on the "fulfillment of a woman's physiological and moral destiny" and undermine the image promoted by the cult of domesticity.

Maternity held not only pleasures, but arrived with a heavy burden of duties. The mother was responsible for the physical and spiritual nurture of her children, preparing them to fulfill their expected roles. And, as Freeling observes in *The Young Bride's Book*, biology alone did not a mother make. "The first requisite" for the job, he asserts, "is a due and entire acquaintance with the physical wants of children" (7). He also advises mothers not to leave infant care to servants. If she does, she "forfeits all claim to the sacred name mother" (7). Nineteenth-century child care was a prolonged task, since children lived longer with their parents than they had in earlier centuries. However, if the father was the strict "earthly legislator" of his family, the mother influenced through tenderness and affection. A contributor to the *American Lady's Preceptor* (1813) asserts "There are no ties in nature to compare with those which unite an affectionate mother to her children, when they repay tenderness with obedience and love" (31, qtd. in Epstein 77). John Abbott's *The Mother at Home* (1834), aimed at "mothers in the common walk of life ... looking eagerly for information respecting the government of their children" (1), spells out these tasks, offering practical advice and examples. Abbott shows particular interest in the inculcation of obedience; this he lists as the mother's first duty towards her children. A clergyman himself and, according to his own words, the result of a mother's careful nurturing, he starts his discussion by extolling her continued influence over her children: most ministers, for example, owe their salvation and their religious vocation to the pious prayers of their mothers. This benign influence extended to all walks of life: the memory of a mother's prayer often preserved men from destruction. Daughters, though, due to the inherent virtue of the female character, were less prone to sin and appear less prominently in conversion stories. Abbott argues that self-control is the key to maternal success. He asserts that the mother must "subdue her own passions; she must set her children an example of meekness and equanimity; or she must reasonably expect that all efforts to control their passions will be ineffectual" (61–62). Some advice literature even expected the mother's responsibilities to also include sexual education. *The Advocate*, for instance, recommended that mothers sit in the dark, with their backs to their sons to hide their own embarrassment when they talked to them about sexual matters.[11]

The cult inevitably held middle-class women to impossible standards since the ideal home was an ideological construct, not a physical reality. Yet women measured themselves, and were measured by others, against this standard every time they opened domestic novels, advice books, and women's magazines. In the latter publications, stories, illustrations, and advertising combined to reinforce the cult's conventions and standards. The need for constant reinforcing of the domestic ideal indicates that while the reformers saw the *need* for domestic bliss, it was neither easily attainable nor instinctive. John Abbot bluntly states that guidance books are needed since "family government" is "generally so defective" (61). It is, of course, difficult to judge to what extent nineteenth-century women actually believed in or adhered to the role prescribed for them, for the most part, by men. Yet some journals voice the frustration of women who fell short of the ideal. One frustrated diarist, the New Englander Mehitable Dawes Goddard, who at age nineteen (in 1815) had read didactic texts in order to "form" herself "to confer happiness in domestic life," confessed, at age thirty-five, that she often wished herself "a smarter body, & able to be a first rate mother, wife, mistress, & every thing — sometimes am quite discouraged on this matter." And the reason for her failure lay within herself: "the difficulty is I do not look above for support — am apt to depend on myself — oh that I could sincerely ask for aid — so many important duties press upon me I am almost bewildered" (Qtd. in Cott 75). Ironically, the very qualities we value today, self-sufficiency and self-dependence, stand in the way of Goddard's success as a mother and wife, or so she thinks. Florence Nightingale, in contrast, although hardly a "typical" Victorian woman in her choice of career, had no such desire to try to live up to the standards of the cult. She rejected its pernicious nature: the family and its demands were vicious forces taking her away from what really mattered to her. One of the things Nightingale attacks is the family's lack of consideration for its members. She writes, "The family uses people, *not* for what they are, nor for what they are intended to be, but for what it wants them for — its own uses" (Qtd. in Gorham 126). To Nightingale, the domestic myth offered no sanctuary, only enforced labor.

Letters and journals from domestic women writers exhibit the same preoccupation with marriage as advice literature does, yet they also record the discrepancy between the cult's promise and reality, thus affirming the need for improvement. Stowe, for instance, promoted the institution's *spiritual* usefulness. Like many of her contemporaries, she saw marriage as an answer to the religious confusion of her time. What she sought in marriage, her journals reveal, was an "exemplification of religion": her daily duties and sacrifices become a means to the spouses' salvation (Mintz 129). Yet Stowe also expected companionship and attention from their relationship, only to find her husband not only neglecting these needs but focusing on her faults, constantly criticizing her. In a letter to her husband she writes "when both parties begin to stand for their rights & to suspect the other of selfish exaction there is an end of every delicate & refined affection & a beginning of coarse and brutal selfishness" (Qtd. in Mintz and Kellogg 57).[12]

Child's letters to and about her husband attempt to present a loving relationship, but the reader registers that the onus of making the relationship work seems to rest solely on the wife's shoulders, despite protestations to the opposite. In words evoking those of Anne Bradstreet, she writes about her loneliness and weariness when they are apart, and presents her David as an exceptional husband. In a letter to him dated July 28, 1836, she writes: "You and I are like two drops of quick-silver placed a few inches apart on a level surface — there is a continual restlessness and agitation, till at last they are together, in spite of the perfect level." She then continues, "you have been to me a most kind, considerate, and forgiving husband.... How many times have you guided me when I was wrong! How many times have you strengthened me, when I have been weak! How often restored me to my balance, when I have been perverse and unreasonable! God bless you, my best-beloved friend! How I *do* want to fold you to my heart" (*Letters* 51).

She presents her concern for her husband's well-being as innate, not learned. She is, she writes to her friend Francis Shaw on Aug. 2, 1846, "naturally very affectionate and domestic." However, to Shaw she also expresses her ambivalent attitude towards marriage, voicing its repercussions in her professional and financial life. She candidly admits, "The strong necessity of loving has been the great temptation and conflict of my life." And this, she emphasizes, results not from her own spiritual shortcomings; she observes "I sincerely believe that few women are more pure-minded than myself" (*Letters* 229). Her letters, though, show that this "pure-mindednesss" (i.e., piety) by no means guarantees a successful marriage — no amount of it could lessen the effects of her husband's character deficiencies. And Child certainly never remained within the confines of the home. She not only became the *de facto* breadwinner but engaged herself eagerly in the fight against various forms of social injustice, for instance slavery. She also legally separated her *financial* affairs from his in order to protect her own income from his creditors, but their marriage remained legally intact (*Letters* 199).

Even if her own marriage remained intact — perhaps due to the long separations— there were times when she admits to being "out of sorts with matrimony" (*Letters* 63). And her marital problems may be the reason behind her tolerance for divorce. In a society where marriage extended into the beyond, Child in a letter dated Jan. 15, 1847 bluntly observes, "when people *are* incongruous and mutually *feel* that they are, it is the wisest and best thing to separate let society say what it may. Nay, *I* go so far as to consider it positively *wrong*, under such circumstances, to live together in the married relation" (*Letters* 235).

Although she never married, Catharine Sedgwick's autobiography, written for her great-niece Alice Minot, reveals that the author well knew the dangers marriage held for women. As Mary Kelley points out in her introduction to the autobiography, *The Power of Her Sympathy*, "Her siblings, female and male, played significant albeit starkly different roles in their sister's decision to remain single" (22). To Catharine, Eliza's and Frances's marriages served as "cautionary tales" which "made tangible a gender hierarchy in which women were relatively powerless" (23). Referring to letters from her two older sister, Sedgwick makes this abundantly clear, although the two marriages appear completely opposite in nature. Eliza, calm and domestic, the mother of twelve children, was "the steady light of her home" (85) in a caring marriage. However, her husband was also of "the old pattern — resolute, fearless, enduring, generous, with alternations of tenderness and austerity ... that were trying to the gentle disposition and unvarying and quiet devotion to duty of my sister" (88). Thinking back on Eliza's short life (she died of a stroke at age 54), she briefly, but succinctly sketches the ambiguous role of the nineteenth-century married woman: "Oh, dear sister, what a life of trial, of patient endurance, of sweet hopes, heavenly affections, keen disappointments, harsh trials, acute sorrows and acute joys then opened upon you! What a life of truth, fidelity, faith, labor and love you lived" (84). Still, the marriage did not encourage emulation.

Neither did her sister Frances's: Sedgwick saw it in a sinister light. Due to severe spousal abuse, Frances "endured much heroically" in her marriage (85). Although she never admits that some of the fault might lie with Frances herself — she had a volatile character and was given to emotional excesses — Sedgwick presents a woman who cannot have been the easiest person to live with. Frances was "excitable, irritable, enthusiastic, imaginative.... No sphere could bound or contain Frances's interests or affections" (85). Despite this portrayal, Sedgwick puts the blame for the marriage's failure on the husband only. In a letter to her sister Eliza, dated Dec. 1, 1822, she describes her brother-in-law as "*brutal* in his conduct to her (Frances)," claiming that he "has for a long time rendered her miserable": he is "oppressive" and "essentially diabolical" (Kelley 23). Accurate or not, Sedgwick's words make her unmarried state more than understandable. Yet her sisters' experiences did not lead to negative literary representations of marriage.

Although not given to critiquing the marriages of his siblings, Cooper shared the preoccupations of his contemporaries regarding matrimony. That is, in his journals, letters, and novels he repeatedly discusses and asserts the importance of marriage, both as the foundation of society and a means to temper male impetuousness. And he obviously had the good sense to not take the male prerogative too far: in keeping with his beliefs, he had resigned his commission in the United States Navy upon marrying Susan De Lancey. His private writings reveal his strong sense of familial commitment and duty, not only to his wife and children but also to the families of his brothers.[13] Many letters attest to his deep affection for his wife — and to his respect for her opinions: in literary matters she is his "tribunal of appeals" and his "female mentor," influencing his literary and financial decisions.[14] Private papers show that the Cooper family, as James Grossman has observed in his 1949 Cooper biography, "had one of those thoroughly happy old-fashioned marriages in which the husband's formal rights of mastery were rigidly respected and the wife, through her delicate sensibilities and the other arts of love, had her way. Susan's way was always in her husband's interests, and the gracefulness of her management left full room for the play of his independent vigor" (16). In other words, it was a marriage that at least outwardly appeared to conform to the ideal of the cult of domesticity — and, more importantly, one where the wife "subtextually" was in control — a pattern Cooper replicated in the conclusions of some of his novels. Mabel Dunham of *The Pathfinder* and Mary Pratt of *The Sea Lions*, for example, both have their husbands change domicile so that they become more domesticated and stay home with their wives. Mabel moves Jasper Western to the coast; Mary persuades Roswell Gardiner to move inland. House and Belfiglio comment about the blurring of the borders of separate spheres in the Cooper household that "we might rather conjecture that Cooper's own experience in growing up on the frontier caused him to be, like Natty Bumppo, relatively unconscious of sexually assigned roles.... Necessity and common sense, rather than sex, decided who did what just as they had when Cooperstown was still the frontier" (46). Cooper's letters and journals certainly support this assessment, although one of the pieces of evidence presented by House and Belfiglio, the fact that he asked his *wife*, and not his *nephew* William, who was traveling with the family, to break up their household in Florence, to my mind speaks just as much of Cooper's knowledge of and respect for his wife's abilities as an able domestic administrator (and his adherence to the ideas of the cult of domesticity) than it does to the opposite. After all, all aspects of housekeeping, including arranging for a move from one location or country to another, belonged to the wife's sphere of interest; it would not have been delegated to a young, inexperienced nephew. Theirs was also a marriage sustained by religious faith; journal entries show that prayers and Bible readings remained constant throughout their forty-five years of married life. The Coopers' habit of reciting together the prayer from the Episcopal wedding ceremony before Cooper left on even a short business journey stands as a touching example of their faith and their love. It was also the last prayer the two prayed together on the morning of Cooper's death, when Susan added it to their morning prayers.[15] She survived him by only two months.

✻ ✻ ✻

> Mrs. Fletcher received his decision as all wives of that age of undisputed masculine supremacy (or most of those of our less passive age) would do, with meek submission.
> — Catharine Maria Sedgwick, *Hope Leslie*, 1827

With all the attention lavished on marriage and motherhood in advice books, ladies' periodicals, and private papers, one might expect that similar attention would have been paid to these institutions in the domestic novels flooding the market place. However, in most nineteenth-century fiction, marriage and maternal characters are at best marginal: male and female writers alike remove wives and, in particular, the "indispensable" mothers—even from the novels' domestic sphere. Motherless girls were hardly a novelty in literary plots; however, in light of the cult of domesticity's emphasis on the mother's influence on her children, this issue merits inquiry. Why this lack of maternal figures, despite a vast number of domestic novels and female authors? Critics on both sides of the Atlantic have pondered the question. Some argue, as does Marianne Hirsch, that the "female family romance" is based on *fraternal* rather than *maternal* attachments and that the heroine, "determined to shape a different plot for herself, tends not only to be separated from the figure and the story of her mother, but she herself tries to avoid maternity at all cost" (34). Shari L. Thurer observes that the deployment of a motherless protagonist enabled authors "to revise standard patriarchal plots" (207). Others, like Sandra Gilbert and Susan Gubar, have claimed that mothers managed to tell their stories, not overtly, but through gaps and contradictions in the textual representation. Regardless of critical approach, though, a reader of nineteenth-century fiction may discover a somewhat schizophrenic approach to the issue of motherhood, perhaps symptomatic of the authors' ambivalence to their own mothers and to the conventions they felt compelled to use.[16] On the one hand, the cult of domesticity retains its influence: dying or departed wives and mothers are venerated; they are "angelic" and "sainted" personifications of the conventions of the day. *Hobomok*, *Hope Leslie*, and *The Wide, Wide World* all conform to this convention; the authors marginalize and remove wives and mothers, simultaneously sanctifying them by presenting them as possessing superior qualities. On the other hand, nineteenth-century writers often criticize the wives and mothers they actually keep in their texts, showing them as abusive, self-centered, and neglectful, especially of their domestic and maternal duties. Austen's *Pride and Prejudice* and Cooper's *Precaution* fall into this category.[17]

In *Hobomok*, Child discusses three marriages spanning two generations: Mary Conant's two marriages and her parents' marriage. The older Conants' marriage is, the text shows, based on and sustained through female affection and patience. It also manifests a rebellion. In a time when marriage was an economic contract between families, Mary's mother, clearly ahead of her time, subverts patriarchal authority by opting for a marriage to the man she loves, even if this means exile and poverty. In keeping with Victorian notions about a wife's function in marriage, she supports and comforts the embittered and disappointed husband, much like Child herself had comforted her despondent David. Mrs. Conant may insist that "It is the duty of woman to love and obey her husband" (74); however, her support of her husband is not only a matter of duty. The text implies that the marriage, despite hardships due to financial problems, emigration, and the husband's "misanthropy and gloom," succeeds due to Mrs. Conant's patience and her affection for her husband. Child describes the marriage in poetic terms, showing the interdependence of male strength and female dependence: "But the love of woman endured through many a scene of privation and hardship, even after the character of its object was totally changed; and the rigid Calvinist, in that lone place, surrounded by his lovely family, seemed like some proud magnolia of the south, scathed and bared of its leaves, adorned with the golden flowers of the twining jessamine" (8). Mrs. Conant also exerts her influence in more direct ways. Now an invalid, she calms her husband by putting her hand on his arm when his temper flares at his daughter. Her intervention succeeds because "a spirit of tenderness toward his sick wife had survived the wreck of all his kindest feelings" (9). Despite this rather limited tenderness, Mr. Conant rules his family with a hard hand; the text presents him as hard and tyrannical, a far cry from the "kinde and tender helpe-meete" his wife tries to project in a letter to her father (80). (Incidentally, Mrs. Fletcher in *Hope Leslie* describes herself in exactly the same words.) The home is not entirely a "woman's sphere"; the husband decides who gains access, issuing "commands which his wife dared not disobey" (80). Only her imminent death changes this power structure; now the husband takes on female qualities, watching "with the tender solicitude of a mother over her sickening infant" (108). More importantly, Mrs. Conant's death effects a transformation in her husband. His wife's dying has stirred up "those deep recesses of feeling, which had for years been sealed within his soul" (109). Reminding her husband about their "thwarted love," Mrs. Conant exacts a promise that he allow his daughter to marry Charles Brown, thereby ensuring his compliance to their marriage at the end of the narrative. Female love has tempered male rigidity; or rather, it has released repressed male emotions.

Child says little of Mrs. Conant as parent, although she presents the invalid as a "gentle and affectionate" mother whose "remembrance of her own thwarted inclinations" leads her to indulge her daughter's wishes (47). Remembering her problems with her own father, she is more willing than her husband to accept a son-in-law from outside their Separatist faith. When Mr. Conant is away, she on one occasion allows Mary to meet her lover Charles unchaperoned, on another occasion she invites him into their home even though she admits, "I know not that I ought to allow this" (74). Despite the positive glimpses she allows of Mrs. Conant, Child also sees the invalid mother as a burden to her daughter; she is "a dead weight" on her daughter's "young life" (74).

Mary's first marriage, although discussed in far less detail than that of her parents, provides more insight into the dynamics of the nineteenth-century marriage, and especially to the complexities inherent in the term "affectionate." Initially, Child takes pains to show that women marry for a multitude of reasons, such as "Sudden bereavement" and "deep and bitter reproaches against her father" (121). Confusion, loneliness, and a desperate need to be loved weigh more heavily on Mary's mind than her affection for Hobomok. When Mary consents to become the Indian's wife, it is on her mother's grave and, declares the narrator, "there was a partial derangement of Mary's faculties ... a chaos in Mary's mind; — a dim twilight, which had at first made all objects shadowy, and which was rapidly darkening into misery, almost insensible of its source" (120). Child, then, emphasizes the despair and depression underlying Mary's decision. She also shows Hobomok's exploiting of Mary's mental confusion — his behavior indicates selfishness disguised as concern. He urges the marriage so she will have no time to change her mind. Furthermore, the wedding does not restore the bride: for several weeks Mary remains in a catatonic state. The narrator explains that "She would lie through the livelong day, unless she was requested to rise; and once risen, nothing could induce her to change her posture" (135). However, Child's text argues that even if mutual love initially is missing, one spouse's love and his suffering on behalf of his beloved begets gratitude, which in turn leads to "something like affection," making conjugal life "something more endurable" (135–36). Child never allows her readers to forget that Mary's love is elsewhere; Hobomok, before removing himself from Mary's life, tells Charles that in her dreams, "the name of the white man is on her lips" (137). The "erotic plasticity" Baym attributes to Mary allows her to give her body but not her soul to her Indian husband (1992 71); a proper Victorian lady gave her heart only once. Interestingly, the text divulges few details about Mary's second marriage, limiting herself to comment that "Brown seldom forgot his promises of forbearance," thus avoiding religious strife within the family (149).

Child also marginalizes Mary's own experience as mother; however, her scanty portrayal of this phase of her heroine's life evokes the cult of domesticity. Mary becomes "the mother of a hopeful son" whose smiles "brought more of pleasure than of pain" (74). The author stresses maternal love: Mary feels "more love for the innocent object, than she thought she should ever again experience" (74). Later, when Hobomok has divorced her and she is about to marry Brown, her maternal concern for her son decides where the family will live. She asserts she cannot go to England because "My boy would disgrace me, and I never will leave him; for love to him is the only way that I can now repay my debt of gratitude" (148).

Nineteenth-century ideas also dictate the novel's treatment of marriage rituals and divorce; Child puts a contemporary grid over such events as Sally Oldham's marriage and Hobomok's marriage to and divorce from Mary. Her nineteenth-century sensibility gets the better of her when she unites Sally and John Collier in a religious ceremony conducted by a clergyman, something the Separatists of 1629 would neither have allowed nor recognized.[18] Hobomok's marriage to Mary is more probable. George Elliot Howard explains that although the Puritans frowned upon interracial marriages, marriage between white persons and Native Americans was not forbidden until 1786. Furthermore, since the Puritans considered marriage a civil contract, the partners could marry themselves just as they made other contracts. However, like all civil institutions, such "self-gifta" (self-marriage) had to be sanctioned by civil authorities (Howard Vol. II. 209). Hobomok's marriage to Mary may have been void on those grounds, although Mary considers it "no less sacred" than other marriages. Curiously, although Hobomok marries Mary in a Native American ceremony, he sees to it that the divorce is authenticated also by white authorities, by the governor of "New Plimouth" (146), thereby enabling her return to the white world. Puritans allowed divorce; it was, after all, Howard observes, "the counterpart of civil marriages." Howard adds that divorce was granted "for various causes, such as desertion, cruelty, or breach of the marriage vow; and usually, though not always, the husband and wife were dealt with as equals before the law" (Howard Vol. II. 330).[19] Child, however, presents a rather unexpected and very thoughtful reason for divorce: the consideration for another's happiness. Hobomok, acutely aware of his wife's longings, divorces her so "that Mary may be happie" (146).

Although much more detailed and melodramatic than *Hobomok*, Sedgwick's *Hope Leslie*, like Child's work, begins and ends with marriage and encompasses two generations. It also simultaneously elevates and marginalizes actual wives and mothers. Paralleling *Hobomok*'s plot, *Hope Leslie* argues for and reinforces the nineteenth-century conception of a fulfilling marriage. The matrimony it envisions at the novel's end for the heroine and hero, Hope Leslie and Everell Fletcher, is one based on common interests, mutual affection, and respect — exactly the kind of relationship the "most indulgent class of our readers, the misses in their teens" could wish for (348). Yet before the readers reach the expected conclusion, Sedgwick discusses — and rejects — Anglican and Puritan ideas of matrimony. Her critique of the patriarchal seventeenth-century marriage is sharper than Child's, perhaps because of the tendency in domestic literature to attack greed. Sir William's actions are financially motivated. Like other parents of his time, he conceives of marriage as a financial matter, arranged by parents, completely ignoring their children's, especially their daughters', feelings. Sir William chooses his nephew William as his only child's spouse solely because the young man carries his name and because Sir William possesses "the common ambition of transmitting his name with his wealth" (7). He perceives marriage as merely an economic arrangement contracted to ensure that a "courtly fortune" — and a name — remains in the family (7). As soon as the prospective groom refuses to give up his Puritan faith, the marriage is off and the prospective bride forced into a loveless marriage. Due to paternal rigidity and greed, what would have been an affectionate marriage ends as an example of thwarted love that, the text argues, leads to an "imbecility of utter despair" and "a total alienation of mind" in the daughter (13–14).

Thwarted love obviously only harms women: William Fletcher soon lets himself become persuaded to marry Mr. Winthrop's ward, an orphan who had, "in the eyes of the elders, all the meek graces that befitted a godly maiden and dutiful helpmate" (14). Appropriately named Martha, for the biblical character more concerned with housekeeping duties than spiritual enlightenment, she serves her husband faithfully, and when he decides to remove to a frontier settlement instead of subjecting himself to a rule he sees as hypocritical, follows him obediently. The narrator comments that she "received his decisions as all wives of that age of undisputed masculine supremacy (or most of those of our less passive age) would do, with meek submission" (16), adroitly and somewhat ironically critiquing her society's views on the role of wives. Fletcher, of course, expects nothing less: he has, in this respect, a successful marriage. Like any properly educated nineteenth-century woman, Martha lets actions demonstrate the depth of her emotions. Sedgwick comments that Mrs. Fletcher "never magnified her love by words, but expressed it by that self-devoting, self-sacrificing conduct to her husband and children, which characterizes, in all ages and circumstances, faithful and devoted woman" (36). This textual representation of love and devotion evokes the one shown by Hobomok, and like his has the same effect on the spouse. Martha's "careful conformity" to her husband's wishes and her "steady love, which hath kept far more than even measure with my deserts" has secured her husband's steadily growing affection, although the narrator observes that his first love "could not be transferred to another" (20). Like Child's text, Sedgwick's asserts that even if love initially is missing, one can learn to "love" or at least respect a spouse who shows love and consideration.[20]

Sedgwick's representation of Puritan family life shows relatively little of Mrs. Leslie and Mrs. Fletcher as mothers and even less of their education. But Martha Fletcher has obviously been raised in strict accordance with Puritan values, whereas Alice has been "educated in retirement, by her mother" (9). Alice, an "angelic spirit" (14) in love with her cousin but forced to marry a man she does not love, endures until the death of her husband. She then takes her daughters and heads for the New World but dies on the transatlantic crossing and is, strictly speaking, never part of the novel's plot. This plot device saves William Fletcher from the temptation to make any kind of choice between his first love and his wife. Sedgwick also removes Martha from the plot in the novel's early stages: the "faithful and devoted woman" dies trying to protect her children during Mononotto's attack on the family home. However, what the narrator allows the reader to see of her character shows that it clearly conforms to nineteenth-century domestic ideals. When William Fletcher is "persuaded to unite himself with her"—an appropriate match as she is John Winthrop's ward—she has, "in the eyes of the elders, all the meek graces that befitted a godly maiden and dutiful helpmate" (14). When her husband decides to accompany Winthrop and his host of Puritans to the New World, she accepts the news, "as all wives of that age of undisputed masculine supremacy (or most of those of our less passive age) would do, with meek submission" (16). But even submission has limits: when she learns that her husband's true love has set out for America, and that the ship has indeed arrived, she may be a "humble wife," but she admits that "it is the nature of a woman to crave the first place" (20). A long letter to her absent husband, reminiscent of Anne Bradstreet's poems, gives the most in-depth impression of Martha Fletcher's relationship to her "good and honoured husband" and to her children. She dotes on them, especially the eldest, Everell; when he comes before her "mind's eye," she admits, she "can see no other object" (32). She boasts to her husband about the other four children: their "three little girls are thriving mightily, and as to the baby, you will not be ashamed to own him.... He is by far the largest child I ever had, and the most knowing" (33). Although not sympathetic to Native American beliefs, her maternal care even extends to Magawisca, whom she instructs in "Mr. Cotton's cathechism" (32). Clearly, she cherishes her domestic life and her marriage.

Not all affectionate marriages offer happiness for the wife and mother. In Warner's *The Wide, Wide World*, Ellen Montgomery's parents ostensibly have married for love and against parental wishes, and the marriage has alienated Mrs. Montgomery from her wealthy Scottish family. Warner's representation of the relationship between the spouses, though, seems strained. The pair lacks mutual respect and understanding, perhaps because only the wife is a Christian. However, the novel makes it clear that although Captain Montgomery is a bad breadwinner and an insensitive husband who is "not readily touched by any thing" (61), he still controls the household and especially his wife, overruling all her objections regarding his treatment of their daughter. When the sick Mrs. Montgomery is unwilling to leave Ellen, correctly fearing she will never see her again if they part, he uses his authority as husband to ensure his wife's cooperation in the matter. Warner paints a negative picture of nineteenth-century fatherhood. Captain Montgomery is a man completely ignorant of conjugal and parental feelings: he is "in happy unconsciousness of his wife's distress and utter inability to sympathize with it" (60). Yet he masks his intentions. When he thinks his wife clings "obstinately" to her child and severs their bond, he ostensibly does so in his wife's best interest. To "the pressure of argument," the narrator observes, "Captain Montgomery added the weight of authority, insisting on her compliance." (60). Mrs. Montgomery, ever the subordinate wife, yields.

Whereas Child and Sedgwick marginalize the mother, Warner allows her more prominence and influence, constantly emphasizing the almost symbiotic attachment between mother and daughter. Mrs. Montgomery, although an invalid, is the most important person in the heroine Ellen's life, carefully shaping her daughter into an angel in the house — and a mirror of her pious and self-sacrificing self. As befits a mother from the heyday of the cult of domesticity, she has the "proper priorities." Ellen reads the Bible and sings hymns; she also nurses her mother and takes care of her own personal belongings. The gifts Mrs. Montgomery buys Ellen before their parting reinforce the indoctrination of the cult's values: Ellen receives a Bible and a workbox, necessary items for a good Victorian girl. Seeking to inculcate Christian values, the mother stresses the reason for her gifts: they will give her (the mother) the "comfort" of knowing that she is providing "everything necessary to the keeping up of good habits" so that Ellen will "be always neat, and tidy, and industrious, depending upon others as little as possible; and careful to improve yourself by every means.... I will leave you no excuse, Ellen, for failing in any of these duties. I trust you will not disappoint me in a single particular" (31–32).

Incidentally, Mrs. Montgomery's illness functions as a powerful means of maternal control. Disobedience and lack of care has an adverse effect on her. Still, her hold on Ellen is stultifying in the extreme. The daughter, strictly speaking, has no life outside the sickroom. Although Warner has Ellen talk about going to school, she is often kept at home. She has no playmates of her own age, instead, she spends hours sitting by her mother's side. On one occasion, when Mrs. Montgomery feels "severely the effects of the excitement and the anxiety of the preceding day and night" and therefore lays motionless on her sofa, Ellen remains immobile by her side, pressing her lips to her mother's hand, "as if they would grow there" (18).

Ellen has no proper childhood; she is an adult in miniature, the dutiful only daughter taking care of an ailing parent. She is expected to devote herself to her mother and make her comfortable in any way she can; her own needs and sorrows have to be suspended. When their physician, Dr. Green, finds his patient weaker, "she isn't quite as well as she ought to be," he suggests that Ellen has not "taken proper care of her," reminding her that her mother "*must* not be excited — you must take care that she is not — it isn't good for her. You mustn't let her talk much, or laugh much, or cry at all, on any account; she mustn't be worried in the least" (19). Curiously, Warner never seems to see these extreme demands for filial devotion as maternal tyranny and child exploitation, unless a reader chooses to read the text as ironic. Instead, her text constantly asserts that the child owes nothing but gratitude and devotion and to a loving and self-sacrificing mother.

The novelist envisions a very different marriage for Ellen and John Humphreys than the one Ellen's parents had: a marriage built on common faith, love, and mutual respect. In a final but unpublished chapter to the novel, Warner imagines the two united in an affectionate, considerate and affluent relationship. When John brings his young bride home, "to the room he called hers," Ellen "noted the multiplied evidences of affection in the thoughtfulness, care, taste, and profusion on every hand displayed" (576). But Ellen not only gets a *room* of her own: John also provides her with "gold and silver pieces and bank bills" to spend exactly as she wishes (582). In this chapter, Warner adds a pragmatic touch; piety, the text asserts, has its worldly rewards.[21] A pious girl can look forward not only to a home in heaven but to an affluent life on earth. Yet the novelist never allows her characters to forget their Christian priorities. John and Ellen's life on earth, she demonstrates, is a *school* for heaven, not an end in itself. For, as John expresses it: "He that doeth the will of God abideth forever ... them that sleep in Jesus will God bring with him" (583).

A woman's duties in marriage and motherhood, as represented in *Hobomok*, *Hope Leslie*, and *The Wide, Wide World*, conform to the conventions promulgated by the cult of domesticity. If these texts are to be seen as vehicles for nineteenth-century socialization of women, the message is unmistakable: they uphold the era's patriarchal notions of family life, asserting the father's right to rule — and tyrannize — his household. All three works perceive of the domestic sphere as the only proper place for women: wives, mothers, and female children rarely venture outside it. Even when circumstance thrusts Ellen Montgomery into the "wide wide world," whether in America or in Scotland, she goes from one domestic situation to another, as had her mother, and their lives are circumscribed and restricted. Even when residing at a hotel, the domestic routine continues. Likewise, Mary Conant exchanges her father's house for a lodge in Hobomok's village and then ultimately returns to her home village as the wife of Charles Brown. Hope Leslie might be rebellious and independent, yet she also adapts to her prescribed role as wife and, one expects, mother. The novels make clear, especially through the depictions of the gentle but oh so short-lived mothers, that the wife defers to her husband, the daughter to her parents. Furthermore, the good wife performs her domestic mission even when she knows her husband is wrong, as does Mrs. Montgomery when her husband forbids her to wake Ellen and prepare the child for her departure to her aunt's farm the following morning. Still, the texts also indicate female disobedience and even subversion in thought and deed: Mrs. Conant, for example, undermines her husband's authority by allowing Charles Brown into their home. Martha Fletcher harbors unkind, bigoted thoughts towards the Natives. Although ostensibly following the cult of domesticity's demands, the fact that the texts allow the mother's thoughts on the matter to be heard shows a certain subversive bent on behalf of the characters.

To the twenty-first-century reader, Child's, Sedgwick's, and Warner's novels provide a rather negative picture of nineteenth-century motherhood. The works present maternal characters that may be loving and self-sacrificing, yet who are ultimately controlling and stultifying, thwarting their daughters' personal development. More importantly, by inculcating piety and domesticity — at times through a heavy dose of guilt — these mother lay the groundwork for patriarchal social conditioning.

❋ ❋ ❋

> Marriage is certainly the natural and most desirable state for a woman, but how few are there who, having entered it, know how to discharge its duties.... On the subject of marrying our daughters, for instance, instead of qualifying them to make a proper choice, they are generally left to pick up such principles and opinions as they may come at, as it were by chance.
> — James Fenimore Cooper, *Precaution*, 1820

One can hardly accuse *Precaution*'s narrator of idealizing matrimony, or of glorifying its maternal characters and their discharging of the duties it entailed. Acutely aware of marital discord and its causes, his terse observations seem to foreshadow Child's words in *The Frugal Housewife*. Both call for better female education in this area because parents clearly neglect to educate their daughters to ensure they "make a proper choice" of a marriage partner. The lack of a systematic female education — i.e., the systematic inculcation of duties and moral values — forms the root of the problem: female education is random and ineffectual, leaving young girls, *Precaution* asserts, to pick up "principles and opinions" at random. On the one hand, Cooper's first novel asserts the importance of marriage, leading its main characters towards it; on the other hand, the marriages described indicate a certain ambiguity as to the outcome of such ventures. They seem more discouragement than encouragement for the reader. But Cooper does not stop there: like his contemporaries, the female domestic writers, he follows a particular strategic trajectory: he valorizes the tradition of marriage while at the same time marginalizing or completely removing wives and mothers from the texts. In this as in other domestic texts, Cooper simultaneously asserts and critiques the popular conventions of his day. His motherless heroines, freed from their controlling and domesticating mothers, can enjoy the world at large, not only the kitchen and the drawing room. Still, as the above quote from *Precaution* asserts, marriage, presented as not only the "natural" but the "most desirable" state for a woman, evokes the arguments found on the pages of Child, Sedgwick, Cummins, and Warner. Like other writers of domestic fiction and advice literature, Cooper lamented the lack of preparation in young women's approach to marriage; like them he attempted to alleviate the situation by subtly redefining the roles of men and women within marriage. As regards marital roles, therefore, his notions are neither "merely conventional," nor do they "invariably support the established society" (Rans 41); rather, they express a desire to disclose the unrealistic paradigm the cult of domesticity prescribed for the nineteenth-century wife and mother.[22] Marriage and motherhood may be "natural" goals for women; however, too deep an absorption in these goals clearly has a negative impact both physically and mentally.

3. Marriage and Motherhood

Cooper, like the author of the article "Marriage" in the November 1832 issue of *Godey's Lady's Book*, advocated not blind female subjection but "equality" and "harmony," that is, he promoted matches founded on affection and mutual respect, not only on "class, property, opportunity, education, social standing" as Rans claims (Rans 41). Cooper saw marriage as the foundation of both private and public happiness and well-being in a rapidly changing society—and the wife as the person most capable of and responsible for achieving this effect. His instinct for realism, though, prevented him from presenting only a flattering image of marriage and motherhood. He knew, as House and Belfiglio have observed, the miseries "attendant on wrong choices—particularly matrimonial ones" (46) and strove to teach his readers to identify and then avoid making similar mistakes.

Like other nineteenth-century domestic writers, he builds his marital edifice on a foundation designed to support the four cornerstones of the cult of domesticity. But whereas the cult merely demands piety, purity, submissiveness, and domesticity, Cooper in addition insists on love, respect, and truth. Throughout his literary career, Cooper consistently demonstrated that a successful marriage depended on a careful blending of these elements. Yet nowhere does he discuss marriage with such eagerness and detail as in *Precaution*. This novel in particular, functions as a virtual manual for marriage and motherhood, furnishing its readers with examples of both good and bad marriages and parents. Furthermore, Cooper diligently instructs his readers as to the *reasons* for each individual relationship's success or failure. He reserves his sharpest criticism for the mothers who fail to instill good Christian values in their children. Cooper would never again attempt such a variety of representations of marriage and motherhood; however, the issues permeate all his novels, even his Leatherstocking tales. Throughout his career the author, as House and Belfiglio have observed, "arranges for all the women ... to be happily married at the end" (46), thus following the literary trends of his day. His heroes and heroines all can look forward to successful marriages, because they share not only affection but moral and social standing. Eager to address all aspects of family life, he also takes on the issue of maternity. Yet where writers like Child, Sedgwick, and Warner—while marginalizing the mother—present dutiful, angelic mothers who faithfully instill Christian and domestic virtues in their daughters, some of Cooper's incarnations fall short of the cult's ideal. His discussion and critique of marriage and motherhood are particularly comprehensive and poignant in *Precaution*; however, the author expresses his opinions on these important issues in other works, for example in *The Prairie, Home as Found, Satanstoe, The Chainbearer,* and *The Wept of Wish-Ton-Wish*.

Precaution's representations of marriage and motherhood have received little serious consideration over the years, even when critics have focused on marriage in Cooper's works. Mostly, the critical attention to the novel has been negative, characterized by an unwillingness to consider Cooper in any other context than that of his later "masculine tales" and his nonfiction.[23] Despite the scathing criticism heaped upon it during the twentieth century, *Precaution* is, as Robert Long points out, "at times surprisingly proficient, and for anyone interested in Cooper's beginnings as an author it is quite revealing" (40).[24] Yet the novel is revealing, not only as "an elaborate exploration of manners" as Long asserts (31), but as an early example of Cooper's link to the cult of domesticity. Cooper's literary *corpus*, and *Precaution* in particular, can, like the works of Charles Brockden Brown, Harriet Beecher Stowe, and Susan Warner, be seen as "surrogate mothers" for a culture not existent in social fact. *Precaution*, therefore, ought to be of profound interest for the student of nineteenth-century domesticity.

In keeping with his day's preoccupation with family life, Cooper's first novel, conceived, as it were, in the bosom of his family, presents itself as a catalogue of successful and not so successful marriages. More importantly, where many domestic writers led their characters no farther than the altar, Cooper takes his characters beyond this threshold, assiduously discussing each relationship's merits and flaws, carefully delineating the reasons for successes and failures. The novel, an entertaining, often even hilarious romp through Regency England, bluntly asserts that Cooper sees marriage as not only a female but as a male concern. As Grossman observes, *Precaution* presents matrimony not as a private union between two people but as "the intense business of a household" (22). This Cooper discusses in a blunt manner; Grossman argues that *Precaution*'s frank discussion of marriage violates "the decencies he is purporting to uphold" (22).[25] Yet the predominant tone in *Precaution* is neither prurience nor indelicacy. Instead, the novel instructs the reader that "If there be bliss in this life, approaching in any degree to the happiness of the blessed, it is the fruition of long and ardent love, where youth, innocence, piety, and family concord, smile upon the union" (393). This statement could stand as a motto for Cooper's works.

If there is less than a "revolution in ideas" in *Precaution*, there definitely is an "embrace of the conventional," to borrow a phrase from Tompkins. Cooper expresses what lay in the minds of nineteenth-century reformers, novelists, and readers. However, his embrace of the conventions of the cult of domesticity is more than a strategy to reach an established audience; it is a clever way of inculcating a Christian moral message. Still,

Cooper goes further than slavishly aping Mrs. Opie's and Jane Austen's novels: he appears to have modeled his plot on Shakespeare's comedies just as much as he has on contemporary novels. There is a disarming Renaissance frankness over the many discussions on marriage. And, if we are to believe the novel's reviews, it certainly did not offend its readers. As Long points out, *Precaution* did "moderately well" in England; it even "went into a second printing" there (18). True to its comedic form, it appropriately ends in a veritable flood of marriages, but only after a series of intrigues, obfuscations, and misunderstandings have been resolved.[26] In keeping with comic conventions, the work intends not merely to amuse, but to 1) teach a value system that will ensure "permanent happiness in wedlock" (121); and 2) enable young women to approach marriage in a professional manner; that is, with precaution and domestic skills.

While the novel is, on one level, a comedy, it is, on another level, a carefully constructed sermon, aimed to simultaneously entertain and above all instruct. Precaution in choice of spouse, a prerequisite to ensure marital happiness, the novel argues, must be based on piety. In this respect, Cooper's representation foreshadows the main concern in Warner's *The Wide, Wide World*. In both works, a successful marriage is a Christian marriage; piety guarantees not only the discharge of marital duty but marital fidelity. There can be no security "against the commission of enormities, but an humble and devout dependence on the assistance of that Almighty Power, which alone is able to hold us up against temptation" (121). Yet where other domestic works might have demanded piety of the heroine only, letting her behavior and prayers transform the hero, Cooper holds the hero to the same standard as he holds the heroine. For both, piety clearly has its rewards; however, the novel emphasizes the effect it has on the wife. The conclusion presents Emily "in the happiest of all stations a female can be in: she is the pious wife of a pious husband, beloved, and deserving of it" (416). Her piety not only ensures marital happiness, it enables her to function in a crisis. When her husband joins his regiment to fight Napoleon, Emily does not despair but trusts in her Maker. And, the narrator piously observes, "It is at such moments as our own acts, or events affecting us, get to be without our control, that faith in the justice and benevolence of God is the most serviceable to the Christian" (393). Furthermore, due to the young couple's piety, the two "are well prepared to meet any reverse of fortune which may occur, as well as to discharge the duties on which they have entered" (416). In this context, the "happily ever after" means storing up goods in heaven. Both spouses are, as Emily's uncle and his servant Peter observe, "as good as angels" and "As good as mankind can well be" (390). None of Cooper's later characters would live up to the standard of Emily and Pendennyss.

Yet if Pendennyss and Emily experience the ideal nineteenth-century Christian marriage, many of the novel's other characters do not. To dramatize the limitations of other relationships, Cooper cleverly juxtaposes the Pendennysses' marriage to those of other characters in his text. In the case of Grace Chatterton and John Moseley, piety in fact drives a wedge between the spouses since John neither shares nor fully understands his wife's piety and therefore attempts to limit her churchgoing. He is not exactly opposed to it, however. Indeed, he claims to "like to hear a good sermon, but not in bad weather" (410), and he cleverly manipulates her, under the guise of kindness, to stay at home in inclement weather. Using her desire to go on a trip to see a waterfall as a bargaining chip, he proposes to drive her if "you will not expose your health again in going to the church on a Sunday, if it rains" (410). The text fully demonstrates that while men may be attracted to a pious woman — for their own selfish reasons — they may not be willing to reciprocate this piety, let alone allow themselves to be influenced by it, thus bringing grief to the spouse and a certain discord to the marriage. Cooper here challenges the assumption, propounded by the cult's adherents, that a pious woman teaches her husband to pray, leading him to salvation. Grace loses at least this round in her struggle to reform her husband; convenience triumphs over conversion. Although the conclusion to their discussion may seem like a compromise, Grace, has, in light of the novel's emphasis on piety, lost more than she has won: she has had to compromise her faith.

What happens, then, when husband and wife have married for worldly considerations only, for transient qualities like wealth and rank, and where the marriage is an economic transaction rather than a love match? Cooper, as categorically as Child and Sedgwick, rejects this conception of marriage. The novel presents the union between young Catharine Chatterton and the aging Lord Herriefield as a disaster for a variety of reasons, the most prominent being parental management, selfishness, lack of common ground, artifice, female greed, and male vanity. Kate has married for rank and position, not love; she "was resolved to be a viscountess" and, more importantly, "her mother was equally determined that she should be rich" (226). Lord Herriefield has married for a different but still wrong set of characteristics: he has been drawn to Kate's beauty and charming simplicity, only to stop loving her when he finds out that it is all artifice. The text chastises Lord Herriefield for his vanity: "It had never struck the viscount as impossible that an artless and innocent girl would fall in love with his faded and bilious face" (395), thereby proving Rowbotham's assertion that men are "too easily fooled by a lovely exterior" (Rowbotham 47). *Precaution*'s narrator tries to counteract the effects of female deceit and male vanity, arguing that "Men are flattered for a season with notice that has been unsought, but it never fails to injure the woman who practices it in the opinion of the other sex, in time. Without a single feeling in common, without a regard to anything but self, in either husband or wife ... a separation must follow, or their days be spent in wrangling and misery. Catharine willingly left her husband; her husband more willingly got rid of her" (395). The reader notices that a broken relationship hurts the wife more than it does the husband, even when the latter's behavior is no less deplorable than that of his wife. Cooper was well aware of the double standard that applies in such cases and refuses to gloss over the circumstances. Kate returns to a quiet life in England with her mother watching her every step, guarding her much more carefully than she had before her marriage. Lord Herriefield, on the other hand, soon after his wife's departure for England leaves for Italy accompanied by "the repudiated wife of a British naval officer" (395–6). *Precaution* does not conclude with this negative image of marriage: Cooper knew the importance of reinforcing his exhortation to engage in the Christian marriage. Instead, he lets the Rev. Dr. Ives have the last word: "...had I a daughter, I would follow a similar course. Give her a delicacy, religion, and a proper taste, aided by the unseen influence of a prudent parent's taste, and the chances of a woman for happiness would be much greater than they are" (503).

Precaution is additionally notable for its criticism of mothers. The novel's cast of characters includes a wide array of bad mothers, most of them belonging to or aspiring to enter the upper classes. The latter, in the character of Mrs. Jarvis, is crassly ridiculed. She fawns over the aristocratic but dastardly Colonel Egerton; whatever he says and does is "always right with that lady" (34). She and her daughters appear in church wearing clothes "carefully selected for the advantageous display of their persons," they "sailed" into their pew, and "the old lady, whose size and flesh really put kneeling out of the question, bent forward for a moment at an angle of eighty with the horizon" (30–31). Even Lady Moseley does not escape chastisement. Already in the opening pages, the narrator comments that she has her "failings ... although few were disposed to view her errors with that severity which truth and a just discrimination of character render necessary" (4). The woman is "religious, but hardly pious; she was charitable in deeds, but not always in opinions; her intentions were pure, but neither her prejudices nor her reasoning powers suffered her to be at all times consistent" (4). This representation is far from flattering, although the narrator comments that "none were ever heard to say aught against her breeding, her morals, or her disposition" (4). He clearly indicates that breeding, morals, and disposition fail to make her a paragon of maternal love and duty. Lady Chatterton, another upper-class mother, fares even worse: she is "really a managing woman in more senses than one" (52). Significantly, her management stops short of instilling proper values in her daughters. To Lady Chatterton, the bottom line is money; the narrator snidely comments that all her considerations of marriage "would have ended with the footing of a rent-roll, provided it contained five figures" (52).

Cooper never again preached about marriage as eagerly as he had in *Precaution*, but the subject never left his mind, as his subsequent literary activities illustrate. *The Prairie*, for instance, presents a hierarchy of marriages just as it presents a hierarchy of daughters. Besides the Bushes, the novel also contains the mandatory upper-class marriage — here between the Creole Inez and the American officer Middleton. It ends with a glimpse of the middle-class marriage of Ellen Wade and Paul Hover. However, Cooper falls rather silent in connection with these marriages, perhaps because of the erotic implications. Ironically, the most "erotic" implications of marriage in the novel concerns Inez and Middleton, yet both of them are, ostensibly, pure and innocent. The novel's plot, moreover, builds on an erotic of delay, since Inez has been abducted on their wedding day; i.e., before the marriage has been consummated. Although never actually mentioned, sexuality is clearly an issue in their relationship: Middleton not only has to rescue his wife, but he has to claim her as his wife — i.e., consummate the marriage — before she can be forced into an interracial marriage. Cooper provides several examples of the young husband's anguish when the Sioux Mahtoree's lust-filled eyes fall on Inez; witnessing the Indian's "fierce joy," for instance, makes Middleton grow cold (270). Both men, then, see Inez primarily as a sexual being, as does the narrator, although the text consistently insists on Inez's piety and otherworldliness.

Ellen Wade's and Paul Hover's relationship follows the same pattern of erotic delay: the young beekeeper for weeks has been trailing the Bush clan to stay near his lover, Ellen, hoping to claim her from her "family." The novel also provides insight into the Middletons' and the Hovers' later life. In keeping with the prescribed role for nineteenth-century wives, female piety and mildness temper male impetuosity. The angelic influence of Inez and Ellen, and the rectitude of Middleton, succeed, "in the process of time," in working a great and beneficial change in Paul's character. Domesticity in this case breeds civic responsibility: Paul ends up, "actually," as "a member of the lower branch of the Legislature of the State where he has long resided" (376).

Cooper is at his best, though, when he describes lower-class families. At first, this may seem surprising, given his respect for upper-class families. Yet liberated from the conventions that dictated a genteel portrayal of upper-class characters, he can indulge in more realistic descriptions, especially of his female characters. A particularly interesting Cooper marriage in this respect is the relationship between Ishmael and Esther Bush in *The Prairie*. The text shows a strong maternal character who decides not only the family's domestic affairs but its relationship to the world outside, claiming a mother's right to do so. Although Ishmael and Esther seem to a certain extent to observe the division into male and female spheres, this marriage is a joint venture. Even on their trek westward across the plains, Esther is clearly a *partner*, not a subordinate. Furthermore, Esther's contribution is needed for the survival of the family in the world at large. She possesses strength, courage, and determination; she has, her husband asserts, "no more fear of a red-skin than of a suckling cub or of a wolf pup," nor is she willing to "part with her cheese and her butter without a price" (63). She has even less fear of authority than her husband. When the latter leaves military service after one season, "without calling on the Paymaster to settle my arrearages," his wife settles them for him. As Esther afterward boasts, she made such use of the pay-ticket "that the States gained no great sum, by the oversight" (63). Life on the frontier, the text argues, blurs gender distinctions, at least among the lower classes. This housewife exerts herself not only in domestic chores, but in defending her family from invaders: "Esther had already, on one occasion, made good the log tenement of Ishmael, against an inroad of savages, and on another, she had been left for dead, by her enemies, after a defence that with a more civilized foe, would have entitled her to the honours of a liberal capitulation" (147). House and Belfiglio see her as a "degraded Amazon" and argue that she is the head of the clan only as long as she has male supporters (46), but Cooper presents her as a woman who clearly can hold her own against any opponent, especially if there is a threat to her children, regardless of male support. She is also the one who demands the family go looking for the missing son, and who feels most acutely the pain of his death. When the family sets out to search for Asa, she takes the lead, claiming a mother's prerogative: "I am leader to day, and I *will* be followed — who so proper, let me know, as a mother to head a search for her own lost child!" (132).

Esther, though, is more than Ishmael's "termagant assistant" (120); she is a sort of lower-class angel in the house. Unlike her husband, she can read, and in possessing "fragments of a bible" she is also the repository of whatever religion has trickled down to the clan. She seeks solace in the Bible; reading "a chapter in that book," Ishmael comments, "always does you good" (142). She is also the one to remind her husband, when Mahtoree wishes to give Ishmael his cast-off wife, Tachechana, of his responsibilities as a Christian father. Only an animal would accept such an obscene offer: "Go back among your children, friend; go, and remember that you are not a prowling bear, but a Christian man, and thank God that you ar' a lawful husband!" (298). Still, Cooper refuses to present her as a truly religious woman. Although she has "long been in the habit of resorting to it (i.e., the fragment of the Bible in their possession) under the pressure of such circumstances as were palpably beyond human redress," she has, the narrator maintains, "made a sort of convenient ally of the word of God, rarely troubling it for counsel, however, except when her own incompetency to avert an evil was too apparent to be disputed" (357).

In 1847, Cooper gave Esther Bush an heiress in the character of Prudence Thousandacres in *The Chainbearer*, the wife of squatter Aaron Thousandacres who is helping himself to the Littlepage family forests. Fiercely loyal to husband and family, she is described as a "tiger's mate," "tiger's dam," and a "tigress" (404); her children are her "brood" (242). However, there is none of the ridicule in the description that Cooper earlier had used in describing lower-class women, for instance, Mrs. Abbott in *Home as Found*, a widow "bewitched of small worldly means, five children, and of great capacity for circulating evidence" (227). Instead, the narrator, Mordaunt Littlepage, expresses a grudging admiration for this strong maternal character.

Again, Cooper allows his readers to *see* Prudence; he provides a realistic description of her physical appearance without resorting to abstract terms. If he intends to show how inferior she is compared to the perfect, but bland, upper class wife and mother, he also manages to bring her to life to a degree he never manages with her upper-class counterparts. Prudence becomes a *person*, not an abstract manifestation of the hardships visited on pioneer women. To the heroine, Ursula "Dus" Malbone, she is "that strange woman, in whom there is so much of her sex mingled with a species of ferocity like that of a she-bear" (417). According to the narrator and hero, Prudence is a "sharp-featured, keen, gray-eyed old woman ... sallow, attenuated, with sunken cheeks, hollow, lack-lustre eyes, and broken-mouthed" (242–43). However, she fulfills the basic demands of the cult of domesticity. She is, for example, first and foremost a conscientious and nurturing mother: "her thoughts were chiefly bent on the cares of her brood; and her charities extended but little beyond them. She had been the mother of fourteen children herself, twelve of which survived. All had been born amid the difficulties, privations, and solitudes of stolen abodes in the wilderness" (242).

That twelve of her fourteen children have survived despite "difficulties" speaks volumes about Prudence's ability to nurture her family. She has "the pride and feeling of a mother, nature having its triumph in her breast as well as in that of the most cultivated woman of the land" (383). The narrator also admires her strength of character and her endurance, observing that she "had endured enough to break down the constitutions and to destroy the tempers of half a dozen of the ordinary beings of her sex; yet she survived, the same enduring, hard-working, self-denying, suffering creature she had been from the day of her bloom and beauty" (242). Prudence comes from strong stock and has survived hardships that would have broken a weaker woman. She has also taught her children obedience and some manners: at dinner, her son Zephaniah and her daughter Lowiny "deported themselves with great modesty at the table" (244). And, although she does not pray for her dying husband herself, she sees to it that "her own 'dying man' ... is not to be forgotten" after Dus has prayed with her uncle (417). She also urges her husband to turn his thoughts from his lumber to eternal matters, toward his "convarsion," a matter which they both, although "children of Puritan parents and a godly ancestry" have delayed long enough (424). Cooper indicates that Prudence over the years has had problems accepting her husband's illegal way of making a living. Predicting she will soon follow him to the grave, she adds, "when we meet together ag'in, I hope't will be where no boards, or trees, or acres can ever make more trouble for us!" (424). However, neither Prudence nor Dus accomplishes this: the squatter dies defiant, with "glary, but still fiery eyes." Mordaunt comments that he had never before "looked upon so revolting a corpse; and never wish to see its equal again" (434).

Although the narrator appears to have problems considering Prudence as fully human — he describes her as clinging "woman-like" to her husband — he acknowledges that she behaves in the appropriate manner. To her husband, she has "always been a faithful and hard-working woman" (423). When she discovers that her husband is not dead, only wounded, she knows how to make the patient comfortable, quietly showing both consideration and affection for her spouse by performing "those duties which naturally suggested themselves to one of her experience.... The whole time she was doing this, her tongue was muttering prayers and menaces, strangely blended together, and quite as strangely mixed up with epithets of endearment ... in a tone that sounded as if Thousandacres had a strong hold on her affections, and might at least have been kind and true to her" (404). At her husband's deathbed, she behaves with stoic strength and composure; however, her calmness covers deep grief. She sits "silent, tearless, moody, and heart-stricken by the great and sudden calamity that had befallen her race, but vigilant and attentive to the least movement in the huge frame of her wounded partner" (418). She neither complains nor acknowledges what goes on around her; she focuses all her attention on her husband: "To him she seemed to be unerringly true; and whatever she may, and must have thought of his natural sternness, and occasional fits of severity toward herself; all now seemed to be forgotten" (418). Although only a minor character in the novel, Prudence may well be one of Cooper's most strongly — and sympathetically — drawn lower-class maternal characters.

The Chainbearer's prequel, *Satanstoe*, presents a protagonist with a close relationship to his mother. To Corny, Madam Littlepage has a tender "gentle nature" (21) but also "good sense" (24). Sending her son off on his first journey to New York City, she is "a tender-hearted parent" but "full of anxiety in behalf of an only child" (46). The novel not only details a mother's love, it also affirms the mother's role as instructor — and women as the tamers of savage males. That Corny, who is unfamiliar with city life, is able to behave appropriately within the Mordaunt family circle is a testimony to her influence. The text also indicates that a mother's love and concern never end. When Corny is about to set out for Albany, and his father provides him with bills and invoices, urging him to "consult them before making any sales" (132), his mother reminds him that the letters of introduction he carries "will probably introduce you to good company, and that is a great beginning to a youth." More importantly, though, she wishes him to "cultivate the society of reputable females." And she explains why: "My sex has great influence on the conduct of yours, at your time of life, and both your manners and principles will be aided by being as much with women of character as possible" (133). And the motherless Anneke is just such a woman. Still, she only improves on the ground work laid by Madam Littlepage.

Finally, *The Wept of Wish-Ton-Wish* holds a special place in the context of Cooper's domestic fiction, being the only one of the novels under discussion not to marginalize the wife and mother. Initially, Ruth Heathcote seems the epitome of the cult of domesticity: as a child she was "one of the mildest and gentlest of the human race" (38); as an adult she is a "gentle" and "faithful wife" (28). Although she has received "new impulses" after becoming wife and mother, her disposition, the narrator confides, "suffered no change in marriage" (37–38). Ruth Heathcote emerges not only as the dutiful housekeeper with a house that displays the family's moral rectitude and social standing, Cooper also reveals less admirable character traits. As a mother she is "tender and anxious," "sensitive," and "affectionate"; she exercises her duties "with the devotedness of her sex"

(28, 63–64, 100). She instructs her children in religion and in more domestic activities such as needlework; the daughters pray and embroider at their mother's knee. The mother of young children, she is also sensitive to the plight of others, such as understanding that the young Indian captive Conanchet "mourneth for its parent" (63). However, Cooper shows that her sensitivity and magnanimity have their limits: her charity, then, does not extend to all God's creatures at all times. Critics have commented on her xenophobia; however, this attitude is consistent with the attitudes toward Indians that emerge in early American as well as nineteenth-century texts. Ruth also feels closer to her own children than to those belonging to friends. Although she has taken in a friend's orphaned daughter, Martha, whom she raises as her own child, she is closest to her own daughter and namesake. Ironically, this devoted mother by mistake saves the life of Martha in an Indian attack and is devastated when she discovers her error: "it was impossible to repress the feeling of disappointment which came over her with the consciousness of the mistake. Nature at first had sway, and to a degree that was fearfully powerful" (180). And after her daughter's disappearance she is "drooping hourly under the sorrow" (266). Later, when Conanchet returns the abducted girl — now his wife Narra-mattah — to her parents, Ruth at first hesitates to recognize her daughter. Holding Narra-mattah at arm's length, she seems "alike unwilling to release her hold, or to admit her closer to a heart which might rightfully be the property of another" (330). She embraces her only when Conanchet "telleth a mother to know her child" (331). Only then do her natural feelings take over: "Ruth could hesitate no longer; neither sound nor exclamation escaped her, but as she strained the yielding frame of her recovered daughter to her heart it appeared as if she strove to incorporate the two bodies into one" (331). However, Cooper shows that a mother's — and grandmother's — "natural feelings" have their limits. At the sight of her biracial grandchild, racial prejudice practically smothers Ruth's maternal instincts: "The innate and never-dying sentiment of maternal joy was opposed by all those feelings of pride that prejudice could not fail to implant, even in the bosom of one so meek" (357). Her reaction is negative: her coldness toward the child is noticeable — and hurtful — to both her husband and her daughter. Aware of their censure, she tries to hide her reactions by "bending her head low, so as entirely to conceal her own flushed face." Furthermore, it takes her husband's interference, and his reminder that "The wisdom of Providence is in this as in all its dispensations" to revive Ruth's "natural feeling." Her husband gently points out her lack of proper maternal feeling: "our daughter is grieved that thou turnest a cold eye on her babe." But Ruth is not beyond redemption. Mr. Heathcote's words make her realize the impact her lapse from her "natural" behavior has on her daughter. Harmony follows: "Ruth herself soon forgot that she had any reason for regret in the innocent delight with which her own daughter now hastened to display the physical excellence of the boy" (357–58). However, through his depiction of Mrs. Heathcote's unwillingness to accept her grandson, Cooper again criticizes the nineteenth-century concept of motherhood: even deeply pious women fall short of the prescribed ideal.

Criticism also enters Cooper's description of the marginalized or absent mother. Like his contemporaries, Cooper marginalized or removed the mothers from his texts to give his heroines the opportunity to develop without stultifying maternal influence. Like them, he showed that the missing mother retained a profound influence on her daughter(s). The death of *The Deerslayer*'s Mrs. Hutter, for instance, has given her daughters, especially the attractive Judith, great freedom; it has also condemned her to repeat her mother's mistakes. Cooper repeatedly emphasizes the daughters' maternal inheritance. Albeit a "fallen woman," Mrs. Hutter has not only taught her daughters to read the Bible, she has provided them with thorough domestic training. In addition, she has furnished them with a level of education not common among frontier people, a circumstance which, ultimately, negatively impacts their lives. Hetty, for instance, speaks "in a low, sweet voice, which nature, aided by some education, had preserved from vulgarity of tone and utterance" (67). Her sister Judith is "singularly handsome and youthful," she has "a pleasant, rich, and yet soft female voice," and she smiles "graciously" at Natty when he first meets her (63). All these feminine graces—more appropriate to the upper-class drawing room than to the Ark or Muskrat Castle—come courtesy of Mrs. Hutter, as does the daughters' illegitimacy and unknown ancestry.

Although mostly physically absent from Cooper's tales, the Victorian mother and her influence surface in other of Cooper's works. Victorian notions of marriage and motherhood permeate Cooper's works as they do the works of female domestic writers. Yet Cooper never presents his readers with a one-dimensional image. Instead, his representations of marriage and motherhood simultaneously assert and undermine the Victorian ideal. On the one hand, the author, in keeping with the Victorian idea that marriage and domesticity are the foundation of society, not only moves his heroes and heroines toward this institution but also provides his readers with a list of criteria essential in securing a good marriage, such as common background, common faith, and common interest. He also creates strong women figures, willing to not only perform their familial duties and defend their families against the wicked outside world but also to defend the family from more physical intruders. On the other hand, by his marginalizing or removal of the mother from his texts Cooper, implicitly critiques these institutions. He does not stop with implied criticism, though: through the representations of greedy, self-centered wives and mothers, he explicitly challenges Victorian idealizations of both marriage and motherhood, providing a more nuanced picture of Victorian domestic institutions.

4

Fatherhood

> Every father is the constituted head of his household. God has made him the supreme earthly legislator over his children, accountable ... to no other power, except in the most extreme cases of neglect, or abuse.
> — Henry Humphrey, *Domestic Education*, 1840

> ...the affection of a parent for his child is never allowed to die.
> — James Fenimore Cooper, *The Last of the Mohicans*

> Every body must have a head, and every society must have subordination. Domestic misrule and anarchy, if universal, would be social chaos.
> —*The Ladies' Repository*, 1871

> And, ye fathers, provoke not your children to wrath: but bring them up in the nurture and admonitions of the Lord.
> — Ephesians 6:4

Much of the research into the cult of domesticity has focused on the lives of mothers and daughters and on the growing separation between public and private spheres of interest in the industrialized Western world. Relatively little interest has been shown in the father's role save as the family's breadwinner: he is a necessary but marginalized fixture in the world of domesticity. Far too many readers of nineteenth-century domestic fiction and advice literature fall into the category Stephen M. Frank describes in *Life with Father: Parenthood and Masculinity in the Nineteenth-Century American North* (1998): they willfully ignore the father's contribution. Frank comments, "A 'father's care,' the phrase rings through nineteenth-century letters and diaries, and yet historians have not heard it clearly" (1). Not merely the family's breadwinner, he also had to provide them with "the character traits necessary to get ahead in life" (Frank 140). Working with letters and private papers of 192 men born between 1800 and 1879, Frank carves a place for hitherto "forgotten family members" (1). Shawn Johansen has a similar objective in *Family Men: Middle Class Fatherhood in Early Industrializing America* (2001). Working with private documents from over ninety families, he paints a nuanced picture of the Victorian father. In their works, the writers reintegrate the father into the domestic *sanctum* and reaffirm the father's rights and obligations within the family.[1]

Both Frank and Johansen are, of course, correct in many respects: studies of nineteenth-century domestic literature often marginalize or present decidedly unflattering images of fathers. Advice books and private papers present a different picture. As the above epigraphs show, fiction and nonfiction alike never ignored this important family member. Manuals consistently sought to persuade its readers of the father's importance — financial, spiritual, and intellectual — within the family circle; letters and journals show eager paternal participation. Frank asserts, "fathers participated actively in child rearing, both when their children were young and as they grew older" (2). The mother might be the domestic *heart*, but the father was its *head*. He had, as Humphrey's statement shows, a God-given dominant position within the family hierarchy. He also had, as Cooper's words indicate, *affection*. These two statements, the one proclaiming the father's divine prerogative as the family's ruler, the other prescribing his obligations to his progeny, present two radically different views of nineteenth-century fatherhood. Humphrey's advice book asserts the father's legal and God-given *rights* vis-à-vis his children; Cooper's lines emphasize a father's *affection* toward his child, expressing a daughter's belief in the nature of paternal love. However, both writers, in a period with a professed belief in separate male and female spheres of interest, find it necessary to insist on the *father's* relationship to his child or children; i.e., on his domestic duties. In Humphrey's Christian vision of family dynamics, the public sphere clearly intersects with the private one; the *paterfamilias* plays a pivotal role in both. Simply by virtue of his masculinity, he is the "earthly legislator over his children," accountable for his actions within the family only to God.[2]

To the twenty-first-century reader, Humphrey's vision of Victorian fatherhood conjures up a grim picture. Not only does the modern reader notice the use of the possessive — it is "*his* household," "*his* children," to do with as *he* sees fit — but civil law cannot intercede "except in the *most extreme* cases of neglect and abuse" (my emphasis). However, as Colleen McDannell points out in *The Christian Home in Victorian America, 1840–1900* (1986), this fact did not encourage paternal abuse. Yes, "the father's authority in the family reflected the authority of God over humanity," but like the benevolent God caring for his children, the father engages in a loving relationship. Adherents to the cult did not envision the father as a brutal despot. Rather, in accordance with the Pauline dictum quoted above, they advocated a more tempered approach to family government. Also, domestic religion was a *joint* although *asymmetrical* venture: both parents served as leaders at the domestic altar. "Domestic writers," she declares, "never intended families to go back to the 'past' when fathers were tyrants in their family" (112). McDannell also highlights another salient fact: the "father's privilege as head of the household" and the "longtime association of domestic order, discipline, and obedience with paternal authority was the model from which writers developed their views on domestic religious leadership" (109). Many advice texts advocated family devotions, where mothers "set the stage for the priestly activities of their husbands.... Formal family prayer, like formal church worship, employed women as domestic acolytes—to prepare, but not to direct" (111).[3]

Fearing that fathers might neglect their family obligations, proponents of the cult of domesticity not only sought to affirm a father's rights; its supporters demanded the father's central and active participation in the social life of the family. Advice manuals aimed at young men temper the image presented by Humphrey. *Titcomb's Letters,* for example, present a male-dominated, yet affectionate household. The narrator asserts, "every child born to you should learn among the first things it is capable of learning, that in your home your will is supreme. The earlier the child learns this, the better." He then adds, "and he should learn, at the same time, from all your words and your conduct, that such authority is the compassion of the tenderest love and the most genial kindness" (224). A father may play with the children "as much as you please ... but keep all the time the reins of your authority steadily drawn, and never allow yourselves to be tifled with" (225). Another advice text, William Cobbett's *Advice to Young Men and (incidentally) to Young Women* (1830),[4] states that children "are the great and unspeakable delight of your youth, the pride of your prime of life, and the props of your old age ... the various blessings which they bring are equally incapable of description" (215). He then warns the father to "act your part well," because "neglect," "ill-treatment," or "evil example" will make children "the contrary of blessings" (215). Interestingly, the first item on Cobbett's list of appropriate fatherly behavior is seeing to it that the child is breast fed. Not only is the mother's milk the most "congenial" to the child, but parents ought not to "overlook the great and wonderful effect that this has on the minds of children." Seeing their mother nursing a new baby, the older children "see with their own eyes the pain, the care, the caresses which their mother has endured for, or bestowed on them" (216–17).

4. Fatherhood

As Cobbett and Holland showed in their books, a successful family life — and fatherhood — was founded on affection, consideration, and forbearance. Both men argue for more male participation in household activities. "The matrimonial duties," *The Young Wife's Book: A Manual of Moral, Religious and Domestic Duties* (1838) reminded its readers, "are *reciprocal*— they consist of mutual forbearance and mutual offices of love and kindness." Even obedience is paid "to the commands of affection," and religion was held out as the obligatory support system: "the matrimonial path is not, any more than another, strewn with thornless roses; and if fate should decree that some of them are to be pointed at our bosom, recollect also that religion, fortitude, and patience will blunt their edge, although they may not be able to heal entirely the wounds inflicted by them" (12). The husband, of course, could remain completely unfamiliar with the practical running of the household, "he must reap the benefit of labours which he must never witness in their progress ... by a proper and methodical arrangement of her business and time, she may always be ready to meet him and his friends in the drawing-room, while the kitchen has not been neglected" (210).

Advice writers had good reason to ply their trade: many men saw family obligations as an unbearable burden, an "encumbrance" (Demos 37), and had no compunction about leaving it behind. Others stayed, but indulged in "beastly drunkenness," "dishonor," and "untruth" (*Titcomb's Letters* 178). The cult sought to change this grim reality. Even if the father belonged to neither of these groups, the potential for neglect remained. Many fathers, busy building their business empires, neglected their own and their families' spirituality, believing financial success alone would absolve them from spiritual obligations. One nineteenth-century commentator, William Alcott, claimed that many businessmen never read the Bible, and that the only book they read at night was their ledger.[5]

Cooper presents a benign vision of nineteenth-century fatherhood, playing up to the readers' sense of love and duty toward their children. Still, there is an unspoken *natural* law enforcing a father's behavior and emotions: God has established the parent-child relationship, imposing a demand for never-ending parental affection. In Cooper, "affection" becomes an eternal parental *duty*. Some outside agency *demands* the constancy of a parent's affection, oblivious to parental inclinations and limitations: it "is never *allowed* to die" (emphasis mine). Nevertheless, Cooper's paternal characters often operate along a trajectory similar to that outlined by Humphrey, Cobbett, and Holland. Like them, Cooper insists on the *father* as the central parental figure in the domestic arena; in fact, by removing the mother from the text, Cooper allows no rival to the father as the head of his household. Still, Cooper emphasizes the father's *duties*—i.e., his *affection*—more than his *legal rights* within the family hierarchy. Furthermore, he has a keen eye for the *weaknesses* of his paternal characters, thus consistently challenging the nineteenth-century concept of omnipotent fatherhood. From *The Spy* and the Leatherstocking tales to *Homeward Bound, Home as Found,* and *Satanstoe,* Cooper's novels consistently present fathers who believe that they act in the best interest of their children out of their professed love for their offspring yet fail in their duties.

A close study of Cooper's texts, and of the works by Child, Sedgwick, Warner, and Cummins, reveals that literary fathers often are oblivious to the fact that their actions are motivated primarily by self-interest. The works discussed in this chapter, primarily concerned with the father-daughter relationship, often show fathers lacking appropriate concern for their progeny's welfare. They may insist on the role of the father as an authoritarian nurturer and educator, but they also consistently show the father as egotistical and self-serving, frequently attempting to shape his daughters to correct his deficiencies.

※ ※ ※

> The having and rearing of children form one of God's ordinances for making you what you should be—what he wishes you to be. They are as necessary to you as you are to them. You can no more reach the highest and most harmonious development of which you are capable without children, than you can develop a muscle without exercise.
> —Josiah G. Holland, *Titcomb's Letters,* 1858

The cult of domesticity not only struggled to bring the father back to the familial fold, insisting on his central position in the private sphere; it also invested the father-daughter relationship with enormous importance, a fact reflected in domestic literature. Again, the relationship was asymmetrical; it focused on the father's *rights* and the daughter's *duties*. Daughters had no rights in this unequal relationship, save the right to receive financial support. The demands on her were severe: the father expected self-abnegation, cheerfulness and gentleness, emotional support, and practical assistance from his daughter; it was her duty to provide these regardless of the physical and emotional costs to herself.

Women's autobiographies—for example those by prominent writers such as Louisa May Alcott, Harriet Beecher Stowe, and Catharine Maria Sedgwick—affirm the daughter's strong ties to the father, consistently emphasizing the importance of the father-daughter bond. The women all describe fathers who, although often absent, maintained a strong and influential presence in their lives. The diarist might write lovingly about her kind, self-sacrificing mother yet clearly saw herself as her *father's* daughter. The writers considered it especially important that their fathers had introduced them to literature at an early age, took interest in their education, and encouraged and delighted in their daughters' intellectual pursuits. Louisa May Alcott tells how her father every morning read aloud to his daughters for an hour; these reading periods remained the most pleasant recollections of her youth. More importantly, Bronson Alcott, as his voluminous, detailed records of his children's upbringing demonstrate, took a keen interest in his daughters' education, often devising educational games to further his educational ends. His efforts had an ulterior motive as well; he was, as Strickland has observed, "motivated in part by his hope that the publication of his extensive observations of their development would eventually establish a reputation for him in philosophy" (Strickland 24). Harriet Beecher Stowe and Catharine Sedgwick, likewise, mention their fathers' positive impacts on their intellectual lives. The Rev. Lyman Beecher, for instance, appears as a very positive influence, especially in encouraging his children to read.[6] In her autobiography, Sedgwick, whose father Theodore Sedgwick, a prominent Federalist politician, served as the Speaker of the House of Representatives during the Washington administration and was thus often absent, writes that her "most vivid childhood memories" consisted of her father's readings from Hume, Shakespeare, *Don Quixote*, and *Hudibras*.[7] Discussing Theodore Sedgwick's participation in family life, she writes, "my father, whenever he was at home, kept me up and at his side till nine o'clock in the evening, to listen to him while he read aloud to the family" (74).

Cooper's journals and letters, as well as the writings of his daughter Susan, attest not only to his deep love of family but to his awareness of his responsibility for his children's education. Biographical evidence shows Cooper as a father very much of the same caliber as Louisa May Alcott's, Harriet Beecher Stowe's and Catharine Maria Sedgwick's. He was, for instance, very concerned with the education of his daughters both in the United States and abroad: the family's European sojourn was at least in part due to this concern. His pleasure in the intellectual pursuits of his daughters spread even further: he proudly and wholeheartedly supported Susan in her writing career. The education of daughters is also a recurrent issue in his domestic novels although he never prescribes any curriculum. Cooper not only stresses that his heroines have received the best education available according to their station, but that it is the fathers' responsibility to see to this education. This concern emerged already in his first novel, *Precaution*: the narrator repeatedly emphasizes Emily Moseley's education that makes her fit for both this life and the next. In his Revolutionary War Epic, *The Spy*, the flawed Mr. Wharton at least worries about his daughters' instruction. When he retires to his Westchester estate, The Locusts, he leaves his daughters in town so that they can finish their education; they only join their father when this has been accomplished and they are fully equipped to take over the running of his household. And in the first of the Leatherstocking tales, *The Pioneers*, Elizabeth Temple returns to Templeton only when the time her father has allowed for her education has come to an end and she is considered capable of assuming her domestic duties.

※ ※ ※

> "Ellen — let me hear you call me father."
> Ellen obeyed....
> "Never let me hear you call me any thing else, Ellen. You are mine own now — my own child — my own little daughter. You shall do just what pleases me in every thing...."
> — Susan Warner, *The Wide, Wide World*

Given the highly sentimentalized notions about paternal rights and responsibilities, and the apparent lack of stability in the rapidly expanding American population, it is perhaps no wonder that writers of domestic fiction consistently chose orphans as protagonists and had their characters search for stable families and father figures. The most popular fictional device of the time was the quest for family connections and belonging. Fictional characters constantly embarked on quests, especially to find a parent or parents, a child or children, or siblings. The quest for family equaled a quest for stability and continuity, an alluring and elusive concept in times of rapid religious, social, and economic changes and an ensuing disruption of family ties. Yet many writers of domestic fiction simultaneously constructed *and* deconstructed the family, insisting upon its importance while removing its core. When the author created a single-parent household, generally the surviving parent was the father. In this respect, the authors responded to the demographic reality: during the nineteenth century, the mortality rate for women greatly exceeded that of men. Harvey Green observes that "Nearly one-third of Massachusetts women born in the United States in 1850 died before they were twenty; eighty percent of that group (that is, twenty-four percent of the total female population) never reached the age of five" (166). Literary fathers fared only slightly better than literary mothers: even when alive and part of the heroines' lives, they often emerged as self-centered, manipulative persons incapable of providing their dependents with stability and security, yet demanding total obedience from their progeny. The latter was especially the case when the dependent child was a daughter and the surviving parent a father. In varying degrees this scenario characterizes much nineteenth-century domestic fiction. Lydia Maria Child deploys the conventional scenario, for instance, in *Hobomok*; and Catharine Sedgwick utilizes it in *Hope Leslie*, works that in subject matter come close to Cooper's frontier novels. Both these works address the father-daughter relationship but present the heroines' fathers in a far less flattering light than Cooper for the most part does his characters. Both texts illustrate the pernicious aspect of the father as his children's earthly legislator: the young girls and women in the texts have tyrannical, inflexible fathers trying to impose their wills on their daughters in connection with marriage and religion. Variants of the father-daughter scenario also inform such later bestsellers as Susan Warner's *The Wide, Wide World* and Maria Cummins's *The Lamplighter*, both published in the decade of Cooper's death.

In *Hobomok*, which some feminist critics see as a "radical revision of the patriarchal script" (Karcher xxxi), Child even doubles the effect of the device, giving the plot an ironic twist by showing paternal rigidity as a universal phenomenon. Due to religious differences between him — a staunch Episcopalian — and his prospective, Puritan son-in-law, Mary Conant's Cavalier grandfather refuses to bless his daughter's marriage to the man she loves. In the next generation, Mary's Puritan father, as inflexible as his own father-in-law, replicates the father-in-law's behavior, rejecting his daughter's Episcopalian lover, Charles. This act, coming soon after the death of her mother, sends the heroine into temporary insanity — and the arms of the Indian Hobomok. Significantly, Mr. Conant has as little success in controlling his daughter as had his father-in-law: both young women choose their mates in defiance of paternal *dicta*. Mrs. Conant opts for poverty and a parent's "lasting displeasure" (8); Mary makes a similar choice when she marries Hobomok. As is the case in many of Cooper's works, the family survivors are the father and the daughter. Child's text presents Mr. Conant as the legal and religious head of his family, issuing commands that his daughter dares not disobey — at least not openly. Preoccupied with his religion, he neither understands the needs of his family nor envisions his dependents as having desires of their own. He is a "stern old man," often in no "pleasant humor," expressing his opinions through Biblical allusions. When his daughter asks visitors from England about the present state of "the scenes of her youth," referring to her idyllic sojourn at her grandfather's manor, her father in a preemptory move attacks what he perceives to be his daughter's shortcomings: her supposed vanity and her lack of proper Christian faith. Mr. Conant clearly does not believe that his daughter adds spirituality or morality to the home. Instead he harps on what he considers to be his daughter's worldliness, trying to shape her into his conception of a spiritual paragon through criticizing her and belittling her interests. Although now "encamped in Elim, beside palm-trees and fountains," she is, he charges, "no doubt looking back for the flesh-pots of Egypt ... willing enough to leave the little heritage which God has planted here, in order to vamp up your frail carcase in French frippery" (9). Although Mr. Conant is tender toward his sick frail wife, the narrator describes this behavior as "oil upon the surface" of a turbulent stream, which "pursued its own course, and a moment after it would boil and fret at every obstruction" (10). When the patriarch finds Brown, his daughter's suitor, with his daughter and wife, he behaves like an enraged, petulant child: he stamps his foot "violently" and points to the door, muttering, "Take my curse with you" after the younger man leaves (183). Paternal stubbornness and pride — combined with Mary's distress at the death of her mother and the believed death of her English lover — prevent any reconciliation between father and daughter, until Charles Brown returns. Only then, with a new, *white*, more suitable husband does Mary return to the Puritan fold, her Indian *intermezzo* erased. Child emphasizes that Mary's marriage to Hobomok — due to Brown's acceptance of her and her child — has no negative impact on her standing in the community once she returns. The novel ends with a reversal of the father-daughter relationship: Mr. Conant becomes a frequent visitor at his daughter and son-in-law's fireside. However, Child leaves us with an open question as to whether the female prerogative dominates. "Disputes on matters of opinion" still seem to be a male prerogative: in these cases Brown, not Mary, shows "forbearance" and brings discussions to "an amicable termination" (149).

In *Hope Leslie*, Sedgwick utilizes variations on the same theme: here, too, fathers attempt to assert their rights as their daughters' earthly legislators, again more from self-interest than from any consideration for their children's feelings. Sir William Fletcher, the first of these fathers and the heroine Hope's grandfather, possesses "the common ambition of transmitting his name with his wealth" and chooses his nephew and namesake William Fletcher as husband for his only child, Alice. However, Hope's grandfather quickly withdraws his choice when he discovers William's newfound religious faith: like Mrs. Conant's stubborn father, he can abide no Puritan in his family's midst. He even resorts to physical force to keep the lovers apart, arriving at the Southampton with "a cavalcade of armed men, in the uniform of the King's guards" to prevent their elopement (13). He succeeds: in "less than a fortnight" he has married Alice, who is far less rebellious than Child's characters, to Charles Leslie, a more suitable — i.e., Episcopalian —candidate (13).

Typically, the book's father figures, with the exception of William Fletcher, Hope Leslie's New England guardian, see a daughter's marriage as something to be decided on and controlled by *men*. This demand transcends race and culture. For example, the relationship between the chief Mononotto and his daughter Magawisca shows that the writer imposes "white" standards also on non-white societies and blithely ignores Native American family structure. Again the reader sees a father who attempts to control his daughter. Like many a white father, Mononotto utilizes every tool of persuasion available to him to ensure Magawisca's compliance in his revenge scheme, in this case evoking the memory of his dead wife and son. Although originally "averse to all hostility" and friendly to the English, after the deaths of his wife and son, he becomes an embittered man who attacks the Fletcher home to achieve his goals: "In this extremity, he determined on the rescue of his children, and the infliction of some signal deed of vengeance, by which he hoped to revive the spirit of the natives, and reinstate himself as head of his broken and dispersed people: in his most sanguine moments, he mediated a unity and combination that should eventually expel the invaders" (57). Dutiful Magawisca can only comply.

Both Child's *Hobomok* and Sedgwick's *Hope Leslie* deliver severe injunctions against the conventional domestic institution of fatherhood. Through their woman-centered plots, they argue that parental rigidity and force, whether deployed for religious, familial, financial, or political reasons, are ultimately destructive to the parent-child relationship. Harsh punishment is visited on the fathers: the texts illustrate that the manipulative patriarch reaps his reward in loneliness and despair. Mary Conant's grandfather loses both his daughter and granddaughter; Mr. Conant sees his daughter elope with the Indian Hobomok. Sir William Fletcher must live with the knowledge that his actions led to his daughter's "total alienation of the mind" (14) and to her physical separation from him. His paternal manipulation receives its ultimate reward when the husband he provides for her dies "in a foreign service," whereupon the widow immediately heads for a new life in America (20), only to die on the voyage across the Atlantic. Mononotto, on the other hand, rescues his children but never manages to rally his broken and dispersed people.

Susan Warner's *The Wide, Wide World*, although written more than two decades later than Sedgwick's, Child's and Cooper's "Indian stories," also shows tyrannical, neglectful, and inconsiderate father figures and levels the most severe criticism at biological ones. Ellen Montgomery's biological father may be a physically attractive man, but he is also unable to provide a proper home for his daughter and sick wife. Furthermore, he dispenses with his daughter as coolly as if she were a parcel, shipping her to his half sister Fortune Emerson whom he relies on to provide for Ellen in his absence. He also appears utterly insensitive to his daughter's—and even his saintly and ailing wife's—emotional needs, allowing them no time together for an affectionate leave-taking. In order to avoid an emotional, tear-filled farewell scene that he would find troublesome, he arranges Ellen's trip without the child's knowledge, then refuses to allow his wife to wake Ellen to say farewell, preferring instead to wake her immediately before she is to leave. Although Captain Montgomery may believe he is doing his best to secure his daughter's future, his emphasis is on his own well-being. His thoughts after having sent Ellen away confirm the negative impression. No expressions of paternal love or regret, let alone loss, ever cross his lips, only a matter-of-fact comment that "Ellen's off—that's one good thing" (64). It comes as no surprise to the reader that he, after his wife's death, transfers the parental rights to his daughter to his Scottish in-laws, nor that he fails to furnish money sufficient for her transatlantic passage.

Once Ellen arrives in Scotland, the pattern of paternal manipulation and control repeats itself. Her Scottish upper-class uncle, Mr. Lindsay, is a better provider than Captain Montgomery; however, he seems just as selfish and insensitive as his predecessor. He attempts to erase Ellen's past and force her to conform to his vision of the perfect daughter. A childless man, he now wishes to possess Ellen completely: she must do as he pleases, even if it goes against her religion, her upbringing, and her pride. In fact, she is allowed no autonomy. Mr. Lindsay clearly sees himself as Ellen's earthly legislator: her only duty is to obey him—unquestioningly. Even the merest hint of opposition triggers his anger, and he uses Ellen's fear of displeasing him to bend her to his will. In a crucial scene following her almost revealing her *real* name to a visitor—she is now, of course, Ellen *Lindsay*—he informs her, "I lay my commands upon you ... that you answer simply according to what I have told you, without any explanation or addition. It is true, and if people draw conclusions that are not true, it is what I wish" (526). He also refers to himself as her "father" and will, he tells her, "have only obedience from you—without either answering or argumenting" (526). Once her obedience has been secured, and he is satisfied he will not "have much difficulty" with her, she meets "with nothing from him but tokens of great and tender fondness" (527). Still, despite his professed love and his affectionate kisses, he clearly treats her primarily as his possession, never allowing her to forget that she now *belongs* to him alone. All other emotional and spiritual obligations have been terminated.

Warner's work also provides a more positive alternative to the fatherhood represented by Captain Montgomery and Mr. Lindsay. Ellen's "American father," Mr. Humphreys, the father of her mentor Alice, has none of the *possessiveness* and arrogance *vis-à-vis* his own child that mark the behavior of Ellen's biological father or her Scottish guardian, who both feel that blood ties justify even the most unreasonable paternal demands. In the novel, the difference in parenting originates in the difference between those who possess Christian faith and those who lack it. The Humphreys act out of their Christian beliefs, values the Lindsay family actively fights and Captain Montgomery at least appears to ignore. Interestingly, Warner chooses to focus on the *effects* of Mr. Humphrey's parenting rather than on his actual instruction; that is, on Alice's and John's behavior both within the family circle and in the outside world. Cooper would have liked Warner's conclusion: Ellen's Christian faith and emotional loyalties cannot be erased despite strong paternal manipulation. Only a Christian father can nurture his children spiritually, making them his enthusiastic emissaries in the wider world.

In Maria Cummins's *The Lamplighter*, another bestseller from the 1850s, the heroine's biological father emerges as a *deus ex machina* toward the end, saving his daughter from drowning and thereby working his way into her affection. However, he is of no importance throughout the preceding narrative, except as a mechanism to launch her into a world of neglect and abuse. To a twenty-first-century reader, Gerty's acceptance of her father in the novel's final pages seems improbable, yet it affirms the sentimental belief that a daughter's love for her parent is instinctive and unconditional. Thus, filial love is a given even when the two are complete strangers. Cummins provides her heroine with proper paternal guidance, though. As Ellen finds a loving, caring father in the Rev. Mr. Humphreys, Gerty finds a home with the old lamplighter, Trueman Flint, also a good Christian father figure. Although the latter can hardly be accused of ulterior motives in his rescue of the orphan girl, he clearly reaps his domestic rewards: Gerty quickly learns to be a good housekeeper and provides her "father" with a proper, clean, and tidy home, a sanctuary to which the old lamplighter can return after work. Whereas good, Christian women had neat and tidy homes, unmarried good, Christian men clearly had not. And, when Flint's health fails, Gertie immediately reverses the parental functions, parenting and caring for him. Cooper envisions similar reversals for the daughters in his novels. *The Pioneers*' Elizabeth Temple arrives in Templeton for this exact purpose; *The Pathfinder*'s Mabel Dunham is expected to provide for her aging parent and takes care of him on his deathbed; *The Chainbearer*'s Dus Malbone cares for her "father" Andries Coejemans, and so on.

The above four woman-centered novels all attest to what their writers perceive as the father's role *vis-à-vis* his daughter. Positing the father as his family's "earthly legislator," the writers show that the father saw himself as *entitled* to his daughter's unconditional love and obedience, regardless of his own treatment of her, be it abandonment, abuse, or neglect. He also expected her to be useful and domestic, qualities that were especially important if the father was a widower. Cooper's novels project a similar image of the father-daughter relationship, repeatedly revealing their deep affiliation to more conventional "domestic" fiction of his day.

※ ※ ※

> 'Tis a sad thing to go into battle with the weight of an unprotected daughter laid upon the heart.
> — James Fenimore Cooper, *The Pathfinder*

Cooper, on the other hand, presents a more benign vision of nineteenth-century fatherhood than his "domestic" counterparts, playing up to the readers' sense of love and duty toward their children. Furthermore, he has a keen eye for the *weaknesses* of his paternal characters, thus consistently challenging the nineteenth-century concept of omnipotent fatherhood. From *The Spy* and the Leatherstocking tales to *Homeward Bound*, *Home as Found*, and *Satanstoe*, Cooper's novels consistently present fathers who believe that they act in the best interest of their children out of their professed love for their offspring, yet who show themselves as incompetent and manipulative.

When Cooper began his literary career with the later so much maligned *Precaution*, the father-daughter relationship was merely a side issue; the author was busy creating a complex web of family configurations and interactions. If this novel is the "seedbed for Cooper's novels of manners" (Darnell 14), in it also lies the seeds for Cooper's treatment of the family and his investigation into nineteenth-century fatherhood. The author intentionally furnishes the heroine with a weak, ineffectual, and somewhat self-centered father. In this respect, he follows the lead of his literary predecessor and model, Jane Austen, especially her portrayal of the indolent and passive Sir Walter Elliot in *Persuasion*, or perhaps Mr. Bennet in *Pride and Prejudice*.[8] Sir Edward Moseley, Cooper's first *paterfamilias*, may be a congenial and thoughtful host, a model of deportment, and a financially responsible parent, but he is somewhat feckless when it comes to family rule: "Nature had not qualified Sir Edward for great or continued exertions, and the prudent decision he had taken to retrieve his fortunes, was perhaps an act of as much forecast and vigor as his talents or energy would afford; it was the step most obviously for his interests, ... but had it required a single particle more of enterprise and calculation, it would have been beyond his powers" (3–4).

Sir Edward's behavior toward his daughters is, as befits a member of the *ton* accustomed to leaving the responsibility for child care to nurses, nannies, and governesses, civil, but rather distant. Furthermore, for some undisclosed reason, he has "relinquished" his parental control of his daughter Emily entirely. Acting *in loco parentis*, his widowed and childless sister Mrs. Wilson has shaped her charge into an angel in the house-in-training. Neither Sir Edward nor Lady Moseley possesses the spiritual qualities needed to mold Emily's character; however, they at least see to it that she receives the best possible education, always a favorite issue for Cooper. In Sir Edward, Cooper creates a father who, despite certain limitations as a parent, accepts his role and his responsibilities. He is wise, or at least competent, inasmuch as he delegates his paternal duties to persons more able to perform them. Also, unlike Cooper's later father figures, Sir Edward does not manipulate his daughters to further his own schemes. Neither tyrannical nor abusive, Cooper's first fictional father receives less criticism than his successors.

With *The Spy*, Cooper's representation of nineteenth-century family dynamics takes root on American soil. His family assortment becomes less complicated: instead of the wide variety of family configurations he had created in *Precaution*, Cooper now concentrates on a very limited number of representative samples. He also moves toward a more detailed exploration of the father-daughter relationship, an exploration which reveals the male egotism frequently underlying the concept of paternal rights and responsibilities. Beginning with this novel, the following paradigm remains prominent throughout Cooper's career: in his amputated families, 1) the father nurtures and educates his daughter (or, to be more precise, he has her educated); 2) the father's activities frequently endanger the daughter; and 3) ultimately the father-daughter relationship is reversed: the daughter emerges as the father's housekeeper, nurturer, and spiritual guide. While Cooper never explicitly accuses fathers of neglecting to fulfill their assigned tasks, his choice of family configurations, problems, and resolutions certainly questions prescribed gender roles. In doing so, Cooper challenges the patriarchal family itself. James Grossman writes in his 1949 Cooper biography that "Cooper has always something of the novelist's vision that sees more than it means to" (215). In my opinion, Cooper's texts certainly seem to *say* more than its writer, bound by the literary conventions of his time, can afford to let them say directly. Although his texts in no way demonstrate the subversive ambivalence later so successfully deployed by for instance Nathaniel Hawthorne, Cooper, through his choice of markedly weak and ineffectual fathers, manages to assert the importance of fatherhood while simultaneously undermining it.

In *The Spy*, Mr. Wharton, a gentleman of independent means, is alone with his daughters Frances and Sarah. His wife is dead and his only son is an officer in the British army. Set in Westchester, New York, in 1780, the novel's opening pages show a weary traveler, Mr. Harper (George Washington in disguise), finding shelter at the Whartons' rural retreat, The Locusts. An "old gentleman" welcomes Harper to his comfortable fireside where "three ladies ... seated at work with their needles" provide an appropriately domestic atmosphere (5). The scene projects domestic tranquility, affluence, and contentment worthy of an illustration in a ladies' magazine: the father enjoys his pipe, the ladies their embroidery. Interestingly, Cooper chooses to describe the group in a very imprecise manner, drawing the readers in by implying that they—either from personal experience or from their reading of various domestic novels—need no specific details. They *know* what distinguishes ladies and gentlemen. His words are almost impersonal when he describes the host, focusing neither on his physical nor his psychological features but on his behavior, clothes, and physical surroundings. Mr. Wharton, the narrator observes, "by his manner, dress, and everything around him, showed that he had seen much of life and the best of society" (5). In keeping with the author's idea, manifestations of class, manners, dress, and deportment, not physical features, mark gentlemen and ladies.[9]

Yet Cooper, often so busy asserting the superiority of the upper classes, quickly downplays his respectful treatment of Mr. Wharton by declaring that the gentleman possesses a "natural imbecility of character," a statement which certainly undermines Ellis's assertion that Cooper in his works consistently presents an idealized image of the gentry. And the text does not stop there; this character flaw was, at least in Mr. Wharton's youth, so pronounced that it made him unfit for the military career his father had planned for his only son (15). His character has not improved over the years. The novel repeatedly shows him as a weak man, incapable of making decisions and equally incapable of protecting his children from the marauding Skinners, the bigamist British Colonel Wellmere, and Revolutionary troops ready to hang his only son. He thus fails noticeably both as the family's "earthly legislator" and as protector. He lacks the qualities of firmness, moral superiority, and piety that the cult of domesticity saw as essential to successful fatherhood.

However, Mr. Wharton's "natural imbecility of character" does not make him less of a manipulator. Pointedly, the text presents a father who carefully, but deliberately uses his daughters for his financial purposes. Not only are the daughters, in accordance with the cult of domesticity's tenets, expected to function as surrogate wives, administering their father's household, they are also expected to safeguard the father's estate. One might argue that the safety of the family estate ultimately will benefit the daughters, but Cooper denies Mr. Wharton even this expression of paternal consideration. Ruthlessly, he lays bare the true motivation for Mr. Wharton's removal to the neutral ground of Westchester: it is a strategic move to secure his worldly possessions and his reputation in case the Revolutionary forces prove victorious. Although loyal to the British cause at least in his heart, he feigns neutrality in order to emerge politically untainted and financially solvent from the war regardless of its outcome. The narrator explains how Mr. Wharton, "after making a provision against future contingencies, by secretly transmitting the whole of his money to British funds ... determined to continue in the theatre of strife, and to maintain so strict a neutrality as to insure the safety of his large estate, whichever party succeeded" (17). A fatherly concern for his daughters' education — "he was apparently engrossed in the education of his daughters" (17) — provides him, or so he thinks, with an excuse for remaining in New York City during the British occupation, an excuse which does not compromise his claim to neutrality. However, he immediately leaves the city when he realizes that his continued residence there jeopardizes his reputation — and might endanger his estate. Significantly, Mr. Wharton himself cannot draw this conclusion on his own; rather, a relative, "high in office in the new State," has to point out "that a residence in what was now a British camp, differed but little, in the eyes of his countrymen, from a residence in the British capital" (17). Mr. Wharton removes to the country.

The love of worldly goods eclipses Mr. Wharton's love for his children: his daughters function as strategic weapons to be deployed to safeguard his estate. The act of leaving the daughters behind in the city, ostensibly for their "education," illuminates the father's egotism. Because of Sarah's beauty, their house becomes a "fashionable lounge" for the city's British officers, thus reinforcing the family's link to the British cause and their claims to British protection. This connection is strengthened by Sarah's engagement to Colonel Wellmere, a liaison the father strongly encourages. To further secure his financial survival and his claim to neutrality, he consents to the younger daughter Frances's engagement to her cousin Peyton Dunwoodie, a major in the Revolutionary forces. Again, paternal self-interest rules; fears of financial loss in case of British defeat dictate the father's behavior. Parental consent, the narrator informs the reader, was "extracted by the increasing necessity which existed for his obtaining republican support, as by any consideration for the happiness of his child" (302). Although the narrator a few lines later will comment that Mr. Wharton loves his children more than he loves his wealth, the actions and motivations he attributes to his character contradict this statement. Self-interest not only constitutes the basis of Mr. Wharton's character, it also shapes his relationship to his daughters. Daughters, Mr. Wharton's behavior demonstrates, exist primarily to be used in various paternal schemes, as housekeepers and/or links between families and nations so that the father's estate remains intact. While asserting the family's importance, then, Cooper's text also critiques fathers and fatherhood. It consistently reveals the egotism and manipulation that might underlie a father's behavior and his relationship to his daughters, making Mr. Wharton a poor role model indeed for the American population. If anything positive can be said about him at all, it is that his weaknesses allow the author to create strong female characters who eventually show themselves to possess the strength of character and the resourcefulness the father sorely lacks.

The ostensibly nurturing, yet manipulative father emerges also in *The Pioneers*: both Judge Marmaduke Temple and the Rev. Mr. Grant, the novel's two fathers, belong to this breed. However, the author scrutinizes these fathers far less severely than he did Mr. Wharton. Authorial leniency does not mean that the characters escape criticism, though: Cooper succeeds in individualizing his characters; we see them "warts and all." Judge Temple, whose achievements and social position resemble those of Cooper's own father, receives his share of negative attention. Although the proprietor of a great estate and a man of "large stature," a "fine manly face," and "expressive, large blue eyes that promised extraordinary intellect, covert humor, and great benevolence" (18), he belongs, strictly speaking, to the "middling sort," not to the upper classes, despite his position as Templeton's leading citizen. He has obtained his status not through descent but through commerce, his alliance with the socially superior Effinghams, and the outcome of the American Revolution. He is, in fact, a *parvenu*, a species much despised and ridiculed by Cooper, for example in characters such as *Home as Found*'s Aristabulus Bragg, *Satanstoe*'s Jason Newcome, and *The Redskins*'s Opportunity Newcome (one of Jason Newcome's descendants).

Cooper exposes the judge's pretensions through his description of both the exterior and the interior of his residence but refuses to let his critique descend into ridicule. The narrator sounds a mite too gleeful when he describes the building as a "superficial construction" with a number of "structural flaws" and comments on the rooms' "incongruity in furniture" only to mitigate his assessment: "there was nothing mean" in the selection (60, 67). Bearing in mind the cult of domesticity's views on the relationship between residence and owner, the text implies that what is said about the house can be said about its owner. However, the narrator provides a significant *caveat*: the judge may have an equally incongruous and "flawed" background but rises above this with his interest in the welfare and development of his community. There is nothing mean in the judge, either, and his behavior *vis-à-vis* his community is clearly paternal. However, like Mr. Wharton, he has his failings; he is stubborn and to a certain extent insensitive to the plight of others. Particularly chilling is his treatment of Elizabeth on Christmas Eve, when he leaves her at home to seek male companionship at the Bold Dragoon. This insensitivity, paired with a somewhat exploitative nature, informs his relationship to his daughter, whom he treats as if she exists solely to complement his existence.

As a supporting member of the cast of characters, the Rev. Mr. Grant receives far less attention, positive or negative, than Judge Temple. Cooper, when introducing the minister to the readers, presents him as a man of breeding who has come down in the world. The narrator gives few specific details when describing him. Mr. Grant is "a meek-looking, long-visaged man ... of a studious complexion.... The character of his whole appearance ... was that of habitual mental care" (48). His clothes are of good quality, but threadbare and rusty, his hat of "extremely decent proportions" (48). He is, in other words, the stereotypical poor clergyman of literature, endeavoring to spread the Episcopal faith on the frontier. As he had with Judge Temple, Cooper provides insight into the minister's personality and family background by describing his residence. It is the very antithesis of Judge Temple's: the floor covered with rag rugs, most of the furniture of the "plainest and cheapest construction" (141). But Cooper quickly emphasizes that despite such poor belongings, there is nothing mean about the room or the persons living there: a few items indicate better times and a more prosperous family background: "There was a trifling air of better life in a tea table and workstand, as well as in an old-fashioned mahogany bookcase" (141).

Yet if there is nothing "mean" in the personalities of the two fathers, each exhibits a noticeable blindness when it comes to domestic affairs. Both Judge Temple and the Rev. Mr. Grant prove oblivious to their daughters' real needs. Or rather, they cannot conceive of their daughters having any needs separate from their own. To each man, the daughter's main purpose in life is to cater to her widowed father's needs, regardless of her own desires. Acting as a surrogate wife, she is to provide the sanctuary to which he will return after his ordeals in the outside world. Cooper's fathers, then, single-handedly enforce the *dicta* of the cult of domesticity: daughters are not expected to have any independent existence; their whole world is the home of the father. The parent's concerns and opinions are also hers, his residence hers for the duration of his life, at least. And, although the cult of domesticity saw matrimony and maternity as a woman's ultimate achievement, Cooper's text shows that not all fathers wished to see their daughters marry and leave home.[10] Judge Temple, for instance, welcomes his daughter home with the words, "See, Bess, there is thy resting place for life" (36), a rather ominous statement to a daughter on the brink of womanhood. Later, when entering the dining room of his home, the judge announces Elizabeth's new function: "My daughter has now grown to woman's estate, and is from this moment mistress of my house" (161). She has returned to Templeton to assume her domestic obligations, not to be married off. To underscore this significant fact, the text shows that Marmaduke Temple has brought his daughter home to a village patently lacking in eligible bachelors.

Judge Temple has brought Elizabeth home to be his companion as well as housekeeper; however, in keeping with Cooper's concept of upper-class behavior, the relationship to his daughter seems rather formal and distant, despite the use of the familiar diminutive "Bess." The narrator supplies the following example of the father's concern for his daughter's emotions: when Elizabeth's mother died a few months after her leaving for school, "he still had enough of real regard for his child not to bring her into the comparative wilderness in which he dwelt until the full period had expired to which he had limited her juvenile labors" (19). The judge's actions may seem considerate, and an expression of his respect for female education; however, he refuses to alleviate her grief and rejects her as a fellow mourner. Also, the father decides when his daughter has had enough education; Elizabeth returns when *he* considers her fully prepared to take over her domestic duties. Yet when she has been installed as mistress of his house, the judge has no scruples about leaving her on the very evening of her arrival, Christmas Eve, never conceiving that, missing her mother, she might find the solitude painful. After having her preside over a groaning dinner table followed by taking her to evensong, he and his male guests quickly desert her for the village pub, "The Bold Dragoon," apparently without a single thought for her well-being. She has been left "either to amuse or employ herself during the evening as best suited her inclinations" (169). She is, in this respect, treated in much the same way as Mistress Pettibone, the housekeeper she has ousted.

The Rev. Mr. Grant similarly subscribes to the judge's opinion of a woman's role within the family: Louisa also functions as her father's housekeeper, catering to his every wish. This role she performs to perfection: "exquisite neatness and comfortable warmth" characterize their modest home. So low is her status in the patriarchal society that she is not invited with her father to meet Elizabeth or partake of the welcome celebration although she is the only young girl of a high enough social standing and education to become Elizabeth's friend. When Elizabeth, happy at having found a friend at Templeton, invites Louisa to her home, Mr. Grant quickly forestalls possible discomfort to himself by gently reminding both Elizabeth and Louisa about a daughter's duties: "Gently, gently, my dear Miss Temple, or you will make my girl too dissipated. You forget that she is my housekeeper, and that my domestic affairs must remain unattended to, should Louisa accept of half the kind offers you are so good as to make her" (131). His daughter's proper sphere is *his* home, *his* "domestic affairs must remain unattended to" if Louisa accepts "half" of Elizabeth's offers. The reader notices the use of the possessive—"my domestic affairs," which diminishes Louisa's status to that of a servant.

The Last of the Mohicans, by comparison, shows few details of domestic arrangements—here are neither groaning tables nor ladies embroidering decorously by a welcoming fire. However, even removed from the visible trappings of domesticity, Cooper's ideas of family organization remain: in the family-centered "domestic" plot of the novel, the reader encounters the familiar father-daughter relationship. The reader also receives a lesson in how fatherhood and affection for one's children can impair a man's professional life when his fear for his family takes precedence over his military career. For, as Cora says, "can daughters forget the anxiety a father must endure, whose children lodge, he knows not where or how, in such a wilderness, and in the middle of so many perils?" (61). Still, this pain is self-inflicted: Munro selfishly allows the two young women to put themselves in danger to reach him. When Duncan Heyward claims Munro is "a soldier and knows how to estimate" the problems bound to arise when personal duties come into conflict with professional ones, Cora sets down a father's priorities, reinforcing his central position within the family: "He is a father, and cannot deny his nature" (61). And a father's "nature" demands that he be with his daughters even if this demand conflicts with his professional life.

Cooper takes pains to present a loving and very emotional father. However, all this sentiment weakens the parent: in the end Colonel Munro, an officer of "gigantic frame" and hair "bleached with years and service" (165), ends up a broken man weeping "scalding" tears over his daughters' footprints (216). The novel shows the difficulty, even impossibility, of trying to reconcile familial and professional duties. However, unlike another military father, Sergeant Dunham of *The Pathfinder*, Munro feels so secure in his military role than he can allow himself the luxury of *showing* love and emotions, receiving his daughters Alice and Cora with open arms and tears when they finally reach Fort William Henry. Indeed, tears appear to come easily to the officer, sometimes rolling, "unheeded," to the floor. This is hardly the behavior one expects from a seasoned soldier. But this welcome takes place only after he has almost had the daughters killed, believing them to be part of a French attack. The scene, appropriately set in a dense mist, would have made an effective cliffhanger, but Cooper has to see his heroines reach the arms of the father after spectacular fireworks and danger before concluding the chapter. But if ending the chapter in this manner aims at emphasizing Colonel Munro's stellar paternal qualities, it also succeeds in highlighting the perils of parenting: loss of good sense. When Munro hears Alice's voice and realizes his daughters are approaching the fort, he throws safety and strategic caution to the wind. The thought that the French might have captured the girls—what seems a likely scenario to the reader in light of the siege—apparently never enters his mind. Stopping his subordinates from discharging their rifles, he "rushed out of the mist, and folded them to his bosom, while large scalding tears rolled down his pale and wrinkled cheeks, and he exclaimed, in the peculiar accent of Scotland—'For this I thank thee, Lord! Let danger come as it will, thy servant is now prepared!'" (165). His behavior undermines the fervent boast. His sentiments, fatherly as they may be, carry an almost ironic message: his powerful affection for his daughters and the uncertainty about their fate seemingly impair his effectiveness as an officer. However, once his daughters have been restored to him—at least temporarily—he can again function professionally.[11] Yet the text sends an important message to the nineteenth-century reader. During the heyday of the cult of domesticity, the duty to his family eclipses the duty to his country.

In *The Last of the Mohicans*, Cooper provides a more emotional and sentimentalized version of fatherhood and family relations than he had in his earlier novels, but he frees the daughters from even the vestiges of domestic obligations—Cora and Alice have no domestic duties to perform at the fort. Cooper also allows that even an affectionate father may fail to love his daughters to the same degree. His furious threats against any man who might refuse Cora's hand, when he vehemently states that someone "who would dare to reflect on my child" will "feel the weight of a father's anger" (159), may be read merely as an expression of his deep love for her. However, his words may be a projection of his own ambivalence toward both Cora and her mother, and his feeling of having somehow failed his "ancient and honorable" Scottish family by entering into a biracial relationship while serving in the West Indies. When he accuses Duncan of scorning to "mingle the blood of the Heywards with one so degraded — lovely and virtuous though she be" (159), he is, perhaps, revealing his own subconscious feelings toward Cora's Creole mother. Marrying her "enriched" him, yet he is more impressed with Alice's mother — his Scottish sweetheart — who remained "in the heartless state of celibacy twenty long years" for his sake. This "suffering angel" is obviously more worthy of his affection than his first wife ever was. As Alice is "the image of what her mother was at her years, and before she had become acquainted with grief" — which he had given her (159) — she is clearly more worthy of affection than her dutiful elder sister. But Cooper's discussion of miscegenation does not stop there. In a startlingly "modern" move, he has Munro place himself in the position of victim: his wife's and his daughter's black ancestry, and in fact his own first racially mixed marriage, originate in a curse "entailed on Scotland by her unnatural union with a foreign and trading people" (159). In connection with his first marriage, he mentions neither affection nor love; instead, his "lot" led to the marriage. He regards his first wife as neither a "suffering angel" nor a "saint in heaven" (159). Only the blond Scotswoman elicits such epithets; only *her* daughter comes close to Munro's domestic ideal. He gives his blessing to a relationship between Alice and Duncan Heyward only when he is convinced that the younger man's choice is free of racial motives, and thus is no slur on Cora's heritage (and his own actions). But only the blond daughter appears marriageable, even if social *dicta* decrees that a family's older daughter should be married before the younger ones can do so.

In *The Last of the Mohicans*, Cooper had given his reader an extreme case of paternal sentimentality; in *The Prairie*, he reverts to the case of the more overtly manipulative father. Again, the heroine is the child of a widower, here a Creole (of Spanish descent), a Louisiana planter of good family. However, the novel's Don Augustin de Certavallos, the heroine Inez's father, receives less favorable treatment than Munro does. Although Cooper treats him with much the same decorum and respect he for the most part reserves for socially prominent characters, he allows a certain negative tone and a xenophobic prejudice towards this character color his narrative — the man is not as "white" as the Scotsman. Initially, though, Cooper's characterization appears positive: Don Augustin's sense of family appeals to the author, himself a lifelong "family man" (Paul 40). Cooper stresses Don Augustin's pride in his blue-blooded origins and ethnic inheritance, a pride the man sees no reason to broadcast yet seeks to instill in his daughter. Although his name is scarcely known outside his own town, he is proud of the fact that it "in large scrolls of musty documents" is "enrolled among the former heroes and grandees of Old and New Spain" (157). He is extremely wealthy — the novel mentions that Inez is the "richest heiress on the banks of the Mississippi" (158) — and Don Augustin never allows his daughter to forget her family's importance. His pride keeps him apart from possible visitors, and he is "seemingly content with the society of his daughter, who was a girl just emerging from the condition of childhood into that of a woman" (157).

Don Augustin, then, lives selfishly in the past, refusing to admit that the society around him is changing. He not only keeps aloof from others, the narrator also describes him as "haughty and reserved" (157). Even his courtesy depends on "the forms of that station, on which he so much valued himself"; he lives up to his duties as a gentleman (157). He is a snob, a recluse, and he is excessively proud of his Spanish and Catholic heritage. Supposedly, Don Augustin has "all the feelings of a father"; however, Cooper undermines this rather vague assertion by admitting that these feelings "were smothered in the lassitude of a Creole" (163). Don Augustin's "lassitude" — his weariness or even debility — overrules his feelings for his daughter. Furthermore, like Mr. Wharton, he has no scruples about using his daughter for his own purposes.

But where Mr. Wharton saw his daughters as instruments necessary to secure his material possessions, Don Augustin sees Inez as a means to expand the Catholic faith and secure the family's spiritual heritage. When he allows Duncan Middleton to first court and then marry his daughter, the text bluntly states that this is due as much to the father's "desire of proselytizing" as to any paternal consideration for Inez's feelings. Don Augustin sees his daughter's marriage to Middleton as a chance for Catholicism to triumph over Protestantism; he is not motivated by any regard for his daughter's happiness. In fact, Inez is merely a pawn to be moved on this religious chessboard; the queen that will check the opponent's moves. The father's religious fervor quite overshadows the "master-passion" between the two lovers, persuading his daughter that it "would be a glorious consummation of her wishes to be a humble instrument of bringing her lover into the bosom of the true church" (159). When Inez is abducted by Abiram White, Don Augustin in turn becomes the victim, seeing her disappearance as God's punishment: it is "a judgment on his presumption and want of adherence to established forms" (163). And, although the newly married Inez is still on her father's estate when she is kidnapped, her father remains ineffectual in securing his daughter's release. Still, despite the negative descriptions, Cooper allows his character a measure of fatherly "nature." Although the congregation believes the pious Inez has been "translated to heaven," Don Augustin cannot quite accept this: "nature was too powerful, and had too strong a hold of the old man's heart not to give rise to the rebellious thought that the succession of his daughter to the heavenly inheritance was a little premature" (163).

Among the so-called "red" novels, Cooper's most dramatic and nicely executed demonstration of paternal self-interest and manipulation manifests itself in Sergeant Dunham in *The Pathfinder*. Unlike Judge Temple, who wants to keep his daughter as a dutiful unmarried companion, Sergeant Dunham arranges to have his daughter Mabel brought to the fort where he is stationed with the express purpose of seeing her married—to his best friend Natty Bumppo. Even the trek to the scouting outpost, ostensibly to keep house for her father, is part of his campaign to see the two married—Natty Bumppo and his friend Jasper Western accompany her part of the way. Paternal responsibility clearly matters in this case: Sergeant Dunham has no way of providing for his daughter financially if she were not to marry. Still, Cooper undercuts Dunham's consideration for Mabel's welfare by exposing the secret that the sergeant deliberately encourages a marriage between the two because he expects to benefit from it as well. Although Dunham, blinded as he is by paternal rights, claims he is only making provisions toward his daughter's future, he also sees her marriage as a means of securing his own retirement. Having known Natty for years, he never quite sees his friend as a full-time part of this arrangement; instead he offers the latter a residence between assignments. Typically, Dunham sees it as perfectly natural that a daughter he hardly knows yield to his wishes. He has provided for her education and upkeep; now it is her turn to reciprocate. The sergeant may be "accustomed to judge men's character," but he has no understanding of women, although he claims "a father's knowledge of womankind" (131)—a rather preposterous claim in light of his lack of paternal expertise. Set in his ways, he can conceive of no domestic opposition to his detailed plans. He has designed it all, as he confides in Natty, secure of the scheme's success, his own benevolence, and his military ability: "I've not planned this marriage, my friend, without thinking it over, as a general does his campaign.... As long as I live, Mabel can dwell with me, and you will always have a home when you return from your scoutings and marches" (131). The father's self-interest is obvious: he is more concerned about furnishing himself with a home than about his daughter's happiness. *He*, not Mabel, will have a home and *his* needs will be catered to for the duration of his life. Tellingly, he sees Mabel's desire as identical to his own: "the hussy would never dream of refusing to marry a man who was her father's best friend before she was born" (132). Dunham sees nothing wrong in the noticeable age difference between his daughter and Natty. Even when Natty—a far more sensitive and sensible man than the sergeant—points out that they do not know what Mabel herself prefers, Sergeant Dunham persists, ignoring this question of his daughter's emotions: "I never knew an old man, now, who had an objection to a young wife" (132). He wastes no thoughts on the fact that a young woman could have an objection to an old husband. The narrator knows where to put the blame for this paternal lack of understanding: it is the result not only of the long separation between father and daughter but of the father's military background. The narrator bluntly exposes the father's thought processes, observing that the sergeant, "accustomed to command and to obey, without being questioned himself or questioning others" is too old-fashioned, self-absorbed and insensitive to see that Mabel has opinions that differ from his own. More importantly, though, "he saw many advantages to himself in dim perspective, connected with the decline of his days, and an evening of life passed among descendents who were equally dear to him through both parents" (137–38).

Sergeant Dunham may indeed be his child's supreme earthly legislator; however, the novelist cannot condone this expression of conventional paternal power, instead resolving the marriage plot by marrying her to Jasper Western, her equal in years and social rank. On the one hand, he might characterize the sergeant as only dimly aware of the advantages to himself; on the other hand, however, his descriptions contradict this. He allows the father to state his motivations quite clearly to the man he has chosen for his daughter, revealing the extent of his paternal egotism. The sergeant sees the daughter as an asset he can "manage" (280). The manipulation reaches its high point with the sergeant on his deathbed; his imminent demise gives his efforts at controlling Mabel more urgency—not to mention more hope of success: a good daughter has no choice but to yield to the wishes of a dying parent. In this dramatic scene, Dunham quite literally gives his daughter to Natty, making arrangements for the upcoming nuptials: "I can do no more than give you the girl in this way. I know you will make her a kind husband. Do not wait on account of my death; but there will be a chaplain in the fort before the season closes, and let him marry you at once. Mabel, your husband will have been my friend, and that will be some consolation to you, I hope" (387). Again, the paternal self-interest overrules all else: *he* is the one who matters in the relationship. On his deathbed, he seeks to affirm his preeminence in her mind. And he expects as little opposition from his daughter as he would from any regimental subordinate.

The relationship between the sergeant and his daughter is distant and restrained; when Mabel arrives at the fort, the two have not seen one another for fourteen years. To his credit, Cooper refuses to sentimentalize their meeting; instead, he depicts a notable awkwardness, especially on Mabel's part, appropriate for such a lengthy separation. When father and daughter meet, "the agitated girl found herself in the arms of a parent who was almost a stranger to her" (106). He is of "stern, rigid countenance ... so much more formal and distant" than Mabel had expected, that he effectively curbs any display of daughterly emotion, in public as well as in private (119–20). Sadly, Mabel seems to expect nothing more; he receives her, as she later tells Natty, "as a soldier and a father should receive a child" (119). Yet despite this emotional distance, the prescribed filial obedience is a given.

The manipulative father emerges also in *The Deerslayer*, where Cooper again focuses on the single-parent patriarch, in this case on the trapper Tom Hutter, ostensibly the father of the beautiful Judith and the supposedly simpleminded Hetty. Hutter, another of Cooper's working-class fathers, is hard, bony, and skilled in woodcraft — he can read tracks and footprints almost as well as Natty Bumppo can — introduces himself as a concerned father, worried about the security of his daughters. Although not the girls' biological father, Hutter shows great tenderness toward them, especially toward the "feeble-minded" Hetty. However, Cooper almost at once expresses Hutter's problems with fulfilling his duty as a parent. Like Colonel Munro, Hutter's strength is vitiated due to his concern for his daughters: "Children sometimes make a stout heart feeble," he comments (70). He also admits to an inability to control his family, stating that "these daughters of mine give me more concern than all my traps, and skins, and rights in the country" (70). Hutter's concern for his daughters constitutes his part of a business arrangement: in return for his physical and material protection, the trapper expects, and receives, obedience and domesticity; after the death of their mother, the two girls are in charge of the family's domestic arrangements. Coming at the heels, so to speak, of the release of *The Pathfinder*, the novel presents a father who, like Sergeant Dunham, intends to use his elder daughter to secure his future and livelihood, not hers, by marrying her to the hunter Hurry Harry. Even if the "business" in question is scalping Indians, the father's bargaining chip is the same as the one used by Sergeant Dunham: an attractive, marriageable daughter that he can dispose of at will. Harry March, Hutter tells Hetty, "has as much as promised that he will enter into this job with me, on condition that I'll consent" (92). Neither man, apparently, considers it important to have *Judith's* opinion to the proposed match.

Similar father-daughter dyads also appear in two more overtly "domestic" later novels, *Homeward Bound, Home as Found*, and the first of the Littlepage chronicles, *Satanstoe*. *Home as Found*, like its precursor *Homeward Bound*, allots more central dramatic importance to the father-daughter relationship than *Satanstoe* does. It also contains Cooper's most flattering portrait of a Victorian father. The sophisticated Edward Effingham belongs to the old, landed gentry, living on income derived from land; he is for this reason "attached ... to this world of ours by kindly feelings" and morally superior to his cousin John whose income derives from commerce and speculation (2). Again, a father installs his daughter as the mistress of his household, knowing it is in capable hands. Like many other fathers in Cooper, he has seen to her education himself. Like his ancestor Marmaduke Temple, he sees his daughter's role as that of a domestic administrator relieved of menial tasks. More importantly, Mr. Effingham seems a considerate father who, having raised his daughter as a companion, takes pains to relieve her from traditional household duties. Being "too just to consider a wife or a daughter a mere upper servant," he secures excellent household help (1). Intriguingly, Cooper presents Effingham's decision as not only a means of making his daughter comfortable, but as a means to a job opportunity for others. Liberating the mistress of the house from actual physical housework, he shows, favorably impacts the labor market, providing employment for a person less fortunate than his main character. To release Eve from housekeeping duties, he employs "a very respectable woman, who was glad to obtain so good a home on so easy terms" (2). But Edward Effingham depends on Eve not only for his domestic arrangements, as did Judge Temple, but also for advice and support in religious, financial, and legal matters. In the controversy about the Effingham family pew, he expects and receives his daughter's support, although their combined efforts fail to achieve the desired result.

Satanstoe presents a rather subdued version of the father-daughter relationship, perhaps because it is seen through the eyes of a rather biased Corny Littlepage, head over heels in love with the heroine, Anneke Mordaunt. Since Herman Mordaunt, another widower, of course, wishes his daughter to marry her cousin, the British officer and nobleman Bulstrode, one can understand his formality *vis-à-vis* Corny, although he feels indebted to him for having saved Anneke's life. Yet the reader also witnesses the now so familiar paternal self-interest. Once again, the daughter functions as the mistress of her father's house, creating the prescribed domestic sanctuary from the outside world. Even when Mordaunt has to go to Albany on business, and then into the wilderness to his estate, Ravensnest, Anneke goes with him, providing the necessary feminine touch for his homes away from home. Furthermore, Mordaunt, like Sergeant Dunham, sees the move to the wilderness at least in part as a step in a marriage campaign: bringing her with him is a means to bring Anneke and Bulstrode together without all the distractions of the city. Bulstrode is, according to himself, Mordaunt, and several other of the novel's characters, a prime catch; he is an English nobleman and officer. Nobody, apparently, can envision Anneke as having opinions that differ from her father's in this respect. Bulstrode, for instance, once he realizes that he and Corny are rivals, asserts that he has "proposed to Herman Mordaunt, with my father's knowledge and approbation" (198); he is fairly sure of success since Mordaunt favors his suit. Marriage plans are a male prerogative in their upper-class world: father and suitor discuss and decide a young couple's nuptials. In this specific case, however, the prospective bride has already made her own — noticeably different — choice.

In addition to being both manipulative and self-centered, Cooper's fictional fathers seem peculiarly unconcerned with the physical safety of their precious daughters — despite the narrator's insistence on their great paternal devotion to their children. Repeatedly, young women are dragged into situations filled with all kinds of physical dangers, including sexual threats. Not only in the Leatherstocking tales but also in *The Spy* and *Satanstoe*, Cooper creates fathers who, despite their supposed love for their children, show a blatant disregard for their well-being. By flirting with the thrill of seduction and ravishment, he appeals to the sentiments and hidden fears of his audience. Influenced by the cult of domesticity, educators of every ilk claimed that nineteenth-century women were physically weak, infantile, delicate, pure, and in need of male protection. This belief made every threat against women's bodies and souls more frightening — and titillating. In fact, even when the text downplayed female sexuality, sexual threats lurked within its pages. To the sexually repressed audience, the worst horror remained "a fate worse than death," i.e., the sexual violation of its daughters.

Although Cooper had introduced this issue already in *Precaution*, where the dastardly Colonel Egerton had attempted to assault Mrs. Fitzgerald, it becomes more noticeable as his literary career progresses. From *The Spy* onward, Cooper appears committed to a paradigm to which he would return frequently throughout his career: to put it simply, the actions of his novels' fathers consistently sexually endanger their female offspring.[12] In *The Spy*, Mr. Wharton leaves his daughters behind in New York City when he flees to the country. Chaperoned by their aunt, Miss Jeanette Peyton, they form the nucleus of the metropolis's social life. However, for a young woman, life in the city has its dangers, such as sexual seduction, even in the highest circles. Mr. Wharton appears to have no understanding of the threats to his daughters' virtue. Apparently, he considers their high social rank and a devoted chaperone a strong enough bulwark against any impropriety or sexual exploitation. In the case of his elder daughter's attachment to the libertine Colonel Wellmere, he even encourages the connection. Cooper's text emphasizes the danger of leaving unprotected women behind. Ironically, although Mr. Wharton's actions may be attributed to his "natural imbecility," he seems oblivious to the fact that the visitors to his city residence advertise the sexual availability — and vulnerability — of his daughters. The text explains, "The house of Mr. Wharton became a fashionable lounge to the officers of the Royal army, as did that of every other family that was thought worthy of their notice. The consequences of this association were, to some few of the visited, fortunate; to more, injurious, by exciting expectations which were never to be realized, and, unhappily, to a small number ruinous" (18). Although the narrator adds that "The known wealth of the father and, possibly, the presence of a highspirited brother, forbade any apprehension of the latter danger to the young ladies" (18), the novel clearly shows that "known wealth" and a "highspirited brother" cannot really protect the innocent once the heart is involved. In the case of Sarah, the elder of the Wharton girls, the association proves ruinous when, on their wedding day, Colonel Wellmere is unmasked as a *de facto* bigamist, whose common-law wife has recently arrived in America in search of him. This revelation quite literally ruins Sarah's life, shattering her sanity.

The Last of the Mohicans shows the same preoccupation with fatherly negligence in the face of sexual threats. The narrator keeps his readers aware that the worst threat to Alice and Cora Munro is not to their scalps but to their *virtue*. The female characters appear well aware of this danger and their own vulnerability. When Magua looks at Cora, it is with "such wavering glances, that her eyes sank with shame, under an impression that, for the first time, they had encountered an expression that no chaste female might endure" (116). The father's relief is almost palpable when he realizes that despite their captivity, his "babes" are still as "spotless and angel-like" as when he lost them during the massacre; they have not been sexually assaulted by their captors (260). Cooper thereby brings in a new, revolutionary element into the domestic arrangements of his novels: sexual violation as a means of punishing a father and husband. Magua intends to punish Munro by taking his daughter's virtue; knowing his daughter is Magua's wife will hurt Munro more than actually killing the young woman would. Demanding Cora as his wife, Magua asserts, "in tones of deepest malignancy.... 'The body of the gray-head would sleep among his cannon, but his heart would lie within reach of the knife of Le Subtil'" (116).

Similarly, the fear of suffering "a fate worse than death," especially at the hand of a perpetrator from another race, informs *The Prairie*, where the beautiful Dona Inez incites the passion of not only her husband, but also of powerful Sioux and Pawnee males. The Pawnee Hard-Heart considers her to be of "such rare excellence as to equal all that savage ingenuity could imagine in the way of loveliness" (189); the Sioux Mahtoree desires her: his eyes on her are "long, riveted, and admiring" (216). The attention aimed at his wife clearly dismays Middleton. When, for instance, Mahtoree looks at her, it is with a palpable desire other men can read, and "the heart of Middleton grew cold as he caught the expression of that eye, which the chief turned on the nearly insensible but still lovely Inez" (270).

The issue emerges in *The Pathfinder* as well, where the treacherous Tuscarora Arrowhead wishes to make Mabel his second wife. According to his wife, Dew-of-June, Arrowhead "Talk of paleface beauty in his sleep. Great chief like many wives" (349)—a confession which in its bluntness shocks Mabel. Ironically, this threat originates in Sergeant Dunham's selfish marriage scheme. To accomplish his goal, he unwittingly exposes his daughter to conditions no truly protective father would: a strenuous trek through the potential war zone of the wilderness, exposing them to savage and potentially sexual Mingo attacks; first on her way to the fort, and later at the isolated scouting outpost where most of the soldiers are killed in an Indian raid.

In *The Deerslayer*, Tom Hutter's paternal self-absorption also endangers his Judith and Hetty, although, unlike other Cooper fathers, he fully realizes the danger to which the girls are exposed. He has, he tells Hurry Harry, "three scalps to see to, and only one pair of hands to protect them" (70). His two dwellings, Muskrat Castle and the Ark, show his concern and his foresight: they have been built to avoid Indian attacks. His careful camouflaging of the Ark leaves it so well hidden that neither Deerslayer nor Harry can discover it, although they are looking for it and stop next to it. They may be skilled woodsmen but Hutter's skill here surpasses theirs. However, Hutter's own interest in making money on Indian scalps ends with his capture and endangers his two daughters when they try to free him. Ultimately, then, *this* father's actions also—and his death—endangers his daughters, leading to the destruction of the family he has struggled to maintain. The death of the simpleminded Hetty is one result of his actions; another, perhaps, is the moral death of Judith. Left with no male protector, she succumbs, or so the novel implies, to the attentions of her former suitor Captain Warley, a man she has forcefully denounced earlier. On the last page, when Hawkeye returns to the region, he learns, from "an old sergeant, who had lately come from England" that "Sir Robert Warley lived on his paternal estates, and that there was a lady of rare beauty in the Lodge, who had great influence over him, though she did not bear his name. Whether this was Judith relapsed into her early failing, or some other victim of the soldier's, Hawkeye never knew, nor would it be pleasant or profitable to inquire" (548).

But what other choice would she have had? With few skills, expensive habits, and no desire to marry a Hurry Harry, few options remained And even we see the results of Hutter's flawed parenting: spending the winters at the fort had a negative effect on Judith's morals: it had accustomed her to a lifestyle at odds with her social rank.

Precaution, the Leatherstocking tales, *Homeward Bound*, *Home as Found*, and *Satanstoe*, then, all present father-daughter relationships that both affirm and undermine the cult of domesticity's concept of fatherhood. Although Cooper continually asserts the father's pivotal role in the family, he also consistently reveals the father's egotism and manipulation, traits which implicitly critique nineteenth-century fatherhood. In the absence of mothers, supposedly strong father figures emerge as rather deficient when it comes to protecting their daughters. Even paternal love becomes a drawback, weakening the father not only in his relationship to his daughters but also disrupting his function and effectiveness in the wider world outside the family.

5
Daughters

> Is it asked what moral lessons, so mightily important, can be learned in the nursery and in the kitchen? In return, I may ask, what lessons of instruction are there which may not be learned there, and what moral virtues may not be cultivated?
> — W.A. Alcott, *The Young Woman's Guide*, 1840

> It is the obedient daughter who will make the obedient wife. Obedient! How antiquated! True; almost as old as creation.... If strength and courage are given to man, he must be foremost in action and danger. If feebleness and timidity claim from him support and protection, what is due in return but love and obedience?
> — Mrs. Louisa C. Tuthill, *The Young Lady's Home*, 1847

Mrs. Tuthill's words, which to a twenty-first-century reader may come across as overly sentimental and rather sarcastic, succinctly encapsulate the cult of domesticity's view on the reciprocal nature of the relationship between fathers and daughters popularized in domestic fiction and nonfiction alike. More importantly, her words stress the propriety and universality of the demand for *filial* obedience: the father/daughter interdependency rests on physical differences "almost as old as creation." How can anybody gainsay such a claim? Ostensibly due to greater physical strength, the father must be strong and brave, "foremost in action and danger"; the daughter, weaker weaker and more delicate than her parent in body, supposedly feeble and timid, demands from her parent "support and protection." *His* most prominent characteristics are "strength and courage," *hers* "feebleness and timidity." Interestingly, Tuthill blends the sentimental with the realistic in her exhortation: she presents these family dynamics in terms of a *sentimentalized business arrangement*, a *quid pro quo*; however, the daughter is the debtor, settling a debt owed. The middle-class father has, of course, certain *familial* responsibilities: with his greater physical and fiscal strength, he provides his daughter with shelter and sustenance. She, on the other hand, is bound to him with bonds of *both* affection *and* obligation: she *owes* him love and submission; her affection and compliance with his demands are payment in kind for services rendered. The cult's demand for piety weds this secularized, mercantile obligation to age-old religious beliefs. But most important, this business transaction is presented as a logical and inevitable end result. Considering how the young female benefits from such an arrangement, it is, Mrs. Tuthill implies, merely the least a daughter can do to repay her father's "support and protection."

Yet Mrs. Tuthill's use of the word "if" somehow undermines her argument: the qualification insinuates that the arrangement she extols might lack the universality it purports to express. Tuthill was hardly alone in seeing this lack: the very insistence and urgency with which nineteenth-century fiction and nonfiction alike struggled to disseminate and reinforce this domestic ideal of filial love and submission make the reader suspect that the ideal was neither universal nor easily attained. Nineteenth century advice literature explicitly confirms this suspicion; domestic fiction expresses similar concerns. Yet fiction performed a double task, constructing and deconstructing the cult's ideals, all while operating within the confines of the cult's tenets. This definition of Victorian womanhood becomes especially significant in this context since novels not only provided their readers with vicarious thrills but, more importantly, functioned as an alternative form of female socialization. In fact, some writers had claimed already early in the nineteenth century that their texts were advice aimed at young women who had no mothers to guide them. Accordingly, the novels provided guidance in familial and social matters.[1] Domestic literature, especially texts discussing the father-daughter scenario, registers an equivocal, at times even subversive, response to this obvious demand. While creating daughters who would eventually accept their prescribed role, authors like Child, Sedgwick, Warner, Cummins, *and* Cooper also showed the limitations and individual responses to such societal indoctrination. The daughters populating their pages often struggle against, challenge, and even change accepted ideas of womanhood from *within* the confines of their culture. Each of these novelists creates daughters who, although appearing to follow the cult's precepts, not only rebel against their patriarchal societies but who also invest their prescribed role with an additional, more androgynous, or perhaps at times even "masculine," set of values. Such representations of womanhood implicitly challenged the concept promulgated by the cult of domesticity. This challenge is especially strong in connection with the demands for filial duty and obligation.

5. Daughters

✳ ✳ ✳

> Surely there is no thought sweeter or more tender than that which comes with a baby girl ... the born queen, and at the same time, the servant of the home; the daughter who is to lift the burden of domestic cares and make them unspeakably lighter by taking her share of them.... A family without a girl ... lacks a crowning grace....
>
> — Sarah Tytler, "Girls," 1851

Judging from the prescriptions in the plethora of commencement addresses delivered at women's academies, advice books, magazine articles, and novels flooding the nineteenth-century marketplace, educators and authors alike struggled to construct a hitherto relatively unknown female species. Once constructed, she would be worthy of enclosure within the walls of a domestic utopia: the Victorian home. Even novelists setting their texts in earlier times succumbed to this practice: their representations of, for instance, seventeenth- and eighteenth-century family life have a distinct Victorian flavor. Yet their purpose is not merely to reflect current trends. Baym, in her introduction to the 1995 edition of Maria Cummins's *The Lamplighter*, emphasizes the dual function of Victorian women's literature: "Novels of this type register the problems of reconciling individuation with womanhood. But — and this is critical — these novels do not merely reflect a current ideology of womanhood; they participate vigorously in constructing and analyzing such an ideology" (x). In other words, nineteenth-century domestic works, among them texts by Child, Sedgwick, Cooper, and Warner, simultaneously construct and deconstruct the domestic icon.

To function in this highly idealized and unattainable *milieu*, the ideal daughter was expected to internalize the value system prescribed by the cult of domesticity. The end result of this process was her emergence as a paragon of piety, purity, submission, and domesticity. As such, she was to be both worshipped and utilized by her immediate family. Tytler's words emphasize the daughter's dual status and her function within the home: society expects her to simultaneously play two mutually exclusive roles. On the one hand, she is a "born queen"; on the other, she is the family's "servant." This is a patently untenable position, unless, perhaps, the model is seen in light of Christ's own example, an example held up for emulation. A "handmaid of Christ," she could be a queen yet still be the demure, selfless, religious *ancilla Christi*. Tytler's curious attempt to "sugar-coat" the ideological pill with terms like "queen" and "crowning grace," does little to mask the oppressive domestic reality facing the Victorian daughter.

On the one hand, she was to be elevated and protected from the vulgar outside world threatening her supposedly innate delicacy and innocence; on the other hand, "the little woman-child" was intended to "lift the burden of domestic cares," presumably from her mother's shoulders. Her performance did not stop there, however. She was also expected to offer the whole family a "particular sort of tenderness and spirituality" (Gorham 5), which almost exclusively found its expression in conventional domesticity. Her life was to be devoted to others, her identity based on her domestic functions and her relationship to the males of her family. Her purity and dependence on the family's men were essential facets of her role; their absence was considered unnatural and unfeminine. Nineteenth-century domestic writers—among them Cooper—cast their female characters in this mold, or so it appears, at least on the surface of the texts.

By the time Cooper started his literary career in 1820, this mold was already firmly in place. The ideas described had already crystallized during the latter part of the eighteenth century. The female ideal is succinctly summed up in the Edinburgh physician John Gregory's advice book, *A Father's Legacy to His Daughters* (1774), a work so popular for five decades after its publication that Mary Wollstonecraft singles it out for special critical attention—and attack—in *A Vindication of the Rights of Woman* (1792). Wollstonecraft's rejection of Gregory's text appears in several chapters of *Vindication*. Despite her claims to viewing the author with affection, she intends to "shew [sic] how absurd and tyrannic it is thus to lay down a system of slavery; or to attempt to educate moral beings by any other rules than those deduced from pure reason, which apply to the whole species" (Ch. 2). Damning Gregory with faint praise, she claims, "I respect his heart; but entirely disapprove of the celebrated Legacy to his Daughters" (*Vindication*, Ch. 2).

But this text was not Wollstonecraft's first foray into a field she found ripe for reform: the female education of her day. Five years earlier she had expressed her opinions on the matter, based on her own experience in teaching, in the 1787 advice book *Thoughts on the Education of Daughters*, a text aimed at preventing a repetition of the defects she finds with the female education of her day. In this text, she stresses the usefulness of her work. Although some may think her reflections "too grave" (3), she hopes, "others may not think them so; and if they should prove useful to one fellow-creature, and beguile any hours, which sorrow has made heavy, I shall think I have not been employed in vain" (4). And even when castigating Gregory, showing how his advice will ultimately have a contrary effect, she claims to do it with "affection" (*Vindication*, Ch. 5). Despite this sentiment, though, she does not mince her words. She claims outright that "all the writers who have written on the subject of female education and manners, from Rousseau to Dr. Gregory, have contributed to render women more artificial, weak characters, than they would otherwise have been; and consequently, more useless members of society." Such advice books, she holds forth, "tend, in my opinion, to degrade one half of the human species, and render women pleasing at the expense of every solid virtue" (*Vindication*, Ch. 2).

In Dr. Gregory's popular work, a concerned parent — a bereaved widower — leaves a lasting gift to his daughters: the writer prescribes and provides survival skills for them in the patriarchal society they inhabit. The cornerstones of his construction of womanhood are the ones later deployed by the advocates for the cult of domesticity: piety, propriety, modesty and moderation in "conduct and behavior," honesty, and domesticity. Acutely aware of the problems facing a woman in a patriarchal world, Dr. Gregory explains why his daughters should heed his advice: "you will hear, at least for once in your lives, the genuine sentiments of a man who has no interest in flattering or deceiving you" (6). The book aims at reinforcing patriarchal demands: it delineates what a man, a father, sees as ideal female behavior, and it presents its writer as intent on removing vices he finds particularly odious in women: immodesty, outspokenness, wit, reason, and vanity. Each one of these, the text asserts, may lead a woman into "a dissipated state of life" (12), revealing the author's fear of "dissipation," i.e., female sexual license. Remarkably, Gregory does not promise a life of happiness even if his advice is followed; instead, he emphasizes that a woman's life is "often a life of suffering" (10). Casting woman as martyr — the suffering Mary, the *mater dolorosa*— he projects a grim picture of a woman's situation: she will not even be allowed to voice her complaints when under pressure, nor can she rage against her fate. Instead, she must "put on a face of serenity and cheerfulness" in the face of adversity and "bear ... sorrows in silence, unknown and unpitied" (11–12).

Gregory promotes orthodox religion both as a means to overcome "domestic misfortune" and attract suitors, "even these men who are themselves unbelievers dislike infidelity in you" (23). The sexual issue again rears its head: a want of religious sensibility, Gregory asserts, points to "that hard and masculine spirit, which of all your faults we dislike the most. Besides, men consider your religion as one of their principal securities for that female virtue in which they are most interested" (23). If a man does not want a religious woman, Gregory warns his female readers, they can "be assured he is either a fool, or has designs on you which he dares not openly avow" (23). Even blushing is treated as an innate female — and desirable — quality. Nature, Gregory opines, has made women to blush: "it is the usual companion of innocence" (27). Modesty is "essential" and "will naturally dispose you to be rather silent in company, especially in a large one" (28). Wit, humor, and, strangely enough, even good sense ought to be hidden from the male denizens of the patriarchal world. Dr Gregory condemns wit because it is "flattering to vanity" (30) and also humor because it is "often a great enemy to delicacy, and a still greater one to dignity of character" (31); good sense must be concealed because "men ... generally look with a jealous and malignant eye on a woman of great parts, and a cultural understanding" (32). In other words, women have to erase their personalities; like children, they are to be seen, not heard; their chief function is to satisfy male vanity. One can well understand that the independent, spirited Mary Wollstonecraft rejected such ideas! Still, Dr. Gregory's words had a more profound impact on the burgeoning middle class than had those of Mary Wollstonecraft. *She* called for reason to become the guiding principle in education and social interaction; *he* promotes self-discipline and a certain measure of subterfuge as a means of securing future (married) content, to the extent that he, as Wollstonecraft asserts, "actually recommends dissimulation, and advises an innocent girl to give the lie to her feelings" (Ch. 2).

Concerns identical to those expressed by Dr. Gregory permeate the nineteenth century cult of domesticity and its literary canon. Even if we have no indication that Cooper knew Gregory's work, his reading had surely familiarized him with similar opinions: his texts echo the same *Zeitgeist*. Already in *Precaution*, Cooper had set forth his conviction of women's purity of character, allowing the novel's intrusive narrator to express this belief in the following manner: "The narrator believes that innocency, singleness of heart, ardency of feeling, and unalloyed, shrinking delicacy, sometimes exist in the female bosom, to an extent that but few men are happy enough to discover, and that most men believe incompatible with the frailties of human nature" (101). However, by inserting the word "sometimes," Cooper indicates a rather unfavorable view of womankind.

In her own writing, Cooper's daughter Susan succinctly affirms her father's belief in "the purity of female character." In the introduction to *Pages and Pictures* (1865), she explains: "While this tale [*Precaution*] was written under an assumed name, it must be understood that there were two particulars in which it was perfectly sincere. The author's reverence for the Christian religion, and his respect for the purity of female character, were entirely unfeigned. Throughout a long life he was never known to trifle with either subject" (24). However, unlike Gregory, who had diligently tried to purge his daughters' minds of expressions of wit, humor, and good sense, Cooper refused to subscribe to so limiting a view. In the works following *Precaution*, he allows most of his heroines an ample supply of the qualities Gregory sought to contain.[3] His letters and journal entries also attest to his abiding faith in a woman's intellectual abilities. His wife is his "female mentor," a person capable of not only running his household but of assisting him in his literary work. In a letter to Andrew Goodrich dated June 12, 1820, he calls her "my tribunal of appeals" (*Letters* Vol. I. 43); two weeks later, having sent *The Spy* off to the publishers, he writes that "my female Mentor says it throws *Precaution* far in the background" (*Letters* Vol. I. 44).

Cooper discussed female characteristics in his non-fiction in much the same way as he did in his fictional works. As early as in the 1828 *Notions of the Americans*, Cooper had highlighted the physical and spiritual attractions of the American girl, a model from which he would not deviate noticeably throughout his career. The text's narrator, a young Belgian bachelor, declares that the "distinguishing feature of American female manners is nature," and that women are modest, polite, "decidedly handsome" and "delicate," all epithets easily recognizable from other Cooper texts. The "Belgian" sounds very much like the narrators of *Precaution* and *The Spy* when he concludes: "Indeed, it is difficult to imagine any creature more attractive than an American beauty between the ages of fifteen and eighteen. There is something in the bloom, delicacy and innocence of one of these young things, that reminds you of the conceptions which poets and painters have taken of the angels" (Vol. I. 191). Although supposedly cheerful, happy, and chatty, the American female never tolerates "the language of gallantry" but is "exceedingly apt to assume a chilling gravity at the slightest trespass on what she believes, and, between ourselves, rightly believes, to be the dignity of her sex" (Vol. I. 192–95). In *Notions of the Americans*, the reader thus recognizes the majority of the "females" that populate Cooper's novels: the attractive ones are young, natural, angelic, dignified, decorous, and modest.

The cult of domesticity, though, demanded more of the daughter than the above kind of decorous behavior. Simply put, a daughter was expected to be *useful*. Ironically, this was also Wollstonecraft's intent. Filial usefulness apparently was in short supply in the early nineteenth century; however, writers of advice manuals struggled to amend the situation by providing the guidance others had failed to give. In the slim volume of practical domestic advice, *The Frugal Housewife* (1826), Lydia Maria Child matter-of-factly states that her reason for penning the work is the lack of proper training for daughters. Less academic and philosophical than Mary Wollstonecraft, she baldly states, "the general tone of female education is bad" (91). She then spells out the reason: "The greatest and most universal error is, teaching girls to exaggerate the importance of getting married; and of course to place an undue importance upon the polite attentions of gentlemen" (91). To repair the situation, Child advocates less emphasis on seeing a daughter married and more on developing their usefulness. Young ladies, she writes, "should be taught that usefulness is happiness, and that all other things are but incidental" (92). Child argues forcefully for "domestic education" and elaborates on the term: "By domestic education ... I mean two or three years spent with a mother, assisting her in her duties, instructing brothers and sisters, and taking care of their own clothes. This is the way to make them happy, as well as good wives; for, being early accustomed to the duties of life, they will sit lightly as well as gracefully upon them" (92). The key to a woman's happiness, Child emphasizes, lies in making her not *be*, but to *feel* useful, a significant distinction. And in order to *feel* useful, Child's practical, matter-of-fact text divulges, the young woman needs to observe the practical side of domesticity, cleanliness, and modesty in all their excessively abundant *minutiae*.[4]

Nineteenth-century private documents similarly illustrate the extent to which the male-generated ideal of femininity had been accepted. In a journal entry dated October 21, 1827, Catharine Sedgwick eulogizes her deceased sister Eliza in terms evoking the cult's ideal. Sedgwick writes: "I have known no life that has been from its beginning to its close such a *domestic blessing*. Her discretion, thoughtfulness, and fidelity made her the trust of her parents in her early years— the support of my dear mother through many years of infirmity and sickness. Her discretion, sedateness, gentleness, and diligence were rare virtues in a young girl and qualified her to be an efficient support to her mother" (121). Sedgwick emphasizes that her sister has been an ideal daughter, and that her life has been a life in service to others, a life devoted to their comfort, not her own. But her comment also points out that her good qualities are "rare virtues in a young girl," indicating a sense of the disparity between the cult's ideal and the reality for the nineteenth-century girl. Sedgwick's words confirm what the very proliferation of advice books aimed at middle-class girls and young women indicate: most young women needed to be taught their proper function and place in society.[5]

To fulfill the many obligations descending on her shoulders, the daughter needed to perfect specific habits. First on the list came obedience; fiction and nonfiction alike saw this as THE most valuable quality. Indeed, advice literature attributed a wide variety of problems to the lack of filial obedience.[6] Yet for the daughter it had to be *cheerful* obedience, a rather impossible demand. Once internalized and made part of the self, obedience would make the young girl pliable and allow other necessary qualities such as piety, modesty, decorum, and domesticity to fall into their proper spaces.

❊ ❊ ❊

> Gently, imperceptibly, but most certainly, will she imbue with her own purity and beneficence the atmosphere in which she moves, softening the obdurate, correcting the depraved, and encouraging the timid.
> — *The Young Lady's Book*, 1830

> I would have her as pure as the snow on the mount —
> As true as the smile that to infamy's given
> As pure as the wave of the crystalline found,
> Yet as warm in the heart as the sunlight of heaven
> — S. R. R., "Female Charms," 1846[7]

Nineteenth-century popular fiction and nonfiction alike clothed the heroine in the same garb: modesty, unselfish submission, and piety were her vestments. Physically, she was delicate, frail, pretty, sweet, and generally unassertive, turning to the men in her life — father, brother, husband, or God for help in a crisis. Her behavior and her education were appropriate to her station in life. Shaped for her own social sphere, she was also expected to comfort the males in her life, be they fathers, brothers, or husbands.[8] To avoid any hint of impropriety — i.e., sexual attractiveness and desire — domestic novelists focused on young girls, often on the verge of womanhood — dependent, childlike, and, for the most part, safely undeveloped sexually.[9] Unlike young boys and men, nineteenth-century young girls and women supposedly felt no sexual urges, possibly because their minds had escaped the contagion from the world at large. Because of their otherworldliness, women wielded an immense power over men. They not only tempered a man's sexual urges; their "job description" even contained, as the poet Coventry Patmore wrote, the demand that they "teach men to pray," moving them toward their salvation.

Regardless of whether the mother was alive or not, the father-daughter bond was of the utmost importance: through the role of the father's daughter, the Victorian "idealization of girlhood was most fully expressed" (Gorham 28). Two main types of the father-daughter relationship emerged in fiction and nonfiction. In intact, happy families with a successful father, the daughter's best quality was her gentleness and cheerfulness. Marianne Farningham's *Girlhood* (1869) admonishes daughters to be "sunbeams that make everything glad"; they were also expected to "adorn the household with their ladylike accomplishments" (11, qtd. in Gorham 28). In case of financial or emotional loss, the daughters should provide both emotional support and practical assistance. It was especially important to take care of the father when he was suffering from either physical illness or moral failings. To enable her to fulfill this task, *The Young Lady's Book: A Manual of Elegant Recreations, Exercises, and Pursuits* (1830) advocates "fortitude ... and firmness, resolution, and perseverance in conduct; without these qualities, a woman, however engaging and attractive as a companion, must be found deficient in all the nearer relationships in life, and incapable of fulfilling its more important duties" (27).

Novels, whether written by women such as Child, Sedgwick, Cummins, and Warner, or a man such as Cooper, provided a persuasive means of inculcating these sought-after domestic values, presenting appealing characters whose lives served as a reminder of the importance of proper — i.e., moral and pious — behavior. Even a cursory reading of nineteenth-century domestic literature reveals that Cooper was not alone in focusing on fathers and daughters, nor was he alone in insisting that piety, purity, obedience, and submission constituted inalienable facets of a daughter's character. Her role was, if one judges from the many novels focusing on a father-daughter dyad, obviously significant both to him and his era. Faulting these writers for not providing realistic characters is, as Nina Baym observes in her introduction to the 1995 edition of *The Lamplighter*, "facile" and "their lack of realism is beside the point." She further asserts, "The depictions of women alone in the world invited women readers to scrutinize their own situations and attempted to influence their scrutiny. The form is engaged rather than contemplative; it intends to be useful. The perfect woman ... is neither a realistic character nor a role model. She is an imaginary construct who spurs, provokes, and inspires her audience" (xi). Although Baym here discusses the female *Bildungsroman*, her words are equally appropriate for other woman-centered genres.

One work dramatizing, scrutinizing, and critiquing the father-daughter relationship is Lydia Maria Child's *Hobomok*, published in 1824, a novel that late twentieth-century feminist critics would celebrate as an example of "white women's desire to be recognized and empowered within male-dominated white society" (Baym 1992, 71). Child's work is the forerunner of and perhaps, as Baym asserts, Cooper's inspiration for *The Last of the Mohicans*.[10] Child's text — a domestic version of the frontier tale, set in 1629 New England — projects the author's vision of Early America as seen through nineteenth-century lenses. Despite its title, the novel focuses on a daughter, Mary Conant, who rebels against her father's authority — and religion — not only by falling in love with an unsuitable Englishman, the Anglican Charles Brown, but also by later marrying her Native American admirer, Hobomok, in a native ritual. One could say she comes by this rebellious streak naturally: her mother opposed her own father in a similar manner, marrying her Puritan lover against her aristocratic parent's wishes. Initially, Mary, an only child after the death of her two brothers, comes close to the cult's ideal. The narrator stresses that she is gentle and beautiful, presenting her as a "little blooming fairy," with sparkling eyes, merry voice, and "aerial" feet, worthy of male attention and respect (8, 10). She is also "sylph-like" and easily moved: the text mentions that her eyes "overflowed with the intense, unrestrained gush of youthful feeling" (16). Mary is, in fact, completely otherworldly and fit only for domestic life, i.e., protection, and so "gentle and childlike that a rough word would draw tears from her eyes" (118). Mary has been raised in her maternal grandfather's home — apparently as an act of pity on his part — but she now has, in accordance with the cult's doctrine, been recalled to New England "to watch the declining health of her mother" (9). Little is said about how, and even if, Mary actually performs other domestic duties; things seem to be done, but not necessarily by her. Although set in the year 1629, the novel's characters mimic their nineteenth-century counterparts in behavior. Mary and her mother are *ladies*: at one point, the narrator explains that they "possessed that indefinable outline of elegance, which is seldom entirely effaced from those of high birth and delicate education" (36). Like any Victorian young woman, the heroine has the mandatory subduing effect on males— that is, on all males except her father. The narrator comments that "Even the rough sailors, who were with me, softened their rude tones of voice, and paid to gentleness and beauty the involuntary tribute of respect" (9). And "Whenever Hobomok gazed upon Mary, it was with an expression in which reverence was strikingly predominant" (17). She fails the cult's ideal in two respects only: she embodies a "childish witchery" (12) and an interest in witchcraft, and she lacks the required sense of filial duty and obedience. Chastised by her father for asking about friends and relatives in England, she blushes— but from anger, not from modesty — when she answers him, asserting her selfhood: "A blush, which seemed to partake of something more unpleasant than mere embarrassment, passed over the face of the maiden as she answered, 'It surely is not strange that I should think often of places where I have enjoyed so much, and should now be tempted to ask questions concerning them, of those who have knowledge thereof.'" (9). Her answer, although couched in polite language and expressed in mild tones, nevertheless is tantamount to open rebellion.

More importantly, she does not share her parents' Puritan religion. Having been raised by an Anglican grandfather, she clings to this belief and to her Anglican prayer book, not to her father's much more rigid faith. The text also shows that she dabbles in witchcraft: this and her refusal to accept her parents' beliefs are clearly rebellious acts and not what one would have expected from a seventeenth-century Puritan or Anglican daughter — let alone a Victorian one. Coming across Mary in the middle of the night, the narrator observes her performing a magical ritual, an action forbidden in the Puritan world and therefore clearly a rebellion against patriarchal authority. The keen-eyed and sympathetic voyeur, eager to remind the reader about the young woman's innate innocence, emphasizes it appears to be a task she does not undertake lightly. Knowing the consequences of detection — her actions would certainly lead to accusations of witchcraft — Mary seems "half fearful" of venturing into the woods to perform her ritual. Afraid of being followed, "she cast a keen, searching glance behind, and a long fearful look, at the woods beneath, before she plunged into the ticket" (13). Following her, the narrator witnesses the magic ritual unfold before his eager eyes. Mary halts by a creek, cuts her "little arm" to draw blood, and "dipping a feather in the blood, wrote something on a piece of white cloth, which was spread before her." She then marks a magic circle on the ground, steps into it, circles it three times forwards and backwards, "speaking all the while in a distinct but trembling voice. The following were the only words I could hear,

> Whoever's to claim a husband's power,
> Come to me in the moonlight hour.
>
> And again, —
>
> Whoe'er my bridegroom is to be,
> Step in the circle after me [13].

Remarkably, the magic works: first Hobomok, then Charles Brown show up in answer to her love charm. And although only Hobomok actually steps *into* the magic circle, their order of appearance foreshadows Mary's two marriages.

Mary's rebellion against paternal authority culminates in her rejection of her father after the death of her beloved mother, an event soon followed by the presumed death of her lover, Charles Brown. Instead of taking over her mother's duties like the Victorian good girl was expected to do, Mary neglects her domestic chores and her prescribed role as her father's comfort in a time of mourning. Although she appreciates his kindness, she cannot "attend to" her father and rejects his belated attempts at showing affection. Although Mr. Conant tries to console his daughter by considering her losses from a Christian perspective, Mary cannot reciprocate. Again Child stresses her heroine's despair and anguish, not her willfulness:

"Mary was too absent, too distressed, to receive these tardy proofs of affection with the gratitude which kindness was always wont to excite" (119).

Mary compounds this rebellion against patriarchal *dicta* by committing an even more heinous sin: she marries Hobomok in a native ritual. Still, rather than showing Mary's marriage as a deliberate act of rebellion, Child emphasizes that the heroine's behavior is due in part to the loss-induced trauma she suffers after losing both her mother and her lover. Mary's remembrance of the magical ritual she once performed also appears to play a part in her decision. These circumstances then, and not Mary's struggle for independence, impede any reconciliation between father and daughter. Child thus undercuts any possibility of seeing Mary's behavior as independence by insisting on the heroine's mental instability.[11] There was, the narrator asserts, "a partial derangement of Mary's faculties.... A bewilderment of despair that almost amounted to insanity" (120). In fact, when Hobomok appears at her mother's grave, wishing to make her "happy," there "was chaos in Mary's mind" (121). Life, she feels, has nothing to offer, and remembering "the idolatry he had always paid her, and in the desolation of the moment, she felt as if he was the only being in the wide world who was left to love her" (121).

This is clearly not enough for Child. In order to diffuse Mary's rebellion, the text states, "With this, came the recollection of his appearance in the magical circle. A broken and confused mass followed; in which a sense of sudden bereavement, deep and bitter reproaches against her father, and a blind belief in fatality were alone conspicuous" (121). Apparently utterly forlorn, she turns to Hobomok and offers to be his wife, "if you love me" (121). By emphasizing this explanation of Mary's unorthodox behavior, Child adroitly sets the stage for the character's later acceptance by the Puritan community. Mary's erratic behavior, she implies, is caused by her mental breakdown and her belief in fate, to which she merely submits (123); her behavior is, in other words, not as subversive and rebellious as the reader might be led to believe. As if eager to avoid any hint of impropriety — sexuality and miscegenation — Child continues in the same vein: the report of the native wedding shows the heroine as "listless and unmoved, apparently unconscious of any change in her situation" (125). Later, we learn that "for several weeks Mary remained in the same stupefied state in which she had been at the time of her marriage" (135). When she finally experiences "something like affection" and has a son, it is because Hobomok's love inspires "gratitude" (135). But she "prays for" Brown in her sleep; her husband knows well that "the name of the white man is on her lips" (139).

Furthermore, when Mary eventually returns from the Indian village — and marries Brown the same day — she and her son are accepted into the family and the Puritan society *because* of her *second* marriage, not because she forces others to accept her mixed marriage. Her actions remain passive: even her father's acceptance of her and the suitor he once showed the door comes through the promise his dying wife extracted from him on her deathbed, not through Mary's independent actions. And, once reintegrated into the "white" world, Mary willingly performs the tasks expected of a Victorian daughter, here seen in the reversing of the father-daughter relationship. The grown Mary accepts her responsibility and takes care of her aging father: "A new house was soon after erected near Mr. Conant's; and through the remainder of his life, the greater part of his evenings were spent by that fireside" (149). She is again the devoted daughter, performing the task for which she has been trained.

Catherine Maria Sedgwick's *Hope Leslie*, inspired, Baym asserts, by *The Last of the Mohicans*, offers an "ingenious reversal" of Cooper's text (Baym 1992, 81). A female adventure story, it contains captures, rescues, bloodbaths, and narrow escapes, and, claims Baym, an "Indian perspective" (Baym 1992, 82). However, Sedgwick still utilizes the conventions of domestic novels: she presents the reader with several variants of daughters, most of whom — whether Indian or white — to a certain extent conform to Victorian gender roles. All are expected to, and often do, fulfill their father's bidding. Like *Hobomok* the text presents a genealogy of thwarted love and misplaced filial devotion. Alice, Hope's mother, "deeply afflicted" by the loss of first her mother and then her lover, is forced to marry the man of her father's choice; only the death of father and spouse frees her from her obligations.

The Indian girl Magawisca, strong and resourceful as she is, still identifies with her father and, like the typical middle-class Victorian daughter, cares for him after the death of her mother. Although she commits the most heroic act in the novel by stepping in and saving Everell Fletcher's life in physical defiance of paternal designs — Mononotto severs his daughter's arm, not Everell's head — her father's world remains hers for the duration. Her attempts at tempering her father — an important attribute of the nineteenth-century middle-class female — for the most part go unheeded. When Mononotto and his companions approach the Fletcher homestead, she tries to stop them from killing the family, but to no avail: "she sunk down at her father's feet, and clasping her hands, 'save them — save them,' she cried, 'the mother — the children — oh they are all good — take vengeance on your enemies — but spare — spare our friends — our benefactors — I bleed when they are struck — oh, command them to stop!' ... looking to the companions of her father, who unchecked by her cries, were pressing on to their deadly work" (63). However, neither then nor later at the Mohawk camp can she temper her father's thirst for vengeance. At the very end of the novel, though, Sedgwick leaves her readers with the indication that some change has been wrought in Mononotto, at least temporarily. The return of his children and daughter-in-law—"and, above all, Magawisca"—after the two women's escape from captivity "works miracles" on the now weakened chief. In keeping with middle-class Victorian ideas of a daughter's role and influence on the father's well-being, Magawisca's return brings about the most decisive change in the father. According to the narrator, "his health and strength were renewed, and, for a while, he forgot, in the powerful influence of her presence, his wrongs and sorrows" (339). Despite her Indian background, physical strength, and courage, Magawisca displays proper nineteenth-century middle-class domestic values.

Hope Leslie, on the other hand, clearly deviates from the cult's ideal in her actions: she openly rebels against patriarchal notions of womanhood, subverting conventions she sees as untenable and unjust. A beautiful, lively, spirited, and somewhat spoiled girl, she is physically and mentally active—and dramatically different from both her Puritan peers and her more conventionally minded Victorian readers. Outwardly, though, she is the sentimental heroine personified: she is young, of medium height, "delicately formed" and "endowed ... with the beauty with which poetry has invested Hebe" (122). More importantly, though, she loves the outdoors, delighting in "exploring hill and dale, ravine and precipice" (122). With Hope Leslie, Sedgwick creates a new type of woman, one whose faculties blossom in the new world. For, as Hope herself writes in a letter to the hero, Everell Fletcher: "our new country develops faculties that young ladies, in England, were unconscious of possessing" (98). Sedgwick may emphasize that Hope is a "virtuous and tender woman" (348); however, she also repeatedly demonstrates her heroine's more androgynous, even masculine qualities, such as daring, fearlessness, and "liberty of thought and word" (272), thereby questioning the veracity of the prescribed female nature. Like Mary Conant, Hope Leslie does not share the religion of her Puritan guardians; nor does she really embrace the faith of her late father, an Episcopalian. Instead, she opts for Natural Religion, "the law of virtue inscribed on her heart by the finger of God" (Kelley xxiii).

By juxtaposing Hope Leslie's behavior to that of her "rival," Esther Downing, the woman Everell Fletcher is expected to marry, Sedgwick demonstrates how her heroine deviates from "approved" female behavior. Where Hope Leslie is independent and strong willed, Esther is religious, sensitive, generous, and selfless. She is, in this respect, and exact clone of Everell's own mother. Like Martha Fletcher, she is part of the Winthrop household and she is "disciplined and circumspect" (275). Yet in the context of the novel, Esther also has noticeable shortcomings, such as her blind compliance with the rules imposed by her society. She is, as Governor Winthrop observes, "the pattern maiden of the commonwealth" (272). Whereas Hope Leslie goes her own way, defying her patriarchal society to help Nelema and Magawisca, Esther wholeheartedly accepts and argues for patriarchal guidance and authority, refusing to show mercy and compassion toward Magawisca. Her words emphasize the hard-heartedness underlying religious observance; she cannot oppose "those chosen servants of the Lord, whose magistracy we are privileged to live under" (278). All Everell's arguments to subdue her scruples fail, "she had some text, or some unquestioned rule of duty, to oppose to every reason and entreaty" (278). Furthermore, despite all Esther's admirable qualities, Sedgwick clearly rejects the version of womanhood this character represents: like Everell, the reader finds "there is something unlovely, if not revolting, in the sterner virtues; and particularly when they oppose those objects which he may feel to be authorised by the most generous emotions of his heart" (28). In its place, she posits her "new" version of American womanhood as represented by Hope Leslie, a woman willing to subvert patriarchal *dicta* when the cause is just, a women who need not claim mental derangement due to extraordinary psychological stress in order to explain her unconventional behavior.

Fully aware that Hope Leslie's character and unconventional behavior may seem "improbable" to her nineteenth-century "fair readers," Sedgwick attributes these not to stress but to the young woman's loving and indulgent upbringing, an upbringing that deviates markedly from the one conducted among the Puritans: "it must be remembered that she lived in an atmosphere of favour and indulgence, which permits the natural qualities to shoot forth in unrepressed luxuriance — an atmosphere of love, that like a tropical climate brings forth the richest flowers and most flavorous fruits" (122).

Although Sedgwick surrounds her heroine with father and mother surrogates — a convention in sentimental and domestic fiction — and even a tutor, none of them seem interested in inculcating religious or domestic values in their charge. Still, Sedgwick stops short of promoting a similar upbringing. All this indulgence is not necessarily an advantage, as Sedgwick points out when she describes how Hope has to suffer defeat at Magawisca's trial despite her attempts at liberating the prisoner: "Hope had been accustomed to the gratification of her wishes ... but uniform indulgence is not a favourable school, and our heroine had now to learn ... that events and circumstances cannot be moulded to individual wishes" (275).

For the most part, though, Hope does try to prove one can mold events and circumstances to individual wishes. When Cradock, her tutor, on an outing is bitten by a snake, Hope goes against Puritan mores by appealing to the old Indian woman Nemela for help. Similarly, she rejects the idea of female passivity and obedience when she engineers and executes the plan to spring Nemela from jail when she has been convicted of witchcraft, an act the authorities consider "a bold, dangerous, and unlawful interposition" (120). Ironically, she avoids punishment due to her youth and her dependent status. Her guardian, Mr. Fletcher, on the other hand, is summoned for a "long and private conference" where Governor Winthrop "recommended, for a time, a temporary transfer of his neglected authority to less indulgent hands" (121). This move proves ineffectual: Hope repeats her exploit, this time helping Everell liberate Magawisca from prison. After the latter escape, her youth and charm (and the testimony from the jailer, Barnaby Tuttle) mellow the authoritarian heart. Hope avoids punishment, receiving instead "a private admonition from the Governor, and a free pardon" (343). In *Hope Leslie*, then, more so than in *Hobomok*, the reader sees an attractive young woman challenging the male world — and getting away with it.

Yet, in both novels, the heroines rebel *within* the confines of their societies; they never attempt to dismantle the societies themselves. Furthermore, both novels end with the reintegration of the heroine into society and her acceptance of conventional gender roles, for instance as caregiver. Mary Conant returns not only as wife, but to provide for her ailing father; Hope Leslie provides a home for her aging guardian. Sedgwick writes that "The elder Fletcher remained with his children, and permitted himself to enjoy, to the full, the happiness which, it was plain, Providence had prepared for him. The close of his life was as the clear shining forth of the sun after a stormy and troubled day" (348). Hope also provides for persons outside the immediate family, another duty often performed by the Victorian woman who was expected to provide for the poor and the ailing. She installs her tutor, Cradock, "as a life-member of her domestic establishment," thus becoming, as she had promised, "the child to his old age" (349). Furthermore, she arranges for an annual stipend to the jailer, Tuttle, enabling him to retire and pass his old age with his grandchildren.

The reader notices that whereas the authors of both *Hobomok* and *Hope Leslie* allow their heroines a certain measure of autonomy and rebellion against the patriarchy before marriage and their absorption into the domestic realm, little is said about preparing them for the domestic duties they ultimately will have to perform. This is not the case with two bestsellers of the 1850s, Susan Warner's *The Wide, Wide World* and Maria Cummins's *The Lamplighter*; both works take a far more practical and didactic approach to Victorian womanhood. Written in the decade after the Seneca Falls Women's Conference, the works appear more conventional than Child's and Sedgwick's novels, and even reactionary in their implications. They are, so to speak, simultaneously the victory chant and the swan song of the cult of domesticity, a frantic blossoming of domestic values before the cult's decline. The death knell has not yet rung: both works seek to not only present but to inculcate the cult's ideals of Christian womanhood. As examples of the female *Bildungsroman* they clearly emphasize female education; they show the process that shapes an angel in the house. On the one hand, they describe the many obstacles, the most formidable being selfishness, willfulness, and abuse, that a young girl has to traverse in order to arrive at true womanhood. On the other, they assert that a Christian grounding is not enough: the young girl has to receive *practical* domestic training at the hands of a mother or a surrogate mother. Physically, Ellen appears to be the embodiment of Victorian daughterhood, she is attractive, delicate, sweet, obedient — and resolute. Although they are living in a hotel and somebody else does the actual cooking, *The Wide, Wide World*'s Ellen Montgomery has her domestic duties: each afternoon she prepares her mother's tea. Ellen's tea-making is designed to show the book's young readers the value and reward of domesticity. The narrator emphasizes Ellen's delight in performing this task, observing that "To make her mother's tea was Ellen's regular business. She treated it as a very grave affair, and loved it as one of the pleasantest in the course of the day" (13). The narrator does not stop here, though; instead, she proceeds to instruct her young readers in how to make tea and how to toast bread the correct way. In words reeking of saccharine sentimentality, she presents the tea ceremony as an expression of filial love, pleasing both mother and child. The narrator comments that "It was a real pleasure; she had the greatest satisfaction in seeing that the little her mother could eat was prepared for her in the nicest possible manner; she knew her hands made it taste better; her mother often said so" (13).

Ellen's domestic initiation — or rather, a cruel version of it — continues at her practical and hard-hearted aunt Fortune Emerson's house. Fortune Emerson — the name itself is a wonderful rebuke of Ralph Waldo Emerson's philosophy — does everything she can to refashion her niece in her own hardworking image. Ellen, whose domestic chores until this have been limited to prepare afternoon tea for her delicate mother, now faces the harsh reality of farm life and physically harder chores. Predictably, the aunt has no love for the girl put in her charge and seems intent on destroying the groundwork laid by Mrs. Montgomery. Ellen receives a more loving type of domestication — appropriately combined with religious instruction — at the home of the Rev. Mr. Humphreys, her mentor Alice's parent, who becomes her own surrogate father. At the home of her Scottish uncle, Lindsay, her *domestic socialization* continues— her newfound family eagerly attempts to counteract the instruction from her mother, her aunt, and her surrogate family alike. The one is too coarse, the other two too religious to make her acceptable to Edinburgh society.

Like *The Wide, Wide World*, *The Lamplighter* is a female *Bildungsroman* detailing the inculcation of domestic values. Its heroine, Gerty, although in the beginning more like a wild, shy animal than a child, goes through severe mental trials and physical abuse, yet emerges victorious from her ordeal. Like Ellen Montgomery, she is lucky in her surrogate parents. She is rescued at a young age by the lamplighter Trueman Flint and soon thereafter taken in hand by a surrogate mother, Mrs. Sullivan, and a mentor, Emily. As the perfect angel in the house-in-training, she busies herself creating a neat and tidy home for her adopted father. Mrs. Sullivan shows her how to clean up Flint's room, suggesting, "'You could sweep the room up every day; you could make the beds, after a fashion, with a little help in turning them; you could set the table, toast the bread, and wash the dishes. Perhaps you would not do these things in the best manner at first; but you would keep improving, and by and by get to be quite a nice little housekeeper'" (27). Moreover, when Gerty witnesses True's "astonishment" and "pleasure" when she succeeds at this, the day becomes "a memorable one in Gerty's life, one to be marked in her memory as long as she lived, as being the first in which she had known *that* happiness— perhaps the highest earth affords— of feeling that she had been instrumental in giving joy to another" (27–28). Ultimately she also reverses the father-daughter relationship, taking care of Flint until his death. Gerty also ultimately becomes close to her biological father, who appears at the end of the book and saves her from drowning. Although he at first keeps his identity hidden, Gerty is drawn to him, and the novel ends with the mandatory happy ending.

Women's literature, then, whether historical novel or contemporary *Bildungsroman*, valorized filial duty, family life and domestic, menial tasks. Such works also instructed the readers in modesty, unselfish submission, and piety, all specific qualities needed for the Victorian daughter. Cooper's novels attempt to inculcate a similar set of values.

※ ※ ※

> We are both motherless; but that aunt — that mild, plainhearted, observing aunt, has given you the victory. Oh! how much she loses, who loses a female guardian to her youth. I have exhibited those feelings which you have been taught to repress.
> — James Fenimore Cooper, *The Spy*

Cooper's "domestic" heroines, although at times just as rebellious as Mary Conant and Hope Leslie, and at times as selfless as Gerty and Ellen, go through no trials of the kind described in the female *Bildungsroman*. Nor do his novels depict the cruelty and blatant child neglect chronicled by, for example, Cummins and Warner. Packed with violence without — Indian and Revolutionary warfare as well as danger on the high seas — it demonstrates harmony within: Cooper's parents heap neither cruelty nor physical or mental abuse on his heroines. True, Cooper promotes a family that may be dysfunctional and amputated, but the family is usually physically and psychologically nonviolent. More importantly, although neither overtly didactic nor preoccupied with the process of character formation, his works present persuasive models of female behavior and deportment.[12] Ironically, although perhaps not intended to provide examples for emulation, Cooper's texts on one level function as teaching aids for the burgeoning middle class eager to adopt the lifestyle and manners of the upper classes.[13] Through his novels, the reader may be able to recognize gentlemanlike and ladylike behavior. Cooper, unlike Warner and Cummins, is not interested in the educational process *per se*, but in the *end result*; the daughters in his novels appear to have accepted their societal and familial roles. With the exception of the aunts in *Precaution* and *The Spy*, female mentors and teachers are barely mentioned in the texts.[14] Cooper's heroines emerge as fully developed as Athena from their creator's forehead — ready to show readers the qualities and behavior possessed by the women especially suited to help construct a democratic society.

Cooper's treatment of the daughter and the father-daughter relationship and familial obligations parallels the treatment the topic receives in the works of Child, Sedgwick, Warner, and Cummins. That is, his works call for *filial* rather than *parental* affection and obligation. Yet Cooper never, for all his consistent deployment of the conventions of the cult of domesticity, conceived of the Victorian daughter as exclusively domestic, fit only to lead a rarified life within the confines of the home. Instead, he posited a different, even subversive notion of womanhood: he created daughters who incorporate both feminine and masculine character traits. This vision of the Victorian daughter is especially noticeable in *The Spy*, the Leatherstocking tales, *Homeward Bound* and *Home as Found*. His "females" may be pious, emotional, and inflamed by filial duty; however, for the most part, they also possess "masculine" qualities such as intelligence and physical endurance. Moreover, in a time when writers increasingly sought to confine women within the home, Cooper showed that women might actually relish and thrive on danger and exertion in the wilderness.

Much criticism has, over the years, been directed at Cooper's representations of "females," their relevance to his works often stubbornly ignored or even rejected. James Russell Lowell's "A Fable for Critics" (1848), poking fun at the entire American literary establishment, pronounced Cooper's heroines to be interchangeable stereotypes, declaring, "The women he draws from one model don't vary / All sappy as maples and flat as the prairie."[15] Lowell did not limit his critique to the females: he found a similar lack of imagination in Cooper's male characters, of course, they are all, he claims, "Natty Bumppo / decked out in dye." Later in the century, W. D. Howells, although admitting he did not remember much of Cooper's writings, nevertheless asserted they lacked the presence of "one genuine heroine" (Qtd. in Warren 90). Leslie Fiedler in *Love and Death in the American Novel* (1966) characterized them as "wooden ingenues" and saw them as Cooper's subconscious "revenge upon the sex" (18). Fiedler must have overlooked Elizabeth Temple, Cora Munro, and Mabel Dunham, to mention a few! Even the so often ridiculed Alice Munro has her adventurous side — she is willing to face physical hardships and even danger to reach her father at Fort William Henry. Joyce C. Warren in *The American Narcissus: Individualism and Women in Nineteenth-Century Fiction* (1985), taking her cue from Fiedler, among others, finds Cooper's heroines "conventional and lifeless ... dependent, emotional, and totally selfless" (92). Kay S. House in *Cooper's Americans* (1965) gave a rather negative reading of his female characters, describing them as "generally his poorest characters and most burdened by the conventions of the time" (14). However, seventeen years later, in collaboration with Genevieve Belfiglio, House gives a much more positive reading of Cooper's works, this time based on Gayle Graham Yates's three paradigms of feminist thought. In "Fenimore Cooper's Heroines" (1982) House and Belfiglio assert: "The 'equalitarian mode' which carries with it an 'unspoken acceptance of the masculinist framework' can be found throughout Cooper's career as can surprisingly enough and perhaps for reasons we have failed to consider, the androgynous paradigm which challenges the conventionally assigned roles of men and women" (42). Although House and Belfiglio still see Cooper's women as social, but "peripheral" to the novels' actions, their reading nevertheless presents most of them as strong and capable. Even Nina Baym in "The Women of Cooper's Leatherstocking Tales" (1971) gives a strong position to Cooper's women characters, arguing that they are "of central social significance" because marriage is the matrix of his romances (697).

Moving a step beyond House and Belfiglio's assessment, I assert that Cooper, despite his emphasis on his heroines' piety, modesty, filial devotion and obedience, creates strong female role models, women characters who from within its confines challenge and even subvert patriarchal authority. His heroines are by and large resourceful, capable, and inventive, often fond of the outdoors and even fascinated by horror. Albeit not as woman centered as the works of his contemporary women writers, his works nevertheless expand the female sphere; on his pages women are not restricted to kitchen and drawing room. Cooper accomplishes this by creating daughters who stretch — but do not rupture — the boundaries of their culture. Central to this process of liberation is the displacement of the daughter(s) from the drawing room to the wilderness — or to the more sophisticated societies of Europe.[16] More than half a century before Henry James's Isabel Archer, Cooper presents a woman who seems her precursor, the well-educated and well-traveled Eve Effingham of *Homeward Bound* and *Home as Found*. In the same works, he also has an American heiress, Grace Van Cortland, marry an English nobleman — a development utilized by his literary heirs.

Not surprisingly, the death of the mother allows the daughter more freedom: in the absence of a stultifying mother, who was expected to instill proper feminine and domestic values in her daughter, the motherless daughter has to craft a new, and in many ways freer, life for herself. On the one hand, she has to take over her mother's functions, providing spiritual, psychological, and physical support to her father; on the other hand, the father often removes his daughter from the domestic arena into the wilderness, opening up for the development of more adventurous, masculine faculties. Still, while appearing to assert the cult's ideal of female "frailty" and sentimental father-daughter relations, Cooper consistently shows heroines stretching the confines of their culture. By insisting on the daughter's "masculine" characteristics, he implicitly subverts the prescribed role for the Victorian daughter.[17]

In his initial literary venture, the domestic novel *Precaution*, Cooper had produced his first portrait of the ideal "Cooper" daughter. The novel's heroine, Emily Moseley, captured at the very cusp of womanhood, emerges as the very embodiment of the early nineteenth-century ideal of femininity. If the cult of domesticity saw piety as the basis of a woman's character, it had found an avid advocate in Cooper, as witnessed by his portrayal of Emily. Emily, fresh from the schoolroom, is the stereotypical Victorian heroine: she is pious, perceptive, delicate, and reserved. Cooper's portrayal evokes Dr. Gregory's words to his daughters, and Mary Wollstonecraft's reflections on female educations, especially as regards proper religious observance: not only piety but decorum and modesty are key elements in Emily's religious habits. On entering the village church, she "glided behind her companions with a face beaming with a look of innocence and love. As she sank in the act of supplication, the rich glow of her healthful cheek lost some of its brilliancy; but on rising it beamed with a renewed lustre, that plainly indicated a heart touched with the sanctity of its situation" (30). She is also young, on the threshold of womanhood, another prerequisite for an ideal daughter. This is Cooper's portrait of his first heroine: "She was artless, but intelligent; cheerful with a deep conviction of the necessity of piety; and uniform in her practice of all her important duties ... familiar with the attainments suitable to her sex and years." Physically, "she was of the middle size, exquisitely formed, graceful and elastic in her step, without, however, the least departure from her natural movements; her eye was dark blue with an expression of joy and intelligence; at times it seemed all soul, and again all heart; her color was rather high, but it varied with every emotion of her bosom; her feelings were strong, ardent, and devoted to those she loved" (83–84). The reader easily recognizes the cornerstones of the cult of domesticity: the heroine has all the prerequisite qualities: pious, pure, submissive, and domestic, she appears as well prepared for life here on earth as for "that which comes hereafter" (84). Certain incongruities, to be sure, mark Cooper's discussion, especially as regards female education. The narrator, for example, never explains why a surrogate mother, Mrs. Wilson, educates Emily but not her other siblings, yet one would assume they are in equal need of appropriate parenting. Incidentally, Mrs. Wilson sounds as if she were a composite of Dr. Gregory and Mary Wollstonecraft. Furthermore, although the narrator emphasizes Emily's spiritual beauty, this beauty is not innate, but an artifact; it has been carefully cultivated. On the one hand, Emily is presented as "artless"; on the other hand, the narrator repeatedly asserts that this artlessness depends on training. The heroine's artlessness and her "deep conviction of the necessity of piety" are the direct results of "the discreet guidance of her aunt"; they are not inherited characteristics.[18]

Mrs. Wilson's guidance also has other benefits: it enables Emily to recognize other people's strengths and weaknesses. Although young and innocent, Emily is able to look beyond an appealing exterior to discern a person's real character. She is the first of the novel's young women to realize that Colonel Egerton, although an aristocrat and "genteel in his deportment," lacks sincerity, the "one thing, without which no one can be truly agreeable" (15). She also gravitates toward the hero Denbigh—a.k.a. the Earl of Pendennyss—when no one in the family knows his background, because she recognizes that he is "sincere and ingenuous" (68). However, where later Cooper heroines appear capable of judging a man's character on their own, *Precaution* consistently shows Mrs. Wilson as influencing her charge, moving her toward making what she considers to be the correct choices for a young woman. When the mentor doubts Denbigh's character, for instance, she immediately takes action by "considering the shortest and best method of interrupting his intercourse with Emily, before he had drawn from her an acknowledgment of her love" (207). Emily, devoted to and dependent upon her aunt for guidance, obeys. The heroines that follow Emily are to some extent all variations on this theme. Cooper never relinquished the idea that the heroine should be pious, pure, perceptive, and devoted to her loved ones. He would, however, add more masculine characteristics to the feminine stereotype of the cult of domesticity if circumstances demanded it.

In *The Spy* (1821), Cooper expands his representation of the nineteenth-century daughter, adding to the cast of characters to dramatize which qualities one ought to cultivate, and which one ought to avoid. The two Wharton daughters, Sarah and Frances, are described in conventional, sentimental terms; the author carefully avoiding specifics. They are "in the pride of youth, and the roses, so eminently the property of the West-Chester fair, glowed on their cheek" (5). Their eyes, the narrator writes, display "that lustre which gives so much pleasure to the beholder, and which indicates so much internal innocence and peace" (5). When they first appear in the text, they are in their aunt's company, and all three women are described as delicate and well-bred, as befits women of their social class—and nationality: "There was much of that feminine delicacy in the appearance of the three, which distinguishes the sex in this country; and, like the gentleman, their demeanor proved them to be women of the higher order of life" (5–6).

Cooper initially describes his ladies and gentlemen with due respect, using abstract rather than concrete traits, focusing on qualities like "innocence," "peace," and "delicacy" and their deportment rather than on physical features. The novel's heroine, Frances Wharton, like Emily Moseley, is pious, pure, and devoted to her family; spiritually and physically she conforms to the prevailing female stereotype. The younger of two sisters, she wants "some months to the charmed age of sixteen" (18), has "a face of infantile innocency" (9) but is also a budding beauty, with an "abundance of ... golden hair," "native humor" (16), and eyes "dancing with the ardor of national feeling" (19). Her filial devotion is unalloyed. She, not her elder sister functions as Mr. Wharton's companion: when her father is detained for a month, she accompanies him into captivity; like the good daughter, she supports her parent in times of trouble. Mr. Wharton explains that "Fanny would not suffer me to go alone ... this little girl was my companion in captivity" (23). Upon her brother Henry's arrest, she again has to support the parent; although feeling miserable herself. As a good Victorian girl, she accepts "a duty imposed on her by filial piety," behaving with prescribed self-abnegation (234). Her father may refer to her as a "little girl"; however, aware of the father's shortcomings, she is the one who consoles and supports him in a crisis. Although Frances experiences a crisis of her own — she has broken her engagement to Peyton Dunwoodie — her needs have to be subordinated to those of the parent. The narrator explains the need for daughterly attention: "The removal of his son had nearly destroyed the little energy of Mr. Wharton, who required all the tenderness of his remaining children to convince him that he was able to perform the ordinary functions of life" (234).

Although the younger of the Wharton sisters, Frances helps take care of the family's domestic arrangements, a duty one would expect to be laid on the elder of the two. However, she does not participate in the actual work, she merely directs it. The narrator observes that when the Wharton family has supper with Mr. Harper, the remnants of the meal "soon disappeared under her superintendence" (24). Similarly, when Harvey Birch arrives with his sack, it is Frances who thinks about offering him refreshments: "By her order a glass of liquor was offered to the trader" (33). Her behavior toward Birch indicates both her natural sympathies — which extend to people of all social classes — and her keener perception; although Birch is seen as a pariah by most of the novel's characters, Frances seems to discern his true nature.

But Cooper, not satisfied with having recreated the stereotypical Victorian "good girl," equips Frances with some rather "masculine" qualities. More politically aware than her sister Sarah, she is also more outspoken, and the only one in her family who sides with the revolutionaries. During the dinner with Mr. Harper — George Washington in disguise — she asserts that she longs for peace, "but not at the expense of the rights of my countrymen" (11). Although young, and initially believing the "political opinions ... coupled with sneers on the conduct of her countrymen" dispensed by British guests at her father's home, she has drawn her own conclusions and now listens to British statements "with great suspicion, and sometimes with resentment" (19). She is also the *first* of Cooper's physically adventurous daughters, a young woman who for the love of father and brother endures both detention by the republican forces and the trek through the picket lines to persuade Mr. Harper to help save her brother's life. When describing Frances's expedition to the mountains, Cooper emphasizes how her fraternal love overcomes gender-imposed limitations: she conquers not only the height of the mountain but her own fears. Although she at times shrinks from her mission "with the timidity of her sex and years" (368) and is "repeatedly exhausted with her efforts" and "faint with her exertions," she refuses to yield to these feminine impulses and eventually reaches her objective (370). He repeats this pattern in the Leatherstocking tales.

Sarah appears as a mere foil to Fanny (Frances). Although older, she is more delicate and also more susceptible to male flattery. "Her person," the narrator observes, "was formed with the early maturity of the climate, and a strict cultivation of the graces had made her decidedly the belle of the city" (16). However, she is "thoughtless" (17); in a way, she appears to be closer to her ineffectual father in behavior and tendencies. Incapable of rising to a challenge, she collapses when disaster strikes and she finds out that the man she intends to marry, the British officer Colonel Wellmere, has a common-law wife newly arrived in New York. And, she quite clearly falls short of Cooper's ideal American woman. His next heroine, Elizabeth Temple of *The Pioneers*, comes closer to a female prototype for a new world order.

Elizabeth, like Frances Wharton, possesses both feminine and masculine character traits. Cooper begins his portrayal of Elizabeth by detailing her feminine side: she is dark, beautiful, and commanding. The novel opens with her return to Templeton to take over her mother's duties; she is to manage her father's household. Obviously aware of her new role, she starts her duties even before she reaches the house when she persuades the wounded Oliver Edwards to come with them to have his injury seen to. In the pages that follow, the narrator repeatedly stresses Elizabeth's role as the mistress of her father's house. Her position immediately become clear: she is, as her cousin Richard Jones exclaims, "the heiress" (64). Upon her arrival at the family home, she immediately arranges for a room for the patient, tactfully, but firmly cutting short the majordomo Benjamin Pump's story and makes him attend to his duties: "Very well, Benjamin ... you shall tell me of that, and all your entertaining adventures together; just now, a room must be prepared in which the arm of this gentleman can be dressed" (70). It is also Elizabeth who extends an invitation to Louisa

Grant — overruling, as it were, Louisa's father when he feebly protests that "you will make my girl too dissipated" (131). Whereas Louisa needs paternal consent in order to accept the invitation, Elizabeth clearly does not any need permission to issue it. As mistress of the house, she decides all domestic arrangements, even who will be invited.

The narrator never implies that Elizabeth's stay in Templeton is temporary, i.e., until an eventual marriage: he bluntly states that her stay will be "for life." She, like any good nineteenth-century daughter, will spend her life as her widowed father's housekeeper. Elizabeth's domestic duties are typical of those of any upper middle-class woman of her time; she is the mistress of the house but not involved in any of the practical tasks. Her education in New York has taught her how a women of her position is expected to behave; she looks and acts the part, her features are both "sweet and commanding…. Her mouth, at first sight, seemed only made for love; but the instant that its muscles moved, every expression that womanly dignity could utter played around it with the flexibility of female grace" (66). Remarkable Pettibone, the old housekeeper, boasting she will soon control her young mistress, quickly finds herself unequal to such a task; upon seeing Elizabeth's mien, she realizes "that her own power had ended" (66). Elizabeth has been taught how to govern servants, and when Remarkable meets "the dark, proud eye of Elizabeth … the housekeeper experienced an awe that she would not own to herself could be excited by anything mortal" (169).

Although some critics argue that all Cooper's heroines are religious and routinely resort to prayer in any crisis, the author's portrayal of Elizabeth Temple allows for no such easy characterization.[19] True, Elizabeth goes to church, knows and participates in the Episcopal rituals, and behaves with appropriate modesty and decorum, as witnessed in the novel's rendition of the Templeton Christmas service, yet she can hardly be termed pious. That is, piety is not second nature to her. Significantly, modesty, not religious ardor, dictates her expression of faith. Although she is "accustomed … to the service in the churches of the metropolis," she finds it difficult to transcend the "awkwardness" of the congregation (125). Her modesty prohibits her from participating in the confessions and prayers until Louisa Grant and Oliver Edwards repeat the priest's words. More importantly, in times of crisis her faith seems to fail her. Threatened by the attacking panther, she "did not or could not move. Her hands were clasped in the attitude of prayer, but her eyes were still drawn to her terrible enemy — her cheeks were blanched to the whiteness of marble, and her lips were slightly separated with horror" (309). In times of danger, then, when a pious girl would be expected to turn to God, Elizabeth cannot pray. Later, she admits to her father, "I saw nothing, I thought of nothing but the beast, I tried to think of better things, but the horror was too glaring, the danger too much before my eyes" (326).[20] Even an almighty God pales before more physical and imminent threats.

Yet Elizabeth has not returned to Templeton a domestic automaton to be confined within the home. Cooper takes pains to make her come alive, pairing her sense of filial duty with a certain independence and courage, a joy of life, and an appreciation for the outdoors. She is the first of the family up and about Christmas Day, braving the cold to "gratify her curiosity with a glance by daylight at the surrounding objects" (179). When she and her cousin Richard overhear John Mohegan, Oliver Edwards, and Natty Bumppo discuss the morning's turkey shoot, she decides not only to witness the "ancient amusement"—in Templeton for men only—but to try her chance for the bird, albeit by proxy, the latter a rather unconventional behavior for a young lady. Cooper also repeatedly stresses the Temple family's love of the outdoors: "exercise in the open air was in some degree necessary to the habits of the family" (219). During the winter months, Elizabeth spends hours outdoors, first on the lake in her one-horse cutter; later she explores the area on horseback and even ventures up the mountain on foot.

Her patriarch father may think he has full control over his daughter, but this is clearly not the case in this household. Standing up to patriarchal authority, Elizabeth helps "spring" Natty from jail when he has been sentenced to a prison term for his refusal to obey Templeton's new hunting laws. She also purchases and brings Natty gunpowder. Her rebellion is the more noticeable since her father, Judge Temple, is the town's civil authority and has imposed the punishment on Natty. Although supposedly entering the jail on an errand from her father, who wants to give the Leatherstocking money so he can pay his fine, she does not hesitate to participate in a plot to undermine her father's authority. There is a wry sense of humor as well as a sense of filial duty in her comment to Natty when he is about to escape: "'Stay!' exclaimed Elizabeth. 'It should not be said that you escaped in the presence of the daughter of Judge Temple. Return, Leatherstocking, and let us retire, before you execute your plan'" (391). Once outside the jail, she has no qualms about suggesting how to effectuate a successful escape, suggesting to hide the irrepressible Ben Pump, the other escapee, by putting him in a cart: "'no one will look there'" (392). She is, of course, right.

Cooper repeatedly stresses Elizabeth's good sense — often combined with a humorous treatment of the males surrounding her. Although young, she immediately sees her cousin Richard's love of competition, his self-aggrandizing behavior and his belittling of her father for what it is: an insecure man's constant attempts to stay in the limelight and "secure all the honors" for himself. The reader can almost hear Elizabeth's laughter when she comments on Richard's love of competition: "'It is all very clear, sir,' said Elizabeth; 'you would not care a fig for distinction if there were no one in the world but yourself; but as there happen to be a great many others, why you must struggle with them all — in the way of competition'" (180–81).

Elizabeth's common sense and tact also emerge when she and Louisa head for the mountain with the gunpowder the former has bought for Natty. The scene emphasizes the difference in personality between the two friends. Louisa, allowing herself to be controlled by what the author clearly sees as "idle apprehension of a danger that no longer existed," refuses to cross the bridge, claiming she is "terrified" and not "equal to" climbing the hill with her friend. Elizabeth, on the other hand, chooses action over reflection. Refusing to be influenced by a danger that has already been eradicated, she climbs the road up the mountain where she earlier had been threatened by the panther. Her obligation to the Leatherstocking overrides imaginary fears. Louisa, a person much weaker of body and courage than Elizabeth, remains behind.[21] Still, the heroine never berates her timid friend for her choice, merely comments, "Well, then it must be done by me alone" (398). However, even when intent on helping the Leatherstocking, she does not neglect her self-preservation, at least as regards her own and Louisa's reputation. She posts Louisa to wait for her so that she will not be seen walking abroad alone, a prescription for gossip. Neither will Louisa; she is "out of the observation of the people who occasionally passed." For, as Elizabeth so sensibly remarks: "One would not wish to create remarks, Louisa" (398). An unblemished reputation is a girl's best friend.

In Elizabeth Temple and Louisa Grant, the reader also notices the first appearance in Cooper of what was to become two familiar stereotypes of American fictional womanhood: "the passionate brunette and the sinless blonde" (Fiedler 200). Yet Cooper never deploys these stereotypes in the predictable manner Fiedler ascribes to him in connection with *The Last of the Mohicans*, i.e., as a projection of male ambivalence toward women and female sexuality. He does not, for instance, *punish* all his dark ladies. In *The Pioneers*, Cooper's sympathies clearly lie with Elizabeth, not with Louisa. Although both are young, "just entering upon womanhood," Elizabeth's striking dark looks rivet the narrator and the people surrounding her. She has hair "shining like the raven's wing" and a face that denotes character as well as beauty: "Her nose would have been called Grecian, but for a softly rounded swell that gave in character to the feature what it lost in beauty. Her mouth, at first sight, seemed only made for love; but the instant that its muscles moved, every expression that womanly dignity could utter played around it with the flexibility of female grace" (66). Her expression is "soft, benevolent, and attractive," but her temper "could be roused, and that without much difficulty" (66). The narrator's enthusiastic description of Elizabeth's body also hints at an appreciation for a more mature type of woman. She is young, but Elizabeth is no fainting, fragile child-maiden; instead, her body is "rather full and rounded for her years, and of the tallest medium height" (66). Louisa Grant, albeit blonde, fragile, "affrighted," and dependent, excites the narrator (and the reader) far less than Elizabeth does. As if to emphasize her lack of appeal, the narrator allows the reader to see her only through Elizabeth's eyes and then describes her only in rather conventional sentimental terms. The girl is a "juvenile assistant" during the church service, "light and fragile," with a "meek face," its expression "pale and slightly agitated" but also "sweet and melancholy" (125–26). Like Elizabeth, she is drawn to the hero, Oliver Effingham, but she is no competition for her friend's darker beauty, courage, and independence.

Cooper changed this paradigm of womanhood in *The Last of the Mohicans*, this time allowing the blonde, dependent child-maiden to take center stage and win the technical hero's affection. Yet where he in earlier works had emphasized the heroine's piety and domesticity, Cooper in this novel downplays these elements, focusing instead on expressions of filial duty. The novel contains two portraits of daughters, Alice and Cora Munro, the former perhaps the most maligned of Cooper's "flat and sappy" heroines due to the novel's popularity and various cinematic representations. Often overlooked is the fact that Cooper almost immediately stresses that the two sisters are familiar with the harsh realities of frontier life. He observes, "it was apparent by their dresses, [that they] were prepared to encounter the fatigues of a journey in the woods" (18). The scene when Magua leads the two women from Fort William Henry after the massacre is even more telling, showing respect for female fortitude — and the knowledge that men and women alike share a fascination with horror and evil. Magua, leading the women away, makes them dismount on a cliff overlooking the site of the massacre. If his intent is to shock them into submission, it clearly backfires: neither Cora nor Alice faint or turn away. Instead, "notwithstanding their own captivity, the curiosity which seems inseparable from horror, induced them to gaze at the sickening sight below" (179).

The text contains few direct examples of the daughters' piety, although

Alice, when she thinks they are safe from an Indian attack, casts herself "with enthusiastic gratitude on the naked rock" to offer thanks "to that heaven who has spared the tears of a gray-haired father" (87). Both women are inflamed with filial duty, a duty that has even led them to demand to visit their father at the besieged Fort William Henry. Incredibly, Colonel Munro allows this utterly insane suggestion, thus setting in motion the novel's plot. Throughout, Cora's and Alice's focus is on him, not on their own safety; *they* have urged their visit as a show of support. Cora even admits to a certain filial manipulation, "in a moment of much embarrassment," but justifies their actions with words worthy of a good Victorian daughter, whose chief function was to aid the father in stressful situations: the two girls wanted to prove "that however others might neglect him in his strait, his children at least were faithful!" (61). Motherless, they identify closely with their father and his values: they are daughters of Munro and can boast of a "stock of hereditary courage" to bolster them on their trek (20). Alice, however, also knows that professions of daughterly love can be deployed to other ends: she uses her professed filial affections to attempt to gain Heyward's attention — and succeeds. When Heyward repeats Munro's praise of Cora, she immediately interrupts him, putting herself into the picture: "'And did he not speak of me, Heyward?' demanded Alice, with jealous affection. 'Surely, he forgot not altogether his little Elsie?'"(61). She is obviously a rather self-centered, spoiled girl, she cannot bear that Cora receives their father's praise — and Heyward's attention. Physically, Alice appears to be the reincarnation of Emily Moseley: she is young, blond, blue-eyed, infantile, artless, dependent, and supposedly quite unaware of her physical appeal. No white male in the novel suffers from this misconception, though: the narrator, as well as Munro, Heyward, and Natty, frequently comments on Alice's youth and infantile dependence, qualities the cult of domesticity and, supposedly, men found especially attractive and lovable in women. When he allows the two young women to enter the stage, Cooper deploys conventional, sentimental language to describe Alice. She has a "dazzling complexion, fair golden hair, and bright blue eyes." She appears artless, this behavioral requisite, and the narrator waxes positively poetic when he adds, "The flush which still lingered above the pines in the western sky was not more bright nor delicate than the bloom on her cheek; nor was the opening day more cheering than the animated smile which she bestowed on the youth, as he assisted her into the saddle" (18).

The word "permitted" allows the reader to see a different side of Alice: she is flirtatious and vivacious, a belle who knows how to draw male attention.[22] She is the first of the sisters to speak, she flirts with Heyward and even the socially inept Gamut; she loves being the center of attention. She has her father wrapped around her little finger; he has always been "tender and indulgent" to all her wishes (61). She even embodies a certain measure of resourcefulness, despite her fainting at critical moments. Cora, on the other hand, appears to be her sister's opposite. Instead of deliberately flaunting her beauty, as her sister does, she conducts herself with proper deportment. The narrator comments that she "concealed her charms from the gaze of the soldiery, with a care that seemed better fitted to the experience of four or five additional years. It could be seen, however, that her person, though moulded with the same exquisite proportions, of which none of the graces were lost by the travelling dress she wore, was rather fuller and more mature than that of her companion" (18–19).

Concealment, however, has its own powerful attraction. What is hinted at becomes more attractive than what is actually shown. Besides, what the veil conceals, her traveling attire reveals: "none of the graces were lost" by it. Only when the villain Magua glides by does Cooper allow Cora's veil to open — appropriately by accident. The unveiling reveals not only "an indescribable look of pity, admiration, and horror" (19); it allows the spectators — and the readers — a glimpse of a beauty of a different kind than her sister's, but rather like Elizabeth Temple's: "The tresses of this lady were shining and black, like the plumage of the raven. Her complexion was not brown, but it rather appeared charged with the color of the rich blood, that seemed ready to burst its bounds. And yet there was neither coarseness nor want of shadowing in a countenance that was exquisitely regular and dignified, and surpassingly beautiful" (19). Cora is "fuller and more mature" than her sister and also more thoughtful and reserved (19).

Like many an elder, motherless daughter, Cora functions as a substitute mother who, in dangerous situations, "taught the more timid Alice the necessity of obedience" (60). Cooper stresses that the relationship between the two sisters resembles the relationship between mother and daughter: Cora has always been maternal toward her younger sibling. However, a certain tension soon emerges between the two, at least on Alice's part, in connection with the "technical hero" Duncan Heyward. Alice uses all the ammunition available to a nineteenth-century woman to gain his love: filial duty, piety, innocence, physical weakness. At one point, she clings to the young officer's arm "with the dependence of an infant"; Cora, in the same scene, finds he "can be of no further service" to them (80). She is also extremely manipulative; her fainting spells and expressions of filial duty are intended for male admiration; she has to be the center of attention. The narrator may insist on sibling love; he shows sibling rivalry. Alice would rather manipulate than be manipulated.

Predictably, Alice and Cora are also presented as paragons of purity and virtue, indispensable attributes for the Victorian good girl. However, although Cooper implies that both young women are sexually appealing, he insists that Alice's charms appeal to *white men* only while Cora's richer blood and courage also attract *Native American males* such as Magua and Uncas. He also takes great pains to prevent readers from equating Cora's "impure blood" with *moral* impurity; she is, as her father says, "a maiden too discreet, and of a mind too elevated and improved, to need the guardianship even of a father" (157–8). Yet the possible sexual violation of these virgins looms in the minds of both Munro and Heyward — but not, it appears, in the minds of the women. Where Cora, trying to stay calm, during the first attack asserts that "the worst to us can be but death," Heyward, appropriately "speaking hoarsely," immediately sexualizes the moment, voicing the white male's ultimate fear when white women are threatened: "There are evils worse than death" (80).

Sexuality also infuses the novel's solitary "domestic" scene (i.e., it takes place within the four walls of Munro's living quarters), which shows Munro, Alice, and Cora in the colonel's quarters. Cooper, perhaps wishing to show how childlike, loving, and trusting Alice is, manages to imply just the opposite: instead of portraying Alice as asexual, the text affirms her sexuality. This occurs when Heyward enters his commander's quarters and witnesses the following *tableau* of domestic bliss: the colonel is in a chair, Alice "upon his knee, parting the gray hairs on the forehead of the old man with her delicate fingers; and whenever he affected to frown on her trifling, appeasing his assumed anger by pressing her ruby lips fondly on his wrinkled brow. Cora was seated near them, a calm and amused looker on; regarding the wayward movements of her more youthful sister, with that species of maternal fondness which characterized her love for Alice" (156). Clearly, Cooper, since the father-daughter relationship was by definition asexual, considered this a perfectly innocent expression of family love. As Morton Cohen observes, in the Victorian era "cuddling and kissing children was accepted behavior" (16). Alice is, after all, like any daughter, programmed to cheer her father and make him comfortable. On the other hand, while Munro may refer to his daughters as his "babes" and his "lambs," both Alice and Cora are young, attractive women ready for marriage. Again we have an example of how the author perhaps sees more than he actually means to see. However, Alice plays an active, almost seductive role in the scene; she is not a passive recipient of her father's caresses, nor is she a child. Therefore, her parting her father's hair and "pressing her ruby lips" on his brow suddenly seems more than mere childishness. The term "ruby lips" in particular sexualizes Alice. Her actions are more those of a lover than the actions of a daughter. Intriguingly, both Cora and Heyward emerge as *voyeurs* in this scene; they are outside the intimacy of the couple in the chair. Furthermore, the scene clearly titillates Heyward, through whose eyes the reader witnesses the couple. In contrast, Cora's "maternal fondness" fails to excite Heyward; Alice's "trifling," on the other hand, appeals. The major, having entered unannounced, stands "many moments an unobserved and *delighted* spectator" (156, my emphasis), to this domestic bliss, perhaps contemplating a similar scene with himself in Munro's position. This is not exactly an idle thought: the scene which follows has Heyward admitting to his commander his "pretensions" to Alice. She has, he claims, captured him with her "sweetness," "beauty," and "witchery"—i.e., with her dependence and her sexuality (159). The more mature, maternal, sensible, and resourceful Cora fails this nineteenth-century litmus test of female attractiveness. And it is the image of the blonde, pale, weak and presumably selfless Alice that reverberates in our consciousness, obliterating the other female characters created by Cooper in his long literary career.

Alice's and Cora's kind of attraction—filial devotion combined with physical appeal—also appears in *The Prairie*; here, however, Cooper never gives the father-daughter relationship the prominence he gave it in his earlier work. Instead, he creates a virtual social hierarchy of daughters: Inez Middleton, Ellen Wade, and the Bush daughters all inhabit different rungs on the novel's social ladder. The novel, therefore, provides the reader with a broader insight into the lives of eighteenth- and nineteenth-century women than Cooper's earlier books, especially as regards the lives of those "reared in the hardihood of a migrating life, on the skirts of society" (147).

Although entirely set on the prairies itself, the novel allots limited space to the activities of the latter group. Initially, Cooper mentions the Bush daughters as "several white-headed, olive-skinned faces ... with eyes of lively curiosity and characteristic animation" (13); later, they are "occupied ... around the fire" (20). Strictly speaking, only two of the daughters, Phoebe and Hetty, become individualized—and then in the context of violence, in a scene that emphasizes their masculine qualities, not their feminine ones. When Ellen and the Bush children fear they are about to be attacked by "Sioux-Indians" (the "Indians" turn out to be Natty, Middleton, Dr. Battius, and Hard-Heart), the two girls prove to be Ellen's superiors "in the important military property of insensibility to danger" (147). Cooper attributes their cold-bloodedness to the fact that frontier life has "familiarized them to the sights and dangers of the wilderness" (147) — and to their mother Esther's example. The two girls look to Esther as a role model, not to Ishmael; they want to emulate *her* daring and resourcefulness. Although still girls, they are "young Amazons," characterized by a unique brand of filial devotion. The narrator comments that "the bosoms of the young Amazons were now strangely fluctuating between natural terror and the ambitious wish to do something that might render them worthy of being the children of such a mother" (147). They also, once Ellen disappears to care for Inez, attack the four men: "Encouraging each other to persevere, they posed the fragments of rocks, prepared the lighter missiles for immediate service, and thrust forward the barrels of the muskets with a business-like air, and a coolness, that would have done credit to men practised in warfare" (147). Life on the frontier, the text indicates, at least among the lower classes, blurs the lines between masculine and feminine qualities: one simply does what needs to be done, regardless of gender.

Inez stands at the top of the novel's social structure. Almost the personification of the nineteenth-century daughter, she is pious, young, dependent, and extraordinarily passive. She is sixteen, "just emerging from the condition of childhood into that of a woman ... alive to all the power of youth and beauty" (157). Although Cooper insists on her "natural timidity," he also insists she is "romantic" and "warm-hearted," as well as "soft and amiable" (157–59). An only child, she is devoted to her widowed father; she can wish nothing more of her husband than that he take after her father "in every thing" (183). Her filial devotion and her piety makes her an eager participant in her father's scheme to convert Duncan Middleton to Catholicism: Inez, the text asserts, "thought it would be a glorious consummation of her wishes to be a humble instrument of bringing her lover into the bosom of the true church," fervently praying to be the one to bring him "into the flock of the faithful" (159–60).

In the character of Inez, though, Cooper creates a female image with a clearly erotic appeal. On the one hand, Inez conforms to the domestic ideal in stature and filial duty: she is small, passive, and dependent. On the other hand, she casts a powerful erotic spell on the men she encounters: her dark, Creole beauty keeps not only her husband, but also various Indians completely enthralled. No wonder her captors keep her hidden from the eyes of the young womenless men of the Bush clan. Inez's dark, erotic power leads to a related issue; the fear of suffering "a fate worse than death" informs *The Prairie* to a much stronger degree than it informed *The Last of the Mohicans*. However, this threat is limited to Inez. Furthermore, the threat comes from one direction only, that of the Native

Americans: both Inez and Middleton revolt at the attention the Sioux chief Mahtoree pays her. Already at their first encounter with the Sioux, Inez's effect on Mahtoree makes her young husband decidedly nervous. When Mahtoree first sees Inez, "the look of the Teton was long, riveted and admiring" (249). Later, when he receives them as his prisoners, "a single gleam of fierce joy broke through his clouded brow" at the sight of the "nearly insensible but still lovely Inez." Middleton, fearing a physical follow-up of the chief's gaze, "grew cold as he caught the expression of that eye" (270). His fears are not unfounded: Mahtoree wants Inez for his wife, proclaiming "none shall be greater than she" (289). The metaphor Mahtoree uses to describe Inez is implicitly sexual; "he found a flower on the prairies, and he plucked it, and brought it into his lodge" (291). However, in Cooper's novels only "bad" Indians—in this case the Sioux who are depicted as the Mingos of *The Prairie*—harbor sexual thoughts toward white women. In the case of the Pawnee Hard-Heart, one of the novel's "good" Indians, Cooper repeatedly emphasizes the man's respect and admiration for Inez. Although the young Indian cannot keep his eyes off Inez, he nevertheless responds to her as any decent white man ought to respond to such a superior being:

> While speaking to the trapper he suffered his wandering glances to stray towards the intellectual and nearly infantile beauty of Inez, as one might be supposed to gaze upon the loveliness of an ethereal being. It was very evident that he now saw, for the first time, one of those females, of whom the fathers of his tribe so often spoke, and who were considered of such rare excellence as to equal all that savage ingenuity would imagine in the way of loveliness [189].

Hard-Heart may find Inez as entrancing as Mahtoree finds her; however, he studies her as if she were "formed with all that perfection with which the youthful poet is apt to endow the glowing images of his brain" (258). He sees her as an *idol*; Mahtoree, on the other hand, sees her as a *sexual being*.

Occupying the middle ground between these two poles of womanhood—the physically active Amazon and the erotic, but passive Dark Lady—is the orphan Ellen Wade, a rather unlikely addition to the Bush clan. Ellen's link to the Bush clan is tenuous at best: she protests to Natty that "I have no father!" (27). Later, when Dr. Battius refers to Ishmael as "Thy uncle, child," she forcefully rejects this, describing Bush as "my father's brother's widow's husband" (126). It is a relationship she abhors; it is "a tie that chance has formed and which I would rejoice so much to break forever!" (126). Still, although not a daughter by blood, she performs a daughter's duties within the household: she does her share of the domestic chores and takes care of the family's children, "satisfying the often repeated demands which her younger associates made on her time and patience, under the pretences of hunger, thirst, and all the other ceaseless wants of captious and inconsiderate childhood" (146). She is also the only one who takes care of the abducted Inez, "administering to the comforts of one far more deserving of her tenderness" than the children, thereby keeping the Creole's presence a secret (146).

Cooper immediately stresses Ellen's difference from the rest of the group, presenting her as a young woman "who in figure, dress, and mien, seemed to belong to a station in society several gradations above that of any one of her visible associates" (13). Whereas Esther Bush has a "sharp, dissonant voice," Ellen's is "soft toned" and her lips tremble when she speaks out against the others who wants to shoot the approaching trapper. Hers is a voice of reason: she reminds her companions that some of their number are still out scouting; the person they see "may be a friend" (15). Cooper invests Ellen with a host of good qualities: she is, for example, "honest and warmhearted" (146). Compared to the members of the Bush family, she is "vastly their superior in that spirit which emanates from moral qualities" (147). She is also brave and resourceful, drawing on stories of "female heroism" to "prepare her slender means of defence" when faced with a possible enemy attack. Furthermore, she relishes the situation. "Flushing cheeks and kindling eyes" indicate excitement and enthusiasm, not fright. Her defense plan is simple, utilizing the location and available resources: "She posted the larger girls at the little levers that were to cast the rocks on the assailants; the smaller were to be used more for show than any positive service they could perform; while like any other leader, she reserved her own person as a superintendent and encourager of the whole." She then "endeavored to await the issue with an air of composure that she intended should inspire her assistants with the confidence necessary to insure success" (147). Although not sympathetic to a family she is only tangentially connected to, she is always willing to play her part in the efforts to support the Bush family. The narrator observes that "Whatever might be the reasons of Ellen for entertaining no strong attachment to the family in which she has first been seen by the reader, the feelings of her sex, and, perhaps, some lingering seeds of kindness, predominated" (48–49). She does her share of chores, and also is in charge of taking care of the captive Inez.

Cooper never dwells on Ellen's sexuality the way he does on Inez's. Or rather, since she is of a "maturer and perhaps more animated beauty," she supposedly does not have the same appeal to the Indians (189) as the Creole has. Mahtoree does not even notice her until he sees her with Inez, and then he merely wants to give her to one of his warriors; she "may stay in the lodge of a brave, and eat of his venison" (289). Hard-Heart, on the other hand, regards her with "much of the homage which man is made to pay to woman" (189); however, "the more intelligible and yet extraordinary charms of Ellen" cannot hold his attention as well as Inez's dark and erotic appearance does (258).

When Cooper in 1840 returns to the Leatherstocking tales after a hiatus of more than a decade, his love plots involve not his earlier upper-class heroines but lower-class ones, combining, as it were, characters and scenes from the earlier novels. In *The Pathfinder*, Cooper chooses a heroine of the "middling sort"—Mabel Dunham—who, like the Munro daughters, treks through the wilderness to be with her father, Sergeant Dunham at the fort where he is posted. Yet in this novel, Cooper reveals how unreasonable the demand for filial duty can be, especially as regards a daughter's marriage; in doing so, he implicitly rejects the cult of domesticity's notion of unquestioned filial piety. Cooper's text also suggests how unrealistic it is to expect that a father-daughter relationship can be taken up without difficulty after long separations.

To the reader, Mabel is an appealing yet frustrating character who, on the one hand, demonstrates great physical and psychological strength while, on the other hand, living up to Warren's notion of her as belonging to Cooper's "dependent, emotional, and totally selfless" females (Warren 93). Cooper initially stresses her "masculine" qualities, not her domesticity. Introducing her on a journey through the wilderness, he focuses on her physical strength, her love of danger, and her appreciation of the outdoors: unlike her seaman uncle, she treks through the wilderness without apparent problems. Her uncle Cap may consider her "fainthearted, like her mother" (44); Natty Bumppo may refer to her as a "sweet child" and a "tenderhearted" and "feeble" girl (66, 130–31), and Jasper Western, as caught up in gender expectations as his comrades, may claim she is "too tender to walk through swamps" (81); however, Cooper repeatedly demonstrates that the three men often project upon her their own expectations of domesticated womanhood. Mabel, he shows, possesses qualities that are needed for survival on the frontier; she is "spirited," "accustomed to self-reliance," "quick of intellect," and "not altogether without a feeling for the poetry of this beautiful earth of ours" (91, 297, 109). Although all members of the company at this point feel insecure, it is young Jasper Western who begins to tremble, supposedly on Mabel's behalf, at every sound coming from the surrounding woods. The young woman shows much more fortitude. The narrator repeatedly stress her delight in the outdoors. "Were I a man," she tells Pathfinder on a later occasion, "it would be my delight to roam through these forests at will, or to sail over this beautiful lake" (267). More importantly, she has confidence in her own strength; she asserts that she is "active" and "used to exercise" (54). She relishes danger, as her first brush with it proves, facing it with calmness, resolution, and excitement: when the canoe bearing her away from the pursuing Iroquois shoots into the river, "the ardent, generous-minded Mabel felt her blood thrill in her veins and her cheeks flush" (90). Although "only a girl from the towns," she finds the whole experience fascinating, not frightening. The text states that the moment is "the most exciting which had ever occurred in the brief existence of Mabel Dunham ... she could hardly be said to be under the influence of fear, yet her heart often beat quicker than common, her fine blue eye lighted with an exhibition of a resolution that was wasted in the darkness, and her quickened feelings came in aid of the real sublimity that belonged to the scene and to the incidents of the night" (90–91). The dark may hide Mabel's excitement from her companions; however, Cooper asserts that women do not necessarily falter in a crisis. Instead, they react with resolution and self-control, allowing men to fight without having to worry about female faint-heartedness. For, as Mabel tells Jasper, "no foolish fears of mine shall stand in the way of your doing your duty" (91). Significantly, she attributes her fearlessness to her being a "soldier's daughter," just as Alice and Cora do in *The Last of the Mohicans*. A woman with her family background, Mabel asserts, "ought to be ashamed to confess fear" (91). Significantly, the daughter's role model is the father; she identifies with him, not with her deceased mother, even if she has been separated from him for the greater part of her life.

Cooper, though, aware of the lives of his readers, stops short of presenting Mabel as a prototype of a new breed, the new American woman. Instead, his text argues that although a woman may show her fearlessness in a physical crisis, she must also conform to ruling ideas of true womanhood: she must know her place and be pious, selfless, and domesticated. Mabel possesses these qualities. She is also "unsophisticated ... and ingenuous and frank as any warmhearted and sincere-minded girl well would be" (109), displaying a "modest but spirited deportment" (136). Although motherless, she has, under the tutelage of an officer's widow, internalized middle-class domestic ideals and with them the belief in reciprocal family love and filial piety and duty. Yet even a daughter's internalizing of domestic values does not make for a smooth adjustment to family life. Mabel, once she comes face to face with her father after a fourteen-year separation, has problems adjusting to him and fulfilling his desires. Significantly, *she* has to adjust to the new situation, not he; malleability is a female requisite. Influenced by a romanticized view on the father-daughter relationship, she expects intimacy but finds her father unapproachable in public as well as in private and adjusts to the reality. While "her very heart yearned to throw herself on his bosom and to weep at will," Sergeant Dunham's behavior discourages such behavior: "he was so much colder in externals, so much more formal and distant than she had expected to find him, that she would not have dared to hazard the freedom, even had they been alone" (119–20). The real father does not live up to the ideal Mabel has nurtured; the sergeant is obviously too conscious of his own military role and image to allow himself any expression of parental love. The perceptive Mabel understands her father's predicament, interpreting his facial muscles moving as a sign of his emotions; however, she knows she can do nothing to bridge the gap between them. The only thing she can do is to attempt to fulfill her prescribed domestic role.

Although Cooper emphasizes Mabel's many domestic — i.e., feminine — qualities, there are, as in *The Last of the Mohicans*, few actual domestic scenes in *The Pathfinder*; after all, the sergeant has not brought his daughter to the fort to keep house. The sergeant may claim he takes his daughter to the scouting outpost so that she can "make my broth for me" (120); however, the actual cooking is done by Jennie, wife of one of the soldiers. Mabel takes over the domestic chores only when Jennie has been killed, and then, almost instantaneously, reverses the father-daughter relationship by becoming her father's nurse and seeing to it that his last days are comfortable. This she does competently and quietly: "All ... was done earnestly, and almost without speaking; nor did Mabel shed a tear until she heard the blessings of her father murmured on her head for this tenderness and care" (383).

Mabel not only sees to her father's physical needs, but to his spiritual ones: she leads the dying man to God. Although her father initially thinks she is too young to provide him with religious consolation — it "appeared like reversing the order of nature" and reminds him of how poorly he has discharged his paternal duties (389) — Mabel is the only one who does not fail the soldier. Pathfinder, Cap, and Jasper encourage him to pray but cannot pray with him. Only Mabel, "religiously educated ... without exaggeration and without self-sufficiency" actually prays *with* him. Fighting to control her emotions, she tells her father: "I will pray with you, *for* you, for *myself*, for us *all*. The petition of the feeblest and humblest is never unheeded" (440). Her prayer is personal, not "slavishly borrowed," and "of a character which might have worthily led the spirits of angels" (441). It also leads the spirit of her father; hearing her words, the sergeant "felt some such relief as one who finds himself staggering on the edge of the precipice, under a burthen difficult to be borne, might be supposed to experience when he unexpectedly feels the weight removed, in order to be placed on the shoulders of another better able to sustain it" (442). Mabel accomplishes more than her father's consolation, though; she gives him the feeling that he has at least discharged one of his paternal duties: he taught Mabel her first prayer. When he wishes he could pray, she reminds him that he knows one prayer — the Lord's Prayer; "you taught it to me yourself while I was yet an infant" (443). The pious daughter, then, has restored her father's faith.

The father-daughter relationship is central also to Cooper's last installment of the Leatherstocking tales, *The Deerslayer*, the novel Cooper originally had thought of calling *The Girls of the Glimmerglass*. *The Deerslayer* has portraits of two very different daughters, Hetty and Judith Hutter, the one "feeble-minded," homely, pious, and domestic, the other intelligent, beautiful, irreverent, immodest, and, like Cora and Inez, clearly sexual. As he had done in *The Pathfinder*, he chose daughters of the middling sort and again he teased his readers with the possibility of marriage and sexual initiation for his eponymous hero Natty Bumppo. In developing his female characters, Cooper once more relied heavily on the conventions of the cult of domesticity.[23] Hetty, for example, seems to be the embodiment of the cult's ideals; Judith, on the other hand, appears to lack all the values that were considered indispensable for a good Victorian daughter. The denouement of the novel, then, becomes especially poignant if read in the context of the conventions of the cult of domesticity and the nineteenth-century family ideal.

To the twenty-first century reader, though, Judith is an appealing character: beautiful, intelligent, and courageous. Cooper describes her as having a "brilliant and singular beauty" (73), "rich hair," a "spirited yet soft countenance" (95), and a "fine, full, person" (160). She is also "quick-witted" (63) and acts resolutely in a crisis. When an Indian attacker lands on the deck of the Ark, she "rushed from the cabin, her beauty heightened by the excitement that produced the bold act, which flushed her cheek to crimson, and, throwing all her strength into the effort, she pushed the intruder over the edge of the scow, headlong into the river" (79). The incident proves her boast to Harry March that she has "the spirit and experience that will make her depend more on herself than on good-looking rovers" like him (71). Judith does not need to be defended; she can defend herself, at least against Indian violence. However, she cannot properly defend herself against the threat posed by the English officers and her own surfeit of sexuality and paucity of principle: "She had many causes deeply to regret the acquaintance — if not to mourn over it, in secret sorrow — for it was impossible for one of her quick intellect not to perceive how hollow was the association between superior and inferior, and that she was regarded as the play thing of an idle hour, rather than as an equal and a friend" (161). Judith's beauty, intelligence, and courage notwithstanding, Cooper never allows his readers to forget that she is the very antithesis of the female ideal of his day. Although she takes care of Hutter's home with her sister, she has, Harry March observes, "the vagaries": she "has caught more than is for her good from the settlers, and especially from the gallantifying officers" (36). In other words, she lacks modesty and virtue. As Darnell asserts, the term "gallant" is "synonymous with upper-class seducer of lower-class girls" (60). Still, she is not quite a "fallen woman." She is, however, noticeably vain, as witnessed by the articles of clothing and decoration on her side of the sisters' bedroom, arranged solely for show. When sewing, she makes things to ornament herself; Hetty makes some "coarse garment" for her father (147). In addition, Judith always dwells on beauty as a personal merit; after she has pushed an Indian warrior overboard she comments that he is "a good-looking savage" (95). She suggests her part of the rescue plot not only to try to save her father, but also to impress Natty with her filial devotion and her daring. Significantly, Cooper, when he dresses her in red, emphasizes her sexual nature. She is immodest; she transgresses against propriety, the cult of domesticity, and true womanhood.

Ironically, it is the "feeble-minded" Hetty who embodies the qualities prized by the cult of domesticity — and the novel's hero. She is domestic, pure, and excessively pious. The reader notices the narrator's keen interest in Hetty's character when he, on the same page where he rather briefly mentions Judith's "brilliant and singular beauty," spends almost a full page establishing Hetty's less noticeable personality. In all fairness, it must be said that Hetty's mental weakness, although commented on by several characters in the book, seems less serious than it has been represented, notwithstanding Railton's assessment that she is an "imbecile" (Railton 213). The narrator explains that her mind is "just enough enfeebled to lose most of those traits that are connected with the more artful qualities, and to retain its ingeniousness and love of truth." Then he adds, "It had often been remarked of this girl, by the few who had seen her, and who possessed sufficient knowledge to discriminate, that her perception of right seemed almost intuitive, while her aversion to the wrong formed so distinctive a feature of her mind, as to surround her with an atmosphere of pure morality" (66). Hetty has all the requisites of a Victorian good girl. In fact, she seems the very embodiment of the cult of domesticity. And the narrator takes this a step further: he repeatedly stresses her unworldliness as if to foreshadow her demise: Hetty is too good for this world. Is this the case also with the cult she embodies? The younger of the Hutter sisters is "guileless" and "innocent," her expression "calm, quiet, almost holy." She has "a modesty so innate, that it almost raised her to the unsuspecting purity of a being superior to human infirmities" (66). The "perfect neatness" of her side of the sisters' room, with her few coarse garments hanging plainly from pegs, attest not only to her cleanliness and sound housekeeping skills, but to her innate goodness: a clean, well-ordered house denotes a good, moral character. The garments themselves also attest to Hetty's intuitive awareness of her own social rank, yet another required trait for the Victorian good daughter: her side of the room contains nothing "beyond those which Hutter's daughters might be fairly entitled to wear" (43).

Despite her alleged feeblemindedness, she has taken over many of her deceased mother's duties, apparently discharging them admirably. She has, Hurry Harry tells Deerslayer, "a wonderful particular way about a frying pan or a gridiron" (41). And, despite her deficiencies, she would, her father observes, "make a much safer and more rational companion than Jude" (63). Emulating her dead mother, she also provides sanctuary for her father, calming his nerves after the day's hardships by singing to him one of her mother's songs, because "Hutter never listened to this simple strain without finding his heart and manner softened; facts that his daughter well knew, and by which she had often profited, through the sort of holy instinct that enlightens the weak of mind, more especially in their aims toward good" (90–1). Hetty, therefore, is much closer and more devoted to her father's physical and spiritual well-being than Judith is; she has been with him whereas Judith has flirted with the officers at the fort. Hetty also serves as her father's spiritual guide. Her objective is not only to calm her father but to convert him; she challenges his ideas of white superiority and tries to change his mind about the scalping expedition he has planned with Hurry Harry, urging him to abstain from selling "human blood" and see that "you must do to your enemies, as you *wish* your enemies would do to you" (92).

Although Cooper initially presents Hetty as almost exclusively domestic, he also shows that she has a certain amount of initiative and courage: Hetty takes the first step to liberate Hutter and Hurry Harry from the Indians, even without suggestions from Deerslayer. Judith puts her sister's boldness down to filial devotion, explaining that Hetty "has her own ideas of what ought to be done. She loves her father more than most children love their parents" (163). Armed only with her Bible, she leaves the Ark to persuade the Indians to release their captives. Hetty's rescue mission receives a rather ambiguous treatment by Cooper. On the one hand, the text emphasizes her "instinctive caution which so often keeps those whom God has thus visited from harm," adding that the girl was "less governed by any chain of reasoning than by her habits" (166). On the other hand, it shows her as reasoning, albeit naively, that she is safe both among the Indians and the animals of the forest because she is "half-witted": "Neither will harm a poor, half-witted girl" (168). On the one hand, she does not even have sense to sit down in the canoe; on the other hand, she not only knows the forest, but she has sense enough to bring a cloak to cover herself with during the night. However, mentally deficient, she cannot cope fully with the demands of the real world. This becomes abundantly clear when she arrives at the Indian village. She tries to persuade the Indians with words from the Bible, but cannot argue her case convincingly because she fails to see they do not fit within the biblical value system.

The culmination of Cooper's depiction of American womanhood, though, comes in his so-called "Silkstocking tales" *Homeward Bound* and its sequel *Home as Found*, where one finds Cooper's *Notions of the American Gentleman and Lady* (Darnell 70). These are Cooper's first contemporary novels, explicitly designed not only to anatomize and satirize what passes for American "society," but to define "those qualities which distinguish" the American gentleman and lady (Darnell 70). Six decades before Thorsten Veblen, then, Cooper gives a representation of and sharply criticizes the American leisure class. Despite its contemporary setting, *Homeward Bound* and *Home as Found* clearly parallel *The Pioneers*. In all three of these novels centered on the Effingham family, a father brings his daughter, now educated to function as his companion and a surrogate for his lost wife, home to Templeton where she is to take over her domestic duties (*Homeward Bound* delineates the transatlantic voyage). Like her ancestress Elizabeth Temple, Eve Effingham is the mistress of her father's household but liberated from most domestic tasks. In this, the most domestic of Cooper's novels, the author envisions the mistress in a purely supervisory capacity; if Eve is useful, it is, strictly speaking, a facsimile of usefulness. Eve shares "equitably in the good things that Providence had so liberally bestowed" on her father; she has been released "from cares that necessarily formed no more a part of her duties than it would be a part of her duty to sweep the pavement before the door" (2). Eve's domestic duties, Cooper writes, consist of issuing "a few orders in the morning, and to examine a few accounts once a week" (2). Her preferences, not his, dictate who will be invited: although her father issues the actual invitations, he will not invite people his daughter dislikes. In *Homeward Bound* and *Home as Found*, then, Cooper depicts a father-daughter relationship based on reciprocal love and respect, not on paternal supremacy and filial subjugation.

More importantly, though, the novels launch Cooper's vision of a new, improved type of American woman, an ingenious blend of breeding, artlessness, and intelligence. Thus, Eve Effingham, the works' heroine, is appropriately named. She is our first "American Girl"—the Eve of a New World—charming, affluent, articulate, well-educated, and well-traveled, a person "totally without management" (*Homeward Bound* 132). As such, she is a worthy role model for Henry James's Isabel Archer and far her superior in knowledge and intelligence. So obviously perfect is she that D. H. Lawrence comments, "We have learned to shudder at her, but Cooper still admired" (47).

When the reader meets Eve on board the American packet the *Montauk* in *Homeward Bound*, she is twenty and has been educated in Europe since she was eleven. Although she considers herself an American, she is, at least in behavior and tastes, more European than American since she is a product of a European upbringing. More importantly, Cooper creates her, metaphorically speaking, from her father's rib, explicitly to complement her father's character. She is, then, a sort of psychological hermaphrodite, combining both masculine and feminine character traits. On the one hand, Eve is a "fair-haired, lovely, blue-eyed girl," well-bred and with impeccable taste; on the other hand, the text shows her primarily as her father's daughter: she is "a softened reflection" of her father's best qualities. In Eve, Mr. Effingham's "sentiment, intelligence, knowledge, tastes, and cultivation" have been added "to the artlessness and simplicity of her sex and years" (2). The product of this *mélange*, her admirer Paul Powis observes, is a person both "so simple and yet so cultivated; with a mind in which nature and knowledge seem to struggle for possession" (131). The text repeatedly stresses her cultivation: she knows music, art, and languages—French, German, Italian, and impeccable English. Too well-bred "to run into the extravagant freedoms which pass for easy manners in America," she is "natural and unembarrassed in her intercourse with the world, and she had been allowed to see so many different nations that she had obtained a self-confidence ... and great natural dignity of mind" (3). Eve, then, is the ideal genteel female: modest, "artless," and innocent, a paragon of moral superiority and "religious without cant" (132). However, she also sees the ridiculous in situations, laughs easily, and shows a "self-confidence that did her no injury" (133). Cooper, apparently, sees no problem in insisting on artlessness while presenting a character who is so obviously a cultural artifact; on the contrary, his portrayal of Eve attests to the possibility of human improvement.[24]

Home as Found completes Cooper's exaltation of this American paragon. Eve, her cousin Grace Van Cortland observes, is "simple and unaffected as a child, with the intelligence of a scholar; with all the graces of a woman she has the learning and mind of a man" (297). Eve's "masculine traits"—for example her intellectual perfection—can be seen not only in her ability to understand different languages, but also in the depth of her knowledge. As Grace points out, Eve not only *speaks* the different languages, she understands the literature of the countries and the philosophies underlying this literature. Whereas Grace speaks several languages "as the parrot repeats words he does not understand ... Eve Effingham has used these languages as means, and she does not tell you merely what such a phrase or idiom signifies, but what the greatest writers have thought or written" (297). Furthermore, although Eve "thoroughly enjoys everything intellectual"—i.e., masculine pursuits—she behaves with the utmost feminine modesty and decorum (297).

Cooper keeps physical expression of filial love to a minimum, although he on two occasions describes Eve as holding her father's hand in both hers and kissing it tenderly. She will, incidentally, do the same to Paul Powis after they are married—she is obviously not a woman of passion but of sensibility. Eve is devoted to her father; on several occasions she functions as her father's loyal and eloquent supporter. In the dispute over the Templeton church pews, for instance, when Mr. Effingham fails to convince his opponents (Aristabulus Bragg, Steadfast Dodge, and a pair of mechanics), Eve takes over the debate, arguing modestly, yet convincingly against not only the proposed removing of the pews, but also against the idea that "churches are built to accommodate people" instead of "for the worship of God" (188). Significantly, it is *her* arguments the readers hear, not her *father's*. Incidentally only she, not her father, manages to abash "even the ordinarily indomitable and self-composed Aristabulus" (188). Later, when John Effingham informs her about the controversy over the Point, to which she has no legal right herself, Eve tells her father, who has, and does not leave him until she perceives "that things were in the right train" (207).

A survey of Cooper's "domestic" novels, then, proves that the heroines are both indispensable to the plot and rather more assertive than most of the earlier criticism has allowed. Although Cooper insisted on constructing his heroines from the building blocks provided by the cult of domesticity, emphasizing the daughters' piety, purity, and domesticity, he also managed to show that they possessed "masculine qualities" such as independence, courage, physical endurance and intelligence. They even, as in the case of Judith and Hetty Hutter, initiate action; they do not rely on men to act for them or tell them how to act. Seen in the context of the conventions of his day, then, Cooper provided an alternative — even subversive — form of female socialization.

Conclusion

Regardless of aspirations as to the settings of their works—contemporary or historical—writers always remain rooted within their own spatial and temporal context, consciously and subconsciously reacting to the cultural matrix in which they find themselves. To James Fenimore Cooper, Lydia Maria Child, Catharine Maria Sedgwick, Maria Cummins, and Susan Warner, this cultural matrix, the cult of domesticity, provided raw material for their works. Like authors of advice literature, these authors sought to strengthen the role of the American family by providing practical guidance to their readers when it came to appropriate manners and choice of spouse. They chose their settings, characters, and plots according to the tenets of the cult. If they lifted their characters from the drawing room to the frontier, they remained focused on domestic issues, such as family dynamics and courtship, on the pure and domestic heroine and the hero who had proven himself worthy of her love.

Yet something happened at the writing desk. Authors revealed that the prescribed ideal masked a sinister reality. Where the cult sought to create a harmonious, spiritual nuclear family, a bulwark against the pernicious industrialist world and its perceived ability to corrupt the men involved in it, novelists more often than not exposed a decidedly unharmonious American family. The mother, the supposed core of the domestic cult, the person who was supposed to spread her divinely endowed influence on the family's other members, especially the spiritually vulnerable husbands and sons, became relegated to the sidelines. The father, the breadwinner and the family's earthly ruler, emerges as self-centered, manipulative, and ineffectual. The daughters, whose main virtues are piety and obedience, oppose and circumvent paternal *dicta*, showing personal initiative and affirming their right to choose their own mates.

From the first novel to the last, James Fenimore Cooper chose the domestic novel as his literary vehicle. Whether set on the high seas, the frontier, or in the city, his novels are woman-centered and preoccupied with "female" concerns like courtship and marriage, which the author sees as the building blocks of the new nation. Although he has often been accused of creating wooden and lifeless heroines—for some reason, Alice Munro of *The Last of the Mohicans* seems to be the one critics latch on to—his novels show a much wider variety of females, many of them clearly subverting the cult's tenets.

While apparently staying close to the demands of the cult, Cooper's, Child's, Sedgwick's, Warner's, and Cummins's novels demonstrate that the cult's version of the American family is a myth — an unobtainable Utopia in the Western hemisphere. Male and female inability to maintain the family, desertion, manipulation, and neglect are the standards that characterize the nation. The novels have a dual function: they simultaneously construct and deconstruct the cult's image. More importantly, they hold up a hope for a better national future. The authors leave their characters on the very border of a promised land — a domestic Canaan — where the old, outdated ideals have to yield to the new ones.

Chapter Notes

Chapter 1

1. In *The Daughter's Dilemma: Family Process and the Nineteenth-Century Domestic Novel* (Ann Arbor: University of Michigan Press, 1993). Cohen argues that these novels "enact an erotics ... of delay. The plot creates the illusion of a passage into a new life when it really prolongs and elaborates the heroine's life in her family of origin" (26).
2. Katherine Sobba Green, in *The Courtship Novel, 1740–1820: A Feminized Genre* (Lexington: University Press of Kentucky, 1991), outlines these elements of "feminizing." Although her study discusses British courtship novels from Eliza Haywood to Jane Austen, these novels had a transatlantic readership and, in the case of Cooper and other domestic writers, transatlantic imitators.
3. Baym's assertion is equally true for the rest of Cooper's fiction. John Cavelti, in "Cooper and the Frontier-Myth and Anti-Myth" (*James Fenimore Cooper: New Historical and Literary Criticism*, Amsterdam and Atlanta: Rodopi, 1993), observes that Cooper's "favorite subject was the dynastic romance — that is the courtship and marriage of the offspring of great aristocratic families" (151).
4. The "heroine's hero," Kay S. House observes in *Cooper's Americans* (Columbus: Ohio State University Press 1965), was built according to a specific formula. She asserts that "these heroes could be shuffled and dealt back into the novels at random.... The hero and heroine are ... rewarded for their common fidelity to truth, virtues, principles, and ... religious faith" (22).
5. In Harvey Green, *The Light of the Home: An Intimate View of the Lives of Women in Victorian America* (New York: Pantheon Books, 1983), 10–28.
6. In Green. "Proper gifts" included flowers, candy, and books. The two former were perishable, and "no undue significance was attached to them" (14).
7. Sobba Green mentions that two advice books popular in England were *Traité de l'éducation des filles* and *New Year's Gift: Advice to a Daughter*. The first, written by the French nobleman François de Salignac de la Mothe Fénelon, was reprinted in translation five times during the eighteenth century — one of the printers was Samuel Richardson. The work advocated female intellectual growth, again, an important issue for Cooper. The second work, by the Marquis de Halifax, demonstrated to its readers that they were inferior to men in nature and station. Haywood's ideas of female education found its disciples. Clifton J. Furness, in *The Genteel Female* (New York: Alfred A. Knopf, 1931), presents an excerpt from the course catalogue of Bradford Academy, a New England institution designed to "afford, as far as in their power ... every facility for a thorough education" of young women. The academy offered the following courses in 1837, for a tuition of $8.00 a term: History, Philosophy, Chemistry, Geology, Botany, Astronomy, Rhetoric, and Metaphysics (including "attention to Logic, so far as it is made a distinct study"). Moral Recitation, Latin, and

French could be added to this curriculum, "at cost of Teachers" (278–81).

8. Green, 10–13.

9. Quoted in *The Young Lady's Book: A Manual of Elegant Recreations, Exercises, and Pursuits* (Boston, 1830), 397.

10. Eric Sundquist's "Incest and Imitation in Cooper's *Home as Found*" (*Nineteenth-Century Fiction* 32, Dec 1977) focuses on what the author considers "the very heart of the book," the incestuous marriage between Eve and Paul: "not only ... the resolution of the plot hinges upon it, but ... aristocratic incest and inbreeding is the last, and most extreme, bulwark against the mob rule which Cooper found threatening himself and his country" (262–63). Sundquist characterizes Cooper's joining of these two characters as a "stark plunge into incest as a means of saving the honor of Paul and Eve's marriage" and "a last-ditch effort at founding a true and lasting home that will withstand the turmoil of mob democracy" (273). Although Sundquist points to Cooper's use of quotes from Shakespeare's *Hamlet*, I still have problems accepting the marriage as incestuous.

11. House, in *Cooper's Americans*, comments that Cooper, in his treatment of orphans or motherless young women, has something in common with Henry James. That is, "the heroine has beauty, money, freedom from maternal domination, and as much mobility as the historical facts allow." But unlike James's heroines, Cooper's females receive "guidance.... A proper heroine accepts tutelage gratefully, marries successfully, and is obviously destined to become herself a wise advisor; a foolish virgin follows her own inclinations, which lead to death or madness or a symbolic death as a virago" (24–25).

12. William E. Cosgrove, in "Family Lineage and Narrative Patterns in Cooper's Littlepage Trilogy" (*Forum* 12, Spring 1974), argues that Bragg's marriage proposal "is a serious threat to the internal stability of the Effingham family and its aristocratic values" (4). However, Cooper's text, and Eve's thoughts and comments in particular, allow for no such reading. Bragg is too ridiculously *gauche* to be a threat to family stability.

13. According to an article in the March 1870 issue of *Godey's Lady's Book*, young women were told not to play with a man's affection whether they intended to accept or reject a proposal of marriage. (In Green 17).

14. James W. Tuttleton, in *The Novel of Manners in America* (Chapel Hill: University of North Carolina Press, 1972), comments that in *The Pathfinder*, "Cooper's real purpose is to explore the question of whether a man of the hunter class ... can find settlement happiness married to a girl whose manners have been polished by real ladies—the wives of the garrison officer" (16). However, such a reading overlooks the woman-centered narrative.

15. James Grossman, in *James Fenimore Cooper* (New York: W. Sloan Associates, 1949), points out that Natty's future "has been molded in the novels already written of his later life, and there is never any doubt of his choice" (148). Still, Cooper certainly shows that Natty is very much drawn to Judith, thus flirting with the possibility of a different outcome.

16. Joyce Warren, in *The American Narcissus: Individualism and Women in Nineteenth-Century American Fiction* (New Brunswick, NJ: Rutgers University Press, 1984), sees Judith as a person of "strength and intelligence, and the ability to act" (98) and faults Natty who cannot overlook Judith's indiscretions. However, Warren conveniently overlooks the fact that Natty claims his heart has not been touched.

17. In "The Women in Cooper's Leatherstocking Tales" 705. There is no rescue of the two Hutter girls. Only Chingachgook's betrothed, Hist, is a woman worth rescuing.

18. In "The Women of Cooper's Leatherstocking Tales," Baym points to Natty's ambivalence toward Judith. She observes that he is "attracted to Judith's spirit and beauty but profoundly alienated by her radical willfulness" (706). Her lack of "proper" feminine qualities, then, overshadows not only her physical beauty but also her courage and ingenuity.

19. In "*The Deerslayer*: a Democratic Knight of the Wilderness" (*Twelve Original Essays on Great American Novels*. Ed. Charles Shapiro. Detroit: Wayne State University Press, 1958), David B. Davis writes that Judith "seems to typify the American

woman who is forever torn between her enviable freedom and power over men and her passionate yearning for the security of a passive and domestic role.... Judith is hopelessly tainted by the values of an artificial civilization. Regardless of her desire, she must remain alienated from the divine harmony of nature" (7).

Chapter 2

1. *Past, Present, and Personal: The Family and Life Course in American History* (New York: Oxford University Press, 1986), 30.
2. Nancy Cott, in *The Bonds of Womanhood: "Woman's Sphere" in New England 1780–1835* (New Haven, Yale University Press, 1979), explains that various forms of advice literature, sermons, and fiction comprising "a canon of domesticity" started "to flood the literary market in the 1820s and 1830s with a tide that has not yet ceased" (63).
3. Cooper's total corpus of works ranges from novels of manners and Indian tales to sea stories, tales from the Revolutionary War, a utopia, naval history, and travel books. Geographically, they encompass the globe: his novels are set in locations ranging from the North American wilderness to the canals of Venice, from upstate New York to the Antarctic. A study of Cooper's achievements alerts the reader to an impressive series of "firsts": Cooper wrote the first American sea story, the first whaling (or "sealing") story, the first family history, and the first naval history of the United States.
4. Josiah G. Holland, *Titcomb's Letters to Young People, Single and Married* (New York: Scribner, Armstrong, 1858).
5. In *Love and Death in the American Novel* (Revised ed., 1966), Leslie Fiedler claims that Cooper "accepted as literal truth" the idea of "the sacredness of womanhood and the sanctity of every member of the sex.... If he ever groaned beneath the weight of this intolerable burden of an eternally confessed moral inferiority, he never groaned openly and would have been appalled to think his wooden *ingénues* were in fact his revenge upon the sex" (185). Fiedler, providing a Freudian reading of the Leatherstocking tales, eagerly illuminates only Cooper's obsession with violence and his "embarrassment before love" (28). He conveniently ignores that no novelist of the time could really deal openly with love and passion and that a large body of Cooper's texts projects a very different image of the novelist's preoccupations. Fiedler grudgingly allows Cooper some "credit" for innovation, damning him with faint praise in the process. Cora and Alice Munro, the archetypal "passionate brunette" and "sinless blonde," become "the standard form in which American writers project their ambivalence toward women" (200–201). However, Cooper himself deviates markedly from this "standard."

6. In *The American Narcissus: Individualism and Women in Nineteenth-Century American Fiction* (New Brunswick, NJ: Rutgers University Press, 1984), Joyce Warren takes Cooper to task for not providing his readers with representations of strong, independent women. She characterizes even his strongest females—Elizabeth Temple, Ellen Wade, Mabel Dunham, and Eve Effingham—as "dependent, emotional, and totally selfless" (93). Still, Cooper's females clearly stretch the boundaries of nineteenth-century womanhood.

7. Warren, eager to show that individualism equals "disregard for others," claims that Cooper's world is a man's world, and that women are almost completely excluded from it and superfluous to the novels' actions. Supporting her assertions with statements from W. D. Howells, J. R. Lowell, Leslie Fiedler, and Richard Chase, she divides Cooper's women into "fragile child-maidens" and "dependent creatures." She faults Cooper for never allowing his heroines to initiate action, although this is clearly wrong. Ironically, Warren blithely ignores that when Natty Bumppo acts, it is out of concern for others. Good people, his texts show, act for the benefit of society; they do not act in their own self-interest.

8. Quoted in Cott 64.

9. Carroll Smith-Rosenberg's *Disorderly Conduct: Visions of Gender in Victorian America* (New York: Oxford University Press, 1985) challenges the assumption that a woman's whole existence was her own family. She emphasizes the importance of close female friendships, which were

recognized by the nineteenth-century American society as "a socially viable form of human contact — and, as such, acceptable throughout a woman's life" (74).

10. In *Cradle of the Middle Class: The Family in Oneida County, New York, 1790–1865* (Cambridge: Cambridge University Press, 1981).

11. Demos traces the change in nineteenth-century values to the country's industrial growth. This growth led to two opposing cults: the "cult of the 'self-made man'" and the "cult of the home." Since the business world endangered men both physically and spiritually, the home provided the business man with "some emblem of the personal and moral regime that he was otherwise leaving behind" (31).

12. Janet Fishburn, in *The Fatherhood of God and the Victorian Family* (Philadelphia: Fortress, 1989), also points to the connection between the self-made man and the cult of domesticity. She sees the emergence of the cult as the work of "Social Gospel pioneers" who "responded to the social revolution by inventing a formula that offered the possibility of a moral populace, a moral nation, and a hopeful future" (18).

13. Harvey Green's *The Light of the Home: An Intimate View of the Lives of Women in Victorian America* (New York: Pantheon Books, 1983) presents many examples of such symbols, from religious pictures to a cross-shaped hall stand. See pp. 93–111.

14. Warren Motley, in *The American Abraham: James Fenimore Cooper and the Frontier Patriarch* (Cambridge: Cambridge University Press, 1987), examines the issue of authority in *The Prairie* and *The Wept of Wish-Ton-Wish*. However, Motley's interest lies solely with the father-sons relationship. No other family configurations appear significant to the study.

15. Two early essays, Harold H. Scudder's "What Mr. Cooper Read to His Wife" (*Sewannee Review* 36, April 1928) and George E. Hastings's "How Cooper Became a Novelist" (*American Literature* 12, March 1940), discuss and reject Susan Fenimore Cooper's claim that the novel was modeled on the works of Mrs. Opie, documenting instead the textual links to Jane Austen.

16. Hastings quotes Professor Fred Lewis Pattee's 1925 article "James Fenimore Cooper," which characterizes *Precaution* as "the best novel written in America before 1821. Were it republished today as a newly-discovered early work by Jane Austen it would deceive most readers" (23).

17. In *Early Cooper and His Audience* (New York: Columbia University Press, 1986), James D. Wallace attempts to fit *Precaution* into a masculine mold. First, though, he attempts to reaffirm the connection to Mrs. Opie, whose novels "had an established audience," and whose texts "were aggressively moral" (60). Then, he rejects the notion that the novels is about "the consequences of improper training. Instead, it is about Denbigh's ability to create himself in the violent transitions to which his author subjects him" (76). Yet the focus in the novels is on marriage, not on Denbigh's character in particular.

18. Kay S. House and Genevieve Belfiglio, in "Fenimore Cooper's Heroines" (*American Novelists Revisited*, Ed. Fritz Fleischmann. Boston: G. K. Hall, 1982), observe that "Necessity and common sense, rather than sex, decided who did what" (46).

19. Alfred Habegger, in *Henry James and the "Woman Business"* (Cambridge: Cambridge University Press, 1989), charges James with "appropriating" one of the most popular themes in women's fiction. The same charge can be aimed at Cooper.

Chapter 3

1. Barbara Epstein, in *The Politics of Domesticity: Women, Evangelism, and Temperance in Nineteenth-Century America* (Middletown, CT: Wesleyan University Press, 1981), remarks that to the Victorians, "Family life ... was held out as the basis of a respectable life, of a piece with such virtues as economy and self-restraint" (70). Although Epstein makes this assertion on the basis of New England schoolbooks, the values they promoted are those underlying the cult of domesticity. J. A. Banks, in *Victorian Values* (London: Routledge & Kegan Paul, 1981), observes that when the Victorians mentioned "moral restraint" they meant limitation of sexual activity and number of children within the marriage. This, "rather than contraception is likely to

have been the means they would have favoured to prevent conceptions" (74).

2. *Democracy in America*, 2 vols. (New York, 1855). When Tocqueville in 1831 arrived in America, he found the most characteristic trait of the society to be "individualism," a term he coined. This move toward individualism, he believed, had reshaped the American institutions, among them the family (Vol. I. 315, Vol. II. 302–4).

3. In Colleen McDannell, *The Christian Home in Victorian America 1840–1900* (Bloomington: Indiana University Press, 1986). McDannell writes: "women writers ... not only challenged traditional notions of sin and salvation, but they presented an alternative to paternal domestic religion. They accomplished this ... through the informal network of fiction and advice literature" (128–29).

4. Carroll Smith-Rosenberg, in *Disorderly Conduct: Visions of Gender in Victorian America* (New York: Oxford University Press, 1985), shows that the perception of female sexuality changed over the course of the nineteenth century. She asserts, "Highly respected medical writers in the 1820s and 1830s had described women as naturally lusty and capable of multiple orgasms. They defined female frigidity as pathological." But four decades later, medical professionals told husbands that "frigidity was rooted in women's very nature. Women's only desire ... was reproductive" (23).

5. In *Manners and Morals in the Age of Optimism 1848–1914* (New York: Harper & Row, 1966), James Laver writes, "Perhaps there never was another period in history when it would be true to say that the wife was considered theoretically an angel and practically a slave" (143).

6. Catherine Beecher's treatise appeared in almost annual issues between its initial publication in 1841 and 1856.

7. Catherine's sister, Harriet Beecher Stowe, co-authored the book but, as Joseph Van Why points out in his introduction to the 1975 edition, the book was largely Catherine's work. Why comments that Mrs. Stowe's fame as a writer, "and her practical experience as mother of seven children led Catherine to conclude that having her sister as co-author would enhance the reputation and sale of the book. Despite her ... previous works on domestic economy and child care, Catherine was shrewdly aware that the public might question a spinster woman in her late sixties writing authoritatively on such subjects" (7).

8. Judith Rowbotham, in *Good Girls Make Good Wives: Guidance for Girls in Victorian Fiction* (Oxford: Basil Blackwell, 1989), shows how and why it became important for women to become "professional" wives/mothers/housekeepers. She writes, "While a man needed a career to justify and bolster his masculinity, being a woman was a 'career' in itself, and in an age of growing emphasis on professionalism in careers, it became increasingly important for women to be professionals in this gender sense" (12).

9. Beecher and Stowe assert that good manners, "the expressions of benevolence in the personal intercourse" are in short supply in the republic, "especially among the descendants of the Puritan settlers of New England." This defect cannot be removed easily: manners "can be successfully cultivated only in early life and in the domestic circle" (201–2).

10. Stowe uses the same correspondence in *Uncle Tom's Cabin*: good Christians have clean and orderly homes and kitchens. The Quakers who help Eliza have a "large, roomy, neatly painted kitchen" with "rows of shining tin, suggestive of unmentionable good things" (96). The kitchen in the St. Clare mansion, on the other hand, reflects the mistress's lack of moral fiber and domestic ability. It "generally looked as if it had been arranged by a hurricane blowing through it" (148).

11. In Smith-Rosenberg 119.

12. Other Victorians shared the Stowes' views, emphasizing the spiritual aspect of marriage and promoting a truly "holy" matrimony which transcended temporal demands. A. B. Muzzey's *The Young Maiden* (1841) argues that the attractions of matrimony were "mental, not animal. Each loves the other's soul mainly, instead of the body" (191, in Mintz 129). William A. Alcott's *The Young Wife* (1837) exalts marriage as a model of "perfect identity" (358, in Mintz 129).

13. Between 1813 and 1819, all five of

Cooper's brothers died. Some of them died insolvent, and Cooper not only had to pay their debts but also had to support their widows and children. Although his own finances also had suffered, he never neglected his familial duties (Grossman 17).

14. Letters to Andrew Thompson Goodrich, 12th and 28th June 1820.

15. In Grossman 255.

16. Child, Warner, and Sedgwick were, in a sense, all abandoned by their mothers at an early age. Child lost her mother at the age of twelve, Warner lost hers at the age of nine. Sedgwick's mother lived until her daughter was eighteen; however, she was suffering form a mental illness throughout Sedgwick's childhood. None of the writers had children; they were, in other words, not interested in visiting their own experiences on eventual progeny.

17. Other writers went much further in critiquing nineteenth-century mothers. Charles Dickens, for example, mercilessly satirizes Mrs. Jellyby of *Bleak House* who is so wrapped up in her philanthropic project — an African tribe on the left bank of the Niger — that she neglects her domestic duties.

18. In *A History of Matrimonial Institutions* 3 vols. (Chicago: University of Chicago Press, 1904), George Elliot Howard details marriages in Colonial New England. He asserts that "marriage was declared to be not a sacrament, but a civil contract in which the intervention of a priest was unnecessary and out of place." To support his assertion, he quotes Governor Winthrop's comments on a 1647 Boston wedding, in which the groom's pastor had been asked to preach. This he was not allowed to do. One of the reasons for this was that the Puritans "were not willing to bring in the English custom of ministers performing the solemnity of marriage ... but if any ministers ... would bestow a word of exhortation, etc., it was permitted" (Vol. II. 127).

19. Howard adds that "early colonial laws, generally, required that all marriages should be celebrated before a justice of the peace or other magistrate, sometimes under penalty of nullity for those solemnized any other way" (Vol. II. 127–28). The laws changed in 1686, when both ministers and justices of the peace were authorized to perform marriages.

20. Rowbotham comments that respect was "equally, if not more essential" than love in a marriage. She continues, "Respect might engender love in due course.... Authors were perfectly aware that it was possible to feel an emotional attachment where there was no respect, but ... such an emotion was unlikely to be lasting, nor could it induce a woman to look up to her husband" (46).

21. Perhaps this is the reason the chapter remained unpublished. It casts a rather mercenary light on female piety.

22. In *Cooper's Leather-Stocking Novels: A Secular Reading* (Chapel Hill: University of North Carolina Press, 1991), Geoffrey Rans asserts that Cooper's instincts were "always toward realism, however romantic the surface might appear (xi–xii). This instinct for realism hinders a possible union between Cora and Uncas: the writer has no "obligation within the novel to resolve the problem in a way that the society has not yet accomplished, if it ever will" (40).

23. Grossman, for instance, sees it as an "accident in history" that cannot be "adequately explained" (21). Robert E. Spiller, in *Fenimore Cooper: Critic of His Times* (New York: Minton Balch, 1931), dismisses *Precaution* categorically: "Seldom has there been a less promising novel" (74). Donald Ringe, in *James Fenimore Cooper* (New York: Twayne, 1988), pronounces Cooper's first literary effort "indefensible" (23), and James D. Wallace even ridicules possible readers, claiming that "hardly anyone who takes fiction seriously has been able to endure reading it" (72).

24. In Robert Emmet Long, *James Fenimore Cooper* (New York: Continuum, 1990) 30.

25. Grossman attributes Cooper's frank discussion of marriage to "the sheer technical incompetence of a beginner" (22). He asserts that the novel's numerous frank discussions of marriage "is also part of his general failure to understand that thorough discussion of conventions is a means of overthrowing them. In his first novel he went so far in crudeness that, had he accepted its intellectual implications, *Precaution* would have been of the same school as *Man and Superman*, a manifesto of the right to arrive openly at sexual objectives" (22).

Grossman further reveals his negative attitude to Cooper's literary beginnings when he comments, "Cooper is as clumsy as Achilles among the women. *Precaution* is throughout an overloaded tale, one is surprised it achieved even a modest success" (21).

26. Several critics, among them Kay S. House, have pointed to the theatricality of the Leatherstocking tales and Cooper's love of Shakespeare. Yet Cooper's talent, as witnessed by *Precaution*, is for comedy as well as for tragedy. He deftly deploys the conventions of the classical comedy in this work: thwarted love, mistaken identity, and overbearing fathers.

Chapter 4

1. Stephen M. Frank, *Life with Father: Parenthood and Masculinity in the Nineteenth-Century American North* (Baltimore: Johns Hopkins University Press, 1998). Shawn Johansen, *Family Men: Middle-Class Fatherhood in Early Industrializing America* (New York & London: Routledge, 2001). See also Robert L. Griswold, *Fatherhood in America: A History* (New York: Basic Books, 1993)

2. Steven Mintz, in *A Prison of Expectations: The Family in Victorian Culture* (New York: New York University Press, 1983), makes the following observation about the father's role in Victorian society: "the father did not perceive his role as involving pleasing children, but rather as training them, teaching them to respect authority, and fostering a capacity for self-government and self-control" (51).

3. In *The Christian Home in Victorian America*, McDannell discusses the paternal model of family government and religious instruction, showing how the ideal father was expected to read "not only the Bible, but biblical commentaries.... Crucial to paternal participation ... was the association of religion with intellectual knowledge. Father as prophet spoke from his mind and not from his heart" (109–10).

4. The full title of Cobbett's work is *Advice to Young Men and (incidentally) to Young Women in the Middle and Higher Ranks of Life in a series of Letters addressed to a Youth, a Bachelor, a Lover, a Husband, a Father, and a Citizen or a Subject.*

5. In McDannell 113.

6. The insights on Alcott and Stowe come from Mintz (see note 2). In this work, Mintz discusses the families of Harriet Beecher Stowe, Catharine Maria Sedgwick, Samuel Butler, Robert Louis Stevenson, and George Eliot. Although, as Mintz observes, this small selection cannot be considered representative of Victorian society, their life stories "illuminate basic tension and underlying themes that lie at the heart of Victorian family life" (6).

7. Even if she was too young to fully appreciate the readings, Sedgwick in retrospect felt she still benefited from them. In her autobiography she comments, "some glances of celestial light reached my soul, and I caught from his magnetic sympathy some elevation of feeling, and that love of reading which has been to me 'education'" (74).

8. See Chapter 1, note 15.

9. William Ellis discusses Cooper's descriptions of his gentlemen in *The Theory of American Romance: An Ideology of American Intellectual Development* (Ann Arbor: UMI Research Press, 1989). He argues that the lack of physical description denies these characters their humanity: "by abstractly idealizing, he [Cooper] empties the gentry of their humanity" (144–45).

10. Cooper himself had similarly conservative ideas about a daughter's marriage. While in France, he rejected an offer for Susan's hand from a French aristocrat, supposedly because he wished her to remain American. She never married. According to Grossman, "it became his odd joke to speak as if he were her suitor" (247). When Cooper's second daughter, Caroline, asked his permission to marry Henry Frederick Phinney, he was "shocked" (248).

11. Jay S. Paul, in "Home as Cherished: The Theme of Family in Fenimore Cooper" (*Studies in the Novel* 5, Spring 1973), comments that Munro must "reconcile" his "powerful affection for his daughters ... with his military duty" (44).

12. Shirley Samuels, in "Generation through Violence: Cooper and the Making of Americans" (*New Essays on The Last of the Mohicans*. Ed. H. Daniel Peck. Cambridge: Cambridge University Press, 1992), claims that Cooper "tends to bring women

and children to the frontier and violently eliminate them" (104). Yet surprisingly few of his characters actually suffer this fate.

Chapter 5

1. This issue had emerged already in pre–Victorian works. Susanna Rowson, for example, explains that the objective of her work is not to entertain, but to instruct. In the preface to *Charlotte Temple* (1794), Rowson piously hopes to "be of service to some who are so unfortunate as to have neither friends to advise, or understanding to direct them, through the various and unexpected evils that attend a young and unprotected woman in her first entrance into life" (1). Hannah Foster's *The Coquette* (1797) serves the same function. Although Cooper carefully avoids placing his young women in the kinds of situations described by Rowson and Foster, he just as carefully as his literary predecessors instructs his readers in what constitutes proper, modest behavior.

2. Quoted in Gorham, *The Victorian Girl and the Feminine Ideal* (1982) 5.

3. Warren claims that Cooper's heroines have "strong emotions and weak intellect" (97); however, the majority of Cooper's female characters, from Emily Moseley, Frances Wharton, and Elizabeth Temple to Eve Effingham and Judith Hutter, seem to be just the opposite.

4. Sometimes, Child's advice seems rather redundant to twenty-first-century readers but must have appeared progressive to her contemporaries. For example, she, under the heading "General Maxims for Health," admonishes her reader to "Clean teeth in pure water two or three times a day ... be sure to have them clean before you go to bed" (88).

5. Epstein, in *The Politics of Domesticity: Women, Evangelism, and Temperance in Nineteenth-Century America* (1981), writes that advice literature aimed at "the women of the middling classes" (76). Daughters "were urged to obey their fathers as unquestioningly as wives their husbands, both as training for marriage and because they were dependent upon their fathers as they would later be upon their husbands.... Women should show their gratitude for male support and protection with childlike docility and admiring love" (78).

6. Obedience is the first topic John Abbott discusses in *The Mother at Home* (1834). He argues that once obedience has been internalized, all other qualities follow.

7. From *Godey's Magazine and Lady's Book* XXXIII (1846) 52. Quoted in Welter 317.

8. Rowbotham provides the following characteristics of the Victorian "good girl" as she appeared in fiction. She is religious, modest, and submissive "to those in due authority over her" and behaves according to "her station in life." She is educated "as fitting for her station and abilities," able to comfort the males of her family and attend to household affairs (23).

9. Gorham argues that by focusing on the daughter, writers avoided the issue of "active sexuality," which they could not avoid in connection with the mother. She asserts that "unlike an adult woman, a girl could be perceived as a wholly unambiguous model of dependence, childlike simplicity, and sexual purity" (5).

10. In his introduction to *New Essays on The Last of the Mohicans* (1992), H. Daniel Peck argues that Nina Baym's essay "How Men and Women Wrote Indian Stories" shows that Child's and Sedgwick's "women-centered narratives implicitly challenge Cooper's assumptions about sexual, racial, and social roles" (17).

11. Baym argues that Mary's depression and her marriages to Hobomok and Charles Brown are signs of strength and give her value independent of men's plans. However, Child repeatedly stresses Mary's mental weakness; her first marriage is a result of confusion, despair, and loneliness; it is not a conscious rebellion. Furthermore, Mary only returns to white society *after* Brown has reappeared and she has accepted his proposal of marriage.

12. Only in *Tales for Fifteen*, written under the pseudonym Jane Morgan, does Cooper indulge in purely didactic writing. The tale shows the dangers of letting oneself be influenced by false friends, by reading romantic novels, and by creating a romantic make-believe world. Cooper also indicates the process to overcome such temptations. And if *Precaution* is Cooper's

version of *Pride and Prejudice*, perhaps *Tales for Fifteen* can be seen as his *Northanger Abbey*?

13. Cooper's works in this respect resembles the so-called "silver-fork novels" which, although supposedly intended for the upper classes, served as "textbooks" for the growing *bourgeoisie*.

14. In *Cooper's Americans*, Kay S. House points out that Cooper's heroines always have had some mentoring. This guidance they can ignore "if they wish. A proper heroine accepts tutelage gratefully, marries successfully ... a foolish virgin follows her own inclination, which leads to death or madness or a symbolic death as a virago" (24–25).

15. Lowell found a similar lack of imagination in Cooper's creation of male characters, with the exception of Natty Bumppo, who he "has done naught but copy ... ill ever since."

16. In "Fenimore Cooper's Heroines," House and Belfiglio comment that Cooper's heroines "are often inventive, resourceful, alert to natural beauty, energetic (even athletic), and fully aware of who they are and what they want" (46).

17. House and Belfiglio give a very positive feminist reading of Cooper's works. They point out that a device often overlooked in connection with Cooper is "the androgynous paradigm which challenges the conventionally assigned roles of men and women" (42).

18. Cooper's novels, letters, and journals all show his belief in the importance of female education. One of his reasons for traveling abroad in 1826 was to further his children's education.

19. Warren argues that all Cooper's heroines are excessively pious and willing to give up everything — except religious faith — for a man (95–95). This seems to be the case with Mary Pratt of *The Sea-Lions*, but other Cooper heroines defy this description.

20. Warren's assertion that the only thing Cooper's heroines can do in an emergency is pray is clearly an exaggeration.

21. Warren faults Elizabeth Temple and other Cooper heroines for their willingness to help others, not themselves. In order to understand the concept of women in American fiction, she claims it is necessary to explore the effect of transcendentalist-sponsored individualism on nineteenth-century novelists (91). According to Warren, part of Cooper's failure to create strong independent women lies in his acceptance of American individualism. Warren equates individualism with "disregard for others" (94). It seems far-fetched to place Cooper in this specific context: he was hardly a transcendentalist. Also, even Natty Bumppo, the character Warren posits as Cooper's epitome of individualism, can hardly be said to show disregard for others. On the contrary, as the texts of the Leatherstocking tales demonstrate, his life is one in service to others.

22. There is, perhaps, a debt to Shakespeare here. Alice resembles the character Bianca in *The Taming of the Shrew*, like *The Last of the Mohicans*, a tale of two daughters. 23. Donald Darnell, in *James Fenimore Cooper: Novelist of Manners* (Newark: University of Delaware Press, 1993), calls *The Deerslayer* Cooper's "Tragedy of Manners" (58): "the author finds his most tragic effects resulting from a young woman's frustrated social aspirations — the favorite subject of that most civilized of genres, the novel of manners" (59).

24. Or, as House and Belfiglio assert: "Cooper suggests that some of Eve's confidence may come from her association with" her independent French governess (50).

Bibliography

Abbott, John S. C. *The Mother at Home; or, The Principles of Maternal Duty*. Revised and corrected by Daniel Walton. London: John Mason, 1834. New York: Arno, 1972.

Alcott, William A. *The Young Man's Guide*. Boston: T. R. Marvin, 1846.

———. *The Young Woman's Guide to Excellence*. Boston: C. H. Peirce, Binney and Otheman, 1840.

Austen, Jane. *Persuasion*. New York: Bantam Books, 1984.

———. *Pride and Prejudice*. New York: Bantam Books, 1981.

Bailey, Ebenezer, ed. *The Young Ladies' Class Book: A Selection of Lessons for Reading in Prose and Verse*. Boston: Gould, Kendall and Lincoln, 1831.

Banks, J. A. *Victorian Values*. London: Routledge & Kegan Paul, 1981.

Baym, Nina. "How Men and Women Wrote Indian Stories." *New Essays on The Last of the Mohicans*. Ed. by H. Daniel Peck. Cambridge: Cambridge University Press, 1992. 67–86.

———. "The Women of Cooper's Leatherstocking Tales." *American Quarterly* 23 (1971): 696–702.

Beecher, Catherine E., and Harriet Beecher Stowe. *The American Woman's Home or, Principles of Domestic Science*. Hartford, CT: Stowe-Day Foundation, 1975.

Burney, Frances. *Evelina*. Ed. and Intro. by Edward A. Bloom. Oxford: Oxford University Press, 1970.

By a Lady. (Eliza Ware Farrar). *The Young Ladies' Friend*. Boston, 1837.

———. *The Young Wife's Book: A Manual of Moral, Religious and Domestic Duties*. Philadelphia: Carey, Lea, and Blanchard, 1838.

Cavelti, John G. "Cooper and the Frontier-Myth and Anti-Myth." *James Fenimore Cooper: New Historical and Literary Criticism*. Ed. by Wm. M. Verhoeven. Amsterdam and Atlanta: Rodopi, 1993. 151–59.

Child, Lydia Maria. *The Frugal Housewife*. Boston: Marsh & Capen, and Carter & Hendee, 1829.

———. *Hobomok and Other Writings on Indians*. Ed. and intro. by Carolyn L. Karcher. New Brunswick, NJ: Rutgers University Press, 1986.

———. *Lydia Maria Child: Selected Letters, 1817–1880*. Ed. by Milton Meltzer, Patricia G. Holland, and Francine Krasno. Amherst: University of Massachussets Press, 1982.

———. *The Mother's Book*. Boston: Carter, Hendee and Babcock, 1831.

Clark, Robert E., ed. *James Fenimore Cooper: New Critical Essays*. Totowa: Vision and Barnes & Noble, 1985.
Cobbett, William. *Advice to Young Men*. 1830. Preface by George Spater. Oxford: Oxford University Press, 1980.
Cohen, Paula Marantz. *The Daughter's Dilemma: Family Process and theNineteenth-Century Domestic Novel*. Ann Arbor: University of Michigan Press, 1993.
Cooper, James Fenimore. *The American Democrat; or, Hints on the Social and Civic Relations of the United States of America*. 1838. New York: Vintage Books, 1956.
_____. *The Chainbearer; or, The Littlepage Manuscripts*. New York: G. P. Putnam's Sons, n.d.
_____. *The Deerslayer; or, The First War-Path*. Historical intro. and explanatory notes by James Franklin Beard. Albany: State University of New York Press, 1987.
_____. *Home as Found*. 1838. New York: Capricorn Books, 1961.
_____. *Homeward Bound; or, The Chase: A Tale of the Sea*. New York: G. P. Putnam's Sons, n.d.
_____. *The Last of the Mohicans: A Narrative of 1757*. Ed. with a historical intro. by James Franklin Beard. Albany: State University of New York Press, 1983.
_____. *The Letters and Journals of James Fenimore Cooper*. 6 vols. Ed. by James F. Beard. Cambridge, MA: Harvard University Press, 1960, 1964, 1968.
_____. *Notions of the Americans, Picked Up by a Travelling Bachelor*. 2 vols. New York: Frederick Ungar, 1963.
_____. *The Pathfinder; or, The Inland Sea*. Ed. with a historical intro. by Richard Dilworth Rust. Albany: State University of New York Press, 1981.
_____. *The Pioneers, or The Sources of the Susquehanna; A Descriptive Tale*. Historical intro. and explanatory notes by James Franklin Beard. Albany: State University of New York Press, 1980.
_____. *The Prairie: A Tale*. Ed. with a historical intro. by James P. Elliott. Albany: State University of New York Press, 1985.
_____. *Precaution: A Novel*. New York: G. P. Putnam's Sons, n.d.
_____. *Satanstoe, or The Littlepage Manuscripts: A Tale of the Colony*. Intro. by Robert L. Hough. Lincoln: University of Nebraska Press, 1962.
_____. *The Sea Lions*. Lincoln: University of Nebraska Press, 1965.
_____. *The Spy: A Tale of the Neutral Ground*. New York: Current Literature, n.d.
_____. *Tales for Fifteen; or, Imagination and Heart*. New York: Charles Wiley, 1823. Gainesville, FL: Scholar's Facsimile and Reprints, 1959.
_____. *The Wept of Wish-Ton-Wish: A Tale*. New York: G. P. Putnam's Sons, n.d.
Cooper, Susan Fenimore. Introduction and notes. *Pages and Pictures, from the Writings of James Fenimore Cooper*. New York: Townsend,1861. Secaucus, NJ: Castle Books, 1980.
Cosgrove, William E. "Family Lineage and Narrative Patterns in Cooper's Littlepage Trilogy." *FORUM* (Houston) 12 (Spring 1974): 2–8.
Cott, Nancy F. *The Bonds of Womanhood: "Woman's Sphere" in New England 1780–1835*. New Haven: Yale University Press, 1977.
Cummins, Maria S. *The Lamplighter*. Ed. and intro. by Nina Baym. New Brunswick, NJ: Rutgers University Press, 1988.
"Cursory Remarks on a Wife." *Godey's Lady's Book* Vol. 5 (July 1832): 8.
Darnell, Donald. *James Fenimore Cooper: Novelist of Manners*. Newark: University of Delaware Press, 1993.

Davis, David Brion. "The Deerslayer: A Democratic Knight in theWilderness." *Twelve Original Essays on Great American Novels*. Ed. by Charles Shapiro. Detroit: Wayne State University Press, 1958.
Demos, John. *Past, Present, and Personal: The Family and the Life Course in American History*. New York: Oxford University Press, 1986.
Dickens, Charles. *Bleak House*. New York: Bantam Books, 1985.
Elliott, Emory, ed. *American Literature*. Vol. 1. Englewood Cliffs, NJ: Prentice-Hall, 1991.
Ellis, William. *The Theory of the American Romance: An Ideology of American Intellectual Development*. Ann Arbor: UMI Research Press, 1989.
Epstein, Barbara Leslie. *The Politics of Domesticity: Women, Evangelism, and Temperance in Nineteenth-Century America*. Middletown, CT: Wesleyan University Press, 1981.
Fiedler, Leslie. *Love and Death in the American Novel*. New York: Stein and Day, 1977.
Fishburn, Janet Forsythe. *The Fatherhood of God and the Victorian Family*. Philadelphia: Fortress, 1989.
Fisher, Philip. *Hard Facts: Setting and Form in the American Novel*. New York: Oxford University Press, 1985.
Fleischmann, Fritz, ed. *American Novelists Revisited: Essays in Feminist Criticism*. Boston: G. K. Hall, 1982.
Foster, Hannah Webster. *The Coquette, or, The History of Eliza Wharton*. Boston: E. Larkin, 1797.
Frank, Stephen M. *Life with Father: Parenthood and Masculinity in the Nineteenth-Century American North*. Baltimore: The Johns Hopkins University Press, 1998.
Freeling, Arthur. *The Young Bride's Book*. New York, 1849.
Furness, Clifton Joseph, ed. *The Genteel Female*. New York: Alfred A. Knopf, 1931.
Gilbert, Sandra, and Susan Gubar. *The Madwoman in the Attic*. New Haven, CT: Yale University Press, 1979.
Goldsmith, Oliver. *The Vicar of Wakefield*. New York: Lancer Books, 1968.
Gordon, Michael, ed. *The American Family in Social-Historical Perspective*. 2nd ed. New York: St. Martin's, 1978.
Gorham, Deborah. *The Victorian Girl and the Feminine Ideal*. London: Croom Helm, 1982.
Goshgarian, G. M. *To Kiss the Chastening Rod: Domestic Fiction and Sexual Ideology in the American Renaissance*. Ithaca, NY: Cornell University Press, 1992.
Green, Harvey. *The Light of the Home: An Intimate View of the Lives of Women in Victorian America*. New York: Pantheon Books, 1983.
Green, Katherine Sobba. *The Courtship Novel, 1740–1820: A Feminized Genre*. Lexington: University Press of Kentucky, 1991.
Gregory, John. *A Father's Legacy to His Daughters*. Facsimile editing. Intro. by Gina Luria. New York: Garland, 1974.
Grossman, James. *James Fenimore Cooper*. New York: W. Sloan Associates, 1949. Stanford, CA: Stanford University Press, 1967.
Habegger, Alfred. *Henry James and the "Woman Business."* Cambridge: Cambridge University Press, 1989.
Harris, Barbara J. *Beyond Her Sphere: Women and the Professions in American History*. Westport, CT: Greenwood, 1978.

Hastings, George E. "How Cooper Became a Novelist." *American Literature* 12 (March 1940): 20–51.
Henderson, Harry B. *Versions of the Past: The Historical Imagination in American Fiction.* New York: Oxford University Press, 1974.
"Hints on Marriage." *Godey's Lady's Book* Vol. 17 (December 1838): 252.
Holland, Josiah G. *Titcomb's Letters to Young People Single and Married.* New York: Scribner, Armstrong, 1858.
House, Kay Seymour. *Cooper's Americans.* Columbus: Ohio State University Press, 1965.
_____, and Genevieve Belfiglio. "Fenimore Cooper's Heroines." *American Novelists Revisited: Essays in Feminist Criticism.* Ed. by Fritz Fleischmann. Boston: G. K. Hall, 1982. 42–57.
Howard, George Elliot. *A History of Matrimonial Institutions.* 3 vols. Chicago: University of Chicago Press, 1904.
Humphrey, Henry. *Domestic Education.* Amherst, MA: J. S. and C. Adams, 1840.
Johansen, Shawn. *Family Men: Middle-Class Fatherhood in Early Industrializing America.* New York: Routledge, 2001.
Karcher, Carolyn L. " Introduction." *Hobomok and Other Writings on Indians.* By Lydia Maria Child. New Brunswick, NJ: Rutgers University Press, 1986.
Kaul, A. N. *The American Vision: Actual and Ideal Society in Nineteenth-Century Fiction.* New Haven, CT: Yale University Press, 1963.
Kelley, Mary. Introduction. *Hope Leslie; or, Early Times in the Massachusetts.* By Catharine Maria Sedgwick. New Brunswick, NJ: Rutgers University Press, 1987.
Kemble, Frances Anne. *Journal of a Residence on a Georgia Plantation, 1838–1839.* Ed. and intro. by John A. Scott. Athens: University of Georgia Press, 1984.
Laver, James. *Manners and Morals in the Age of Optimism 1848–1914.* New York: Harper & Row, 1966.
Lawrence, D. H. *Studies in Classical American Literature.* New York: Thomas Seltzer, 1923. New York: Doubleday, 1951.
Lawson-Peebles, Robert. "Property, Marriage, Women, and Fenimore Cooper's First Fictions." *James Fenimore Cooper: New Historical and Literary Criticism.* Ed. by Wm. M. Verhoeven. Amsterdam and Atlanta: Rodopi, 1993.
Long, Robert Emmet. *James Fenimore Cooper.* New York: Continuum, 1990.
Lowell, James Russell. "A Fable for Critics." *American Literature.* Vol. 1. Ed. by Emory Elliott. Englewood Cliffs, NJ: Prentice-Hall, 1991. 1905–14.
"Marriage." *Godey's Lady's Book* Vol. 5 (November 1832): 244.
McDannell, Colleen. *The Christian Home in Victorian America 1840–1900.* Bloomington: Indiana University Press, 1986.
McNall, Sally Allen. *Who Is in the House: A Psychological Study of Two Centuries of Women's Fiction in America, 1795 to the Present.* New York: Elsevier North Holland, 1981.
Mintz, Steven. *A Prison of Expectations: The Family in Victorian Culture.* New York: New York University Press, 1983.
_____, and Susan Kellogg. *Domestic Revolution: A Social History of American Family Life.* New York: Free, 1988.
Motley, Warren. *The American Abraham: James Fenimore Cooper and the Frontier Patriarch.* Cambridge: Cambridge University Press, 1987.
Noble, David W. "Cooper, Leatherstocking, and the Death of the American Adam." *American Quarterly* 16 (1964): 419–31.

Packard, Clarissa (Mrs. Caroline Howard Gilman). *Recollections of a Housekeeper.* New York: Harper, 1834.
Patmore, Coventry. *Poems.* London: G. Bell, 1906.
Paul, Jay S. "Home as Cherished: The Theme of Family in Fenimore Cooper." *Studies in the Novel* 5 (Spring 1973): 39–51.
Peck, H. Daniel, ed. *New Essays on The Last of the Mohicans.* Cambridge: Cambridge University Press, 1992.
Pinckney, Colesworth, ed. *The Lady's Token, or Gift of Friendship.* Nashua, NH: J. Buffum, 1848.
Porte, Joel. *The Romance in America: Studies in Cooper, Poe, Hawthorne, Melville, and James.* Middletown, CT: Wesleyan University Press, 1969.
Railton, Stephen. *Fenimore Cooper: A Study of His Life and Imagination.* Princeton, NJ: Princeton University Press, 1978.
Rans, Geoffrey. *Cooper's Leather-Stocking Novels: A Secular Reading.* Chapel Hill: University of North Carolina Press, 1991.
Ringe, Donald A. *James Fenimore Cooper.* New York: Twayne, 1962. Updated edition, 1988.
Rowbotham, Judith. *Good Girls Make Good Wives: Guidance for Girls in Victorian Fiction.* Oxford: Basil Blackwell, 1989.
Rowson, Susanna Haswell. *Charlotte, a Tale of Truth.* 2nd ed. Philadelphia, 1794.
Ryan, Mary P. *Cradle of the Middle Class: The Family in Oneida County, New York, 1790–1865.* Cambridge: Cambridge University Press, 1981.
Samuels, Shirley. "Generation through Violence: Cooper and the Making of Americans." *New Essays on The Last of the Mohicans.* Ed. by H. Daniel Peck. Cambridge: Cambridge University Press, 1992.
Scudder, Harold C. "What Mr. Cooper Read to His Wife." *Sewannee Review* 36 (April 1928): 177–194.
Sedgwick, Catharine Maria. *Hope Leslie, or, Early Times in the Massachussets.* Ed. and intro. by Mary Kelley. New Brunswick, NJ: Rutgers University Press, 1987.
———. *The Power of Her Sympathy: The Autobiography and Journal of Catharine Maria Sedgwick.* Ed. and intro. by Mary Kelley. Boston: Massachussets Historical Society, 1993.
Shapiro, Charles, ed. *Twelve Original Essays on Great American Novels.* Detroit: Wayne State University Press, 1958.
Smith-Rosenberg, Carroll. *Disorderly Conduct: Visions of Gender in Victorian America.* New York: Oxford University Press, 1985.
Spiller, Robert E. *Fenimore Cooper: Critic of His Times.* New York: Minton Balch, 1931.
Stone, Lawrence. *The Family, Sex, and Marriage in England, 1500–1800.* New York: Harper & Row, 1977.
Stowe, Harriet Beecher. *Uncle Tom's Cabin: Or, Life Among the Lowly.* London, n.d.
Sundquist, Eric J. "Incest and Imitation in Cooper's *Home as Found*." *Nineteenth-Century Fiction* 32 (Dec 1977): 261–84.
Thurer, Shari L. *The Myths of Motherhood: How Culture Reinvents the Good Mother.* Boston: Houghton Mifflin, 1994.
Tocqueville, Alexis de. *Democracy in America.* 2 vols. New York, 1855.
Tompkins, Jane. *Sensational Designs: The Cultural Work of American Fiction 1790–1860.* New York: Oxford University Press, 1985.

Tuthill, Louisa. *The Young Lady's Home.* Boston: William J. Reynolds, 1847.
Tuttleton, James W. *The Novel of Manners in America.* Chapel Hill: University of North Carolina Press, 1972.
Tyler, Royall. *The Contrast. American Literature.* Vol. 1. Ed. by Emory Elliott. Englewood Cliffs, NJ: Prentice-Hall, 1991.
Verhoeven, Wm. M., ed. *James Fenimore Cooper: New Historical and Literary Criticism.* Amsterdam and Atlanta: Rodopi, 1993.
Wallace, James D. *Early Cooper and His Audience.* New York: Columbia University Press, 1986.
Warner, Susan. *The Wide, Wide World.* Afterword by Jane Tompkins. New York: The Feminist Press at The City University of New York, 1987.
Warren, Joyce W. *The American Narcissus: Individualism and Women in Nineteenth-Century American Fiction.* New Brunswick, NJ: Rutgers University Press, 1984.
Webster, Hannah Foster. *The Coquette, or The History of Eliza Wharton.* Reprint with an intro. by Herbert Ross Brown. New York: Columbia University Press, 1939.
Welter, Barbara. "The Cult of True Womanhood 1820–1860." *The American Family in Social-Historical Perspective.* 2nd ed. Ed. by Michael Gordon. New York: St. Martin's, 1978. 313–33.
Why, Joseph Van. Introduction. *The American Woman's Home or, Principles of Domestic Science.* By Catherine E. Beecher and Harriet Beecher Stowe. Hartford, CT: Stowe-Day Foundation, 1975.
Wollstonecraft, Mary. *Thoughts on the Education of Daughters with Reflections on Female Conduct in the More Important Duties of Life.* Clifton, NJ: A. M. Kelley, 1972
_____. *A Vindication of the Rights of Women.* New York: Source Book, 1971.
The Young Lady's Book: A Manual of Elegant Recreations, Exercises, and Pursuits. Boston, 1830.
The Young Lady's Own Book. Philadelphia: Key & Biddle, 1833.

Index

Abbott, John S. C. *The Mother at Home or, The Principles of Maternal Duty* 58, 64–65, 180n
"Address on Female Education" 40
The Advocate 64
Alcott, Louisa May 96–97
Alcott, William A. *The Young Woman's Guide* 35, 58, 60, 123
American Lady's Preceptor 64
Austen, Jane 5, 17, 81; *Persuasion* 44; *Pride and Prejudice* 5, 45, 69

Bailey, Ebenezer, ed. *The Young Ladies' Class Book: A Selection of Lessons for Reading in Prose and Verse* 62
Banks, J. A. *Victorian Values* 176n
Baym, Nina 6, 124, 132, 144, 173n, 174n, 180n
Beecher, Catharine E. and Harriet Beecher Stowe: *The American Woman's Home or, Principles of Domestic Science* 61–62, 177n
Belfiglio, Genevieve 79, 143–144, 176n, 181n
Bradstreet, Anne 65
Brooke, Frances 10
Brown, Charles Brockden 80
Burney, Frances 10
By a Lady (Eliza Ware Farrar). *The Young Ladies' Friend* 54
By a Lady. *The Young Wife's Book: A Manual of Moral, Religious and Domestic Duties* 60, 95, 180n

Cavelti, John G. 173n
Child, Lydia Maria 1, 3, 5–6, 10, 13, 37–39, 56, 61, 65–66, 75, 79, 82, 96, 79, 124, 129–30, 180n; *The Frugal Housewife* 43, 61, 78, 129–130; *Hobomok and Other Writings on Indians* 3, 11–13, 14–15, 18, 47, 69–72, 96, 99–101, 132–136
Cobbett, William. *Advice to Young Men* 94–95, 179n
Cohen, Paula Marantz 6, 173n
Cooper, James Fenimore 1–10, 15–19, 37–40, 54–56, 59, 63, 67–68, 90, 95, 124–125, 142–170; *The American Democrat; or, Hints on the Social and Civic Relations of The United States of America* 45–46, 51–52; *The Chainbearer; or, The Littlepage Manuscripts* 2, 51, 79, 86–88, 104; *The Deerslayer; or, The First War-Path* 2–3, 10, 26, 30–33, 46, 49–50, 90, 117–118, 121–122, 163–166; *Home as Found* 3, 10, 15, 20, 25–26, 43, 46, 63, 79, 96, 104, 118, 122, 143–144, 166–168; *Homeward Bound; or, The Chase: A Tale of the Sea* 3, 10, 15, 20, 25, 46, 96, 122, 143, 144; *The Last of the Mohicans: A Narrative of 1757* 3, 10, 46, 92, 111–113, 120–121, 152–156, 171; *The Letters and Journals of James Fenimore Cooper* 129; *Lionel Lincoln* 15, 20; *Notions of the Americans, Picked Up by a Travelling Bachelor* 7–10, 63, 129; *The Pathfinder; or, The Inland Sea* 3, 10, 20, 26–30, 32, 104, 115–117, 160–163; *The Pioneers, or The Sources of the Susquehanna; A Descriptive Tale* 3, 10, 43, 45–46, 48–49, 98, 104,

108–111, 148–152; *The Prairie: A Tale* 3, 46–47, 51, 79, 84–86, 113–115, 121, 156–160; *Precaution: A Novel* 3, 5, 15–20, 25, 38, 43–46, 54–55, 69, 78–84, 98, 104–105, 118, 142, 144–146; *The Redskins* 2, 51; *Satanstoe, or The Littlepage Manuscripts: A Tale of the Colony* 2, 3, 20, 24–25, 46, 79, 88, 104, 118–119, 122; *The Sea Lions* 51; *The Spy: A Tale of the Neutral Ground* 3, 10, 15, 20–25, 46, 96, 105–108, 118–119, 142–143, 146–148; *Tales for Fifteen; or, Imagination and Heart; The Way of the Hour* 38; *The Wept of Wish-Ton-Wish: A Tale* 3, 50–51, 79, 88–90
Cooper, Susan Fenimore 45, 128
Cosgrove, William E. 1, 174n
Cott, Nancy F. 37, 41–43, 65, 175n
Courtship: in Child 11–13; in Cooper 7–10, 15–34; in Sedgwick 13–15
"The Cult of Domesticity" 1–2, 34, 36–37, 40–43, 129
Cummins, Maria S. 1, 3, 5–6, 10, 37, 43, 47, 103–4, 141–142; *The Lamplighter* 3, 43, 47, 124, 132, 147, 170–171
"Cursory Remarks on a Wife" 56

Darnell, Donald 39, 166, 181n
Daughters 123–128, 130–132; in Child 129–130, 132–136; in Cooper 128–129, 142–169; in Cummins 141; in Sedgwick 130, 136–140; in Warner 140–141
Davis, David Brion 174n
Declaration of Sentiments 59
Demorest Monthly Magazine 63
Demos, John 35–36, 42, 58, 95, 175n, 176n
Dickens, Charles. *Bleak House* 178n

Edgeworth, Maria 10
Ellis, William 179n
Epstein, Barbara Leslie 64, 176n
Ernest Linwood 15

Farmingham, Marianne. *Girlhood* 131
Fatherhood 92–95; in Child 99–101; in Cooper 95–98, 104–122; in Cummins 103; in Sedgwick 96–97, 100–101; in Warner 101–103
Fiedler, Leslie 39, 175n

Fishburn, Janet Forsythe 59, 176n
Fordyce, James. *Sermons to Young Women* 8
Foster, Hannah Webster. *The Coquette, or, The History of Eliza Wharton* 10, 180n
Frank, Stephen M. 92–93, 179n
Freeling, Arthur. *The Young Bride's Book* 38, 63
Furness, Clifton Joseph 173n

Gilbert, Sandra, and Susan Gubar 69
Gilman, Caroline. *Recollections of a Housekeeper* 60
Goddard, Mehitable Dawes 65
Godey's Lady's Book and Magazine 7, 38, 55, 56, 63, 180n
Goldsmith, Oliver. *The Vicar of Wakefield* 16
Gorham, Deborah 65, 131, 180n
Goshgarian, G. M. 15
Green, Harvey 2, 7, 38, 43, 58, 63, 98–99, 173n, 174n, 175n
Green, Katherine Sobba 2, 5–6, 10, 38, 173n, 174n
Gregory, John. *A Father's Legacy to His Daughters* 126–129
Grossman, James 39, 45, 80, 174n, 178n, 179n

Habegger, Alfred 47, 176n
Hale, Sarah Josepha 41
Hastings, George E. 176n
Haywod, Eliza 7, 10
"Hints on Marriage" 56
Hirsch, Marianne 69
Holland, Josiah G. *Titcomb's Letters to Young People Single and Married* 38, 42–43, 95–96, 175n
House, Kay Seymour 6, 143, 173n, 174n, 176n, 179n, 181n
Howard, George Elliot 72, 178n
Humphrey, Henry. *Domestic Education* 92–93, 96

Johansen, Shawn 93, 179n

Karcher, Carolyn L. 99
Kelley, Mary 66–67
Kellogg, Susan 65, 177n
Kemble, Frances Anne (Fanny) 59–60

The Lady at Home 62
The Lady's Repository 92
The Lady's Token, or Gift of Friendship 60, 92
Lena Rivers 15
Long, Robert Emmet 80, 178n
Lowell, James Russell. "A Fable for Critics" 143, 181n

"Marriage" 55–57, 79
Marriage and Motherhood 54–65, 69; in Child 65–66, 70–72, 77; in Cooper 67–68, 78–91; in Sedgwick 66–67, 72–75, 77
McDannell, Colleen 93–94, 177n, 179n
Mintz, Steven 65, 177n, 179n
Moore, Edward. *Fables for the Female Sex* 8
The Mother's Assistant and Young Lady's Friend 60
Motley, Warren 44, 176n
Murphy, Shirley. *Our Homes and How to Make Them Healthy* 43

Opie, Mrs. 10, 45, 81

Patmore, Coventry 58, 131
Paul, Jay S. 1, 179n
Peck, H. Daniel 179n, 180n

Rans, Geoffrey 79, 178n
Ringe, Donald A. 2, 37, 178n
Rowbotham, Judith 177n, 178n, 180n
Rowson, Mrs. (Susanna Haswell). *Charlotte, A Tale of Truth* 10, 180n
Ryan, Mary P. 41, 176n

Samuels 179n
Scudder, Harold C. 176n
Sedgwick, Catharine Maria 3, 10, 39, 75, 77, 82, 96–97, 99, 125, 132, 142, 170; *Hope Leslie, or, Early Times in the Massachussets* 3, 13–15, 47, 56, 69–70, 72–75, 77, 100–101, 136–139; *The Power of Her Sympathy: The Autobiography and Journal of Catharine Maria Sedgwick* 66–67, 130

Shapiro, Charles. *Twelve Original Essays on Great American Novels* 174n
Sigourney, Mrs. *Lettters to Mothers* 62
Smith-Rosenberg, Carroll 59, 175n, 177n
Spiller, Robert E. 45, 178n
S. R. R. "Female Charms" 131
Stanton, Elizabeth Cady 54
Stowe, Harriet Beecher 61–62, 65, 80, 96–97, 177n
Sundquist, Eric J. 174n

Thurer, Shari L. 69
Titcomb's Letters to Young People, Married and Single 10, 42–43, 59, 63, 94, 95–96
Tocqueville, Alexis de. *Democracy in America* 56
Tompkins, Jane 49, 80, 177n
Tuthill, Louisa. *The Young Lady's Home* 60, 123–124
Tuttleton, James 174n
Tyler, Royall. *The Contrast* 17
Tytler, Sarah. "Girls" 125–126

Wallace, James D. 16, 45, 176n, 178n
Warner, Susan 1, 3, 5, 10, 15, 37, 39, 43, 47, 75–77, 98, 101–103, 124–125, 142, 170–171; *The Wide, Wide World* 3, 15, 43, 69, 77, 98, 140–141
Warren, Joyce W. 40, 143, 174n, 175n, 180n, 181n
Webster, Hannah Foster. *The Coquette, or The History of Eliza Wharton**
Welter, Barbara 2, 32, 58, 60
Wollstonecraft, Mary 126–128; *Thoughts on the Education of Daughters* 126; *A Vindication of the Rights of Women* 126–128

The Young Lady's Book: A Manual of Elegant Recreations, Exercises, and Pursuits 8, 132, 174n
The Young Lady's Own Book 55

www.ingramcontent.com/pod-product-compliance
Lightning Source LLC
Chambersburg PA
CBHW032102300426
44116CB00007B/857